The Rebirth
of Dialogue

The Rebirth of Dialogue

Bakhtin, Socrates, and the Rhetorical Tradition

James P. Zappen

State University of New York Press

Published by
State University of New York Press, Albany

For information, address State University of New York Press,
90 State Street, Suite 700, Albany, NY 12207

Production by Michael Haggett
Marketing by Susan M. Petrie

Library of Congress Cataloging-in-Publication Data

Zappen, James Philip.
    The rebirth of dialogue : Bakhtin, Socrates, and the rhetorical tradition / James P.
Zappen.
        p. cm.
    Includes bibliographical references and index.
    ISBN 0-7914-6129-7 (alk. paper)
    1. Plato. Dialogues. 2. Socrates. 3. Bakhtin, M. M. (Mikhail Mikhaæilovich), 1895–
1975. 4. Dialogue analysis. 5. Rhetoric. I. Title.
B395.Z37 2004
183'.2—dc22
                                                                                            2004008698

10 9 8 7 6 5 4 3 2 1

Contents

Acknowledgments

My greatest indebtedness—as a reader who knows no Russian and only a little Greek—is to scholars who have labored to translate and to interpret the writings of Mikhail Bakhtin for an English-speaking audience and to scholars in rhetoric, philosophy, and the classics who have endeavored to reconstruct the Socrates of the early Platonic dialogues. I hope that I have used their work wisely in my effort to intermingle *slovo* and *logos*—Russian and Greek and, of necessity, also English words.

Many others have generously provided advice, support, and assistance. Priscilla C. Ross, Director of the State University of New York Press, has thoughtfully and patiently guided me through the editorial process, and the anonymous State University of New York Press reviewers have generously offered helpful and constructive suggestions for revision, for which they deserve more thanks than I can give them here. Frank Farmer, Kay Halasek, Deborah Mutnick, and Filipp Sapienza have shared with me their thoughts and writings on Bakhtin, rhetoric, and composition studies, and Caryl Emerson and R. Bracht Branham have kindly directed me to recent scholarship on Bakhtin and the classics. Richard Leo Enos and Andreas Karatsolis have checked my bibliography and have helped me to document my occasional use of Greek terms.

Laura J. Gurak, Stephen Doheny-Farina, Teresa M. Harrison, and Sibel Adali have shared with me the challenges and the rewards of collaborative research and writing. Current and former graduate students Elizabeth C. Britt, Jennifer Estava Davis, Kevin Hunt, and Terese Monberg have broadened my thinking about Bakhtin, rhetoric, and culture, and research assistants Jennifer Bullard, Mousumi Chatterjee, Carolyn M. Clegg, Sandrine Dincki, Victoria Moore, Huatong Sun, and Ashley Williams have been the cornerstones of the Connected Kids project described in my epilogue. Rensselaer Polytechnic Institute colleagues Cheryl Geisler, S. Michael Halloran, and Merrill D. Whitburn have provided the advice and encouragement and the time and equipment support that was necessary to complete this project. Former colleagues and mentors Winifred Bryan Horner and Richard E.

Young long ago introduced me to the challenges and opportunities in rhetoric and composition studies.

Susan H. Zappen and the library staffs of Rensselaer and Skidmore College have provided bibliographic assistance, Matthew J. Zappen has been my constant editorial consultant, and Gregory J. Zappen has been my expert and always patient technical consultant and graphic designer.

Some of the ideas and several pages of text have appeared in previous publications. I am grateful to the publishers for their permission to use this material, as follows:

James P. Zappen. "Bakhtin's Socrates." *Rhetoric Review* 15:1 (1996): 66–83. Copyright by Lawrence Erlbaum Associates. Used with permission of the publisher.

James P. Zappen. "The Logic and Rhetoric of John Stuart Mill." *Philosophy and Rhetoric* 26:3 (1993): 191–200. Copyright 1993 by the Pennsylvania State University Press. Portions revised and reproduced by permission of the publisher.

James P. Zappen. "Mikhail Bakhtin (1895–1975)." In *Twentieth-Century Rhetorics and Rhetoricians: Critical Studies and Sources,* ed. Michael G. Moran and Michelle Ballif, 7–22. Westport, Connecticut: Greenwood Publishing Group, 2000. Used with permission of the publisher.

James P. Zappen, Laura J. Gurak, and Stephen Doheny-Farina. "Rhetoric, Community, and Cyberspace." *Rhetoric Review* 15:2 (1997): 400–419. Copyright by Lawrence Erlbaum Associates. Used with permission of the publisher.

1

Introduction

Dialogue has suffered a long eclipse in the history of rhetoric and in the history of philosophy. Socrates, its most important early practitioner, left no writings of his own, and his voice has become inextricably merged with the writings of Plato. As a consequence, Socratic dialogue has become little more than a precursor to the dialectic and rhetoric of Plato and Aristotle, and Socratic questioning has come to be seen as a search for answers—a quest for universal definitions that set philosophy and science on a fruitless search for truth.[1] In traditional readings of the early history of rhetoric, the Socrates of early Platonic dialogues such as the *Protagoras* and the *Gorgias* is a practitioner of a dialectical/dialogical method that becomes transformed into the dialectical rhetoric of the *Phaedrus* and the philosophical rhetoric of Aristotle.[2] In traditional readings of the early history of philosophy, he is also a practitioner of a rudimentary form of inductive method in search of universal definitions that becomes refined as a method of argument and persuasion in Aristotle's dialectic and his rhetoric.[3] Thus dialogue has merged almost imperceptibly into dialectic and has become the cornerstone of a dialectical or philosophical rhetoric. Dialogue has reemerged, however, in the twentieth century, in the work of theorists from a range of disciplinary orientations—Mikhail M. Bakhtin, Martin Buber, Hans-Georg Gadamer, and Carl R. Rogers, for example—some of whom have taken an interest in the early Platonic dialogues and their relationship to the rhetorical tradition.[4] Recent scholarship on the early dialogues, moreover, has envisioned a Socrates distinct from the Socrates of the later dialogues, a Socrates more concerned with how we live than with what or how we know, a Socrates who practices dialogue as the only true art of politics and who rejects rhetoric as the dangerous tool of an imperialistic empire.[5] This renewed interest in dialogue offers an opportunity to rethink the

role of dialogue within the rhetorical tradition and to reconstruct a dialogical
(not a dialectical) rhetoric as a rhetoric that is responsive, and accountable, to
other people. This renewed interest offers an opportunity, moreover, to rethink
the very meaning and purpose of public discourse not as persuasion but as an
ongoing exchange in which we test and contest and create ideas in cooperation and when necessary in conflict with others.

Among twentieth-century theorists of dialogue, Bakhtin takes a special
interest in the early Platonic dialogues and in their relationship to the rhetorical tradition. Gadamer writes extensively about the Platonic dialogues, but he
is less interested in the early than the later dialogues.[6] Nonetheless, Gadamer's
reading of the dialogues provides a useful reminder of the importance of questioning as the starting point of dialogue and a reminder also of Plato's ever-
present hand in the shaping of the dialogues, including the early dialogues.[7]
Buber reads Socrates as prototypical of the person who lives the life of dialogue, between I and Thou, but Buber's commentators maintain that Socrates
was a "monological thinker," too much given to "dialectical thought," to provide a model for Buber's life of dialogue.[8] These reservations notwithstanding, Buber provides an important point of departure for contemporary thinking about the possibility of a dialogical rhetoric—a dialogical rhetoric quite
different, however, from Bakhtin's.[9] Unlike other twentieth-century theorists
of dialogue, Bakhtin distinguishes the earlier from the later Platonic dialogues, Socratic dialogue from rhetorical dialogue and Platonic monologue.[10]
In the earlier dialogues, he finds a Socrates who offers alternatives to the traditional view of rhetoric as persuasion. But he also envisions the possibility
of a rhetoric transformed by dialogue, a rhetoric that acknowledges prior
speakers and future answerers—a *dialogized* or dialogical rhetoric.[11]

At first notice, Socrates and Bakhtin might appear to be unlikely sources
for a revisioning of the rhetorical tradition as dialogue, for both are at times
quite openly hostile to rhetoric. In the *Gorgias,* Socrates rejects the rhetorics
of Gorgias and Pericles as equally unjust—Gorgias' carelessly and confusedly, Pericles' thoughtfully and deliberately.[12] In "Discourse in the Novel,"
Bakhtin describes rhetoric as a formal and superficial method of analysis that
hears a mere diversity of voices and misses the "double-voicedness" of rhetorical discourse, its orientation toward both the listeners who answer and react
to it and the prior speakers whose words it transmits and re-accentuates.[13] In
Problems of Dostoevsky's Poetics, however, Bakhtin describes the kind of
double-voicedness that he finds in the earlier Platonic dialogues: the testing
and contesting and creating of ideas that occurs not as a result of a single
speaker speaking but only as a result of a change, and an exchange, of speaking subjects—the drawing forth and juxtaposing of voices and the collision of
voices by which old ideas are challenged and new ideas are born.[14] Bakhtin
probably overstates his distinction between the earlier and the later dialogues,
as R. Allen Harris and Paul Kameen suggest in their Bakhtinian readings of

the later *Phaedrus*.[15] Bakhtin's reading of the earlier dialogues thus might be extended to some of the later dialogues as well. It might also be enriched by concepts that appear elsewhere in his work. Bakhtin's concepts of novelistic discourse—polyphony, hybridization, parody, and carnival—can help to explain *how* Plato's ever-present and artful hand works to re-create the Socrates who appears in the earlier (and some of the later) dialogues.[16] His contextual and extratextual approach to textual analysis—his insistence upon reading texts in relationship to other texts and to their historical and cultural context—can help to explain *why* Socrates engages in testing and contesting and creating ideas.[17] Socrates is not seeking but rather questioning universal definitions because he believes that others uphold definitions that they do not understand, definitions that are grounded in cultural values that they do not question, definitions that are, moreover, in conflict with each other.

The most important of the early dialogues for the study of rhetoric and other forms of public discourse are, of course, the *Protagoras* and the *Gorgias,* and these are also the dialogues that offer the clearest articulations of Socrates' thoughts about the art of dialogue. The texts of these dialogues take on different meanings in different contexts, of course, as they are read in relation to other early dialogues and to their historical and cultural context or in relation to later dialogues such as the *Republic* and the *Phaedrus* and to the dialectic and the rhetoric of the later Aristotle.[18] Read in relation to other early dialogues, the *Protagoras* and the *Gorgias* reveal the persistence of the problem of the relationship of the virtues, and read in relation to the *Laches,* in particular, they reveal the immediate and pressing problem of courage in its relationship to the other virtues or to virtue itself. Read, too, in their historical and cultural context, as Bakhtin insists we read them, these early dialogues show that the problem of the relationship of the virtues is not as much a philosophical problem as it is a cultural problem, not a problem of knowing but a problem of living. It is specifically a problem of cultural conflict between courage and the other virtues, between the traditional Homeric virtue of *aretē* and the newer civic virtues, between the virtue that supports and sustains an unjust empire and the virtues that oppose it.[19] The problem is both historical and contemporary, for the cultural values embedded in the Greek oral tradition persist in the literate tradition of printed texts, and the emergence of Socratic dialogue as a response to the oral tradition finds its parallel in the reemergence of dialogue as a response to the cultural values embedded within printed texts, beginning as early as Bakhtin and extending to recent discussion of the new digital media.[20]

RETHINKING THE SOCRATIC DIALOGUE

Bakhtin's invitation to rethink the Socratic dialogue and its place in the rhetorical tradition is supported by scholarship on the origins and early history of rhetoric and by scholarship that seeks to recapture the Socrates of the early dialogues as the best evidence that we have of Socrates' life and work. Studies of the early history of rhetoric demonstrate that this history is more rich and varied than traditional accounts would have us believe,[21] and studies of the early dialogues identify unique features that distinguish the earlier from the middle and later dialogues.[22] These studies recognize the Socratic art of dialogue as a significant contribution to the development of the arts of public discourse in the Athens of the fifth century BCE.

Studies of the early history of rhetoric demonstrate that both the term *rhetoric* and the disciplinary concepts associated with it were relatively late developments, belonging to the fourth rather than to the fifth century BCE. According to Edward Schiappa, Plato likely coined terms such as *rhetoric (rhētorikē)* and *dialectic (dialektikē)* in the fourth century and thus made possible the coalescence of disciplinary meanings that we have come to associate with these terms.[23] The naming of rhetoric was thus significant because it allowed the discipline of rhetoric to develop, to become the locus for organizing thought and effort around a set of problems concerned with the persuasive *rhētōr*.[24] In the fifth century, in contrast, sophists such as Protagoras and Gorgias regularly used the term *logos* in a broad "predisciplinary" sense to designate speakers and arguers, various forms of argument, different and competing ends or purposes for argument, and different contexts for argument, both political and nonpolitical.[25] Schiappa notes that the few extended fifth-century texts that address issues in persuasive discourse suffice to challenge the now standard accounts of early Greek rhetorical theory.[26] Michael Gagarin believes that these texts challenge even the traditional view that sophistic discourse always aimed only to persuade.[27] According to Gagarin, these texts express disapproval of persuasion as either ineffective or harmful and explore *logos* as a tool for thinking rather than persuasive speaking.[28] G. B. Kerferd maintains, moreover, that Socrates belongs to this same period, that he was considered a sophist by his contemporaries, that he was interested in the same kinds of problems, and that he was in this respect more like the sophists than the later Plato.[29] Thus we might add to the few surviving texts from the fifth century the portrait of Socrates in the early Platonic dialogues, which offers the best evidence that we have of Socrates' life and work, whether or not it happens to present an accurate portrayal of the historical Socrates himself.

Much has been written about the so-called Socratic problem, that is, the problem of weighing and evaluating the sources—Aristophanes, Xenophon, Plato, and Aristotle—and re-creating on the basis of these sources the life and character of the historical Socrates and assessing the significance of his work.[30] The Socrates of the early Platonic dialogues is especially prominent among these sources, not because this Socrates necessarily represents the historical Socrates but because this Socrates is the best evidence that we have of Socrates' intellectual work.[31] This Socrates is traditionally read from the perspective of Plato and Aristotle, just as the early Platonic dialogues are often read from the perspective of the later dialogues, the *Gorgias,* for example, from the perspective of the *Phaedrus.* Thus W. K. C. Guthrie, for example, assesses Socrates' contribution to philosophy from the perspective of those presumed to be most capable of understanding him, that is, Plato and Aristotle:

> For the personal appearance, character and habits of Socrates we may go with confidence to both Plato and Xenophon, and we find indeed a general agreement in their accounts of these matters. But for our chief concern, the contribution of Socrates to philosophical, and in particular ethical, inquiry, I believe it is best to rely primarily on those who were themselves philosophers and so best capable of understanding him. That means in the first place Plato, but also Aristotle in so far as he was a student and associate of Plato and had learned from him the relation of his own thought to the unwritten teaching of his master.[32]

Similarly, the *Gorgias* is traditionally read as an early expression of ideas about rhetoric that reach fulfillment in the later *Phaedrus* and in Aristotle's *Rhetoric.* Thomas M. Conley finds a scathing attack on rhetoric in the *Gorgias* and finds its positive counterpart in the legitimate rhetoric of the *Phaedrus.*[33] George A. Kennedy, conversely, finds suggestions about the positive role of rhetoric in the *Gorgias* and finds their fulfillment and fruition in the later rhetorics of Plato and Aristotle: in the *Phaedrus,* he argues, "Plato goes significantly beyond the suggestions of *Gorgias* about the positive role of rhetoric; he lays the foundation for basic features of Aristotle's *Rhetoric,* and he integrates rhetoric into his other philosophical ideas in a way not attempted elsewhere."[34]

Jacques Derrida, however, envisions an alternative Socrates, a Socrates with a life of his own. In a striking portrait of Socrates and Plato in *The Post Card,* Derrida describes the teleology according to which Socrates always says only what Plato wants him to say and envisions the possibility of reversing the teleology and catching a glimpse of a Socrates who writes what he himself, not Plato, wants him to say.[35] In *Problems of Dostoevsky's Poetics,* Bakhtin offers a brief sketch of a Socrates of the kind that Derrida envisions— the Socrates of the early Platonic dialogues. Bakhtin, of course, reads the early dialogues from the perspective of his own teleology, his attempt to trace the lineage of the dialogue form, a form that he characterizes as "serio-comical" and "carnivalistic" and situates in a line of novelistic development that leads to Fyodor Dostoevsky.[36] Bakhtin finds in the Socratic dialogue the same emphasis upon the dialogic nature of truth—the juxtaposing and testing, the colliding and contesting, the collectively seeking and *birthing* of ideas—that he finds in the Dostoevsky novels.[37]

Studies of the early dialogues support this vision of an alternative Socrates. Thomas C. Brickhouse and Nicholas D. Smith, Terry Penner, and Gregory Vlastos note the differences between the early and the middle and later Platonic dialogues.[38] All agree that the early dialogues are more ethical than philosophical, more concerned with living than with knowing, and less concerned with the exposition of positive doctrine than the middle and later dialogues. Brickhouse and Smith explain that the Socrates of the early dialogues examines not propositions but lives, not what people say or even what they believe but how they live.[39] Others explore the ethical problem in the early dialogues. Arthur W. H. Adkins and Charles H. Kahn, for example, observe the cultural conflict between courage and the other virtues apparent in the early dialogues, especially the *Gorgias,* and Harvey Yunis explains the cultural conflict in the *Gorgias* as a conflict between the Athenian quest for empire and the Periclean rhetoric that sustains it, on the one hand, and Socrates' pursuit of justice and the art of dialogue that nurtures and preserves it, on the other.[40] Still others explore the contribution of the Socratic dialogue to the arts of public discussion. Andrea Wilson Nightingale and Robert Wardy observe Socrates' insistence that his art of dialogue is the only "true political art" since his art alone is capable of improving people's lives.[41] Brickhouse and Smith and Penner explain the Socratic art of dialogue as a kind of exhortation or teaching, distinct from the Platonic view of rhetoric as persuasion.[42] As Penner observes, while the later Platonic dialogues identify persuasion with appeals to emotion, the earlier Socratic dialogues maintain that persuasion can only be teaching, that is, bringing people to understand, for themselves, though with the aid of Socratic questioning, what is or is not the case.[43]

BAKHTIN, DIALOGUE, AND THE RHETORICAL TRADITION

The distinction between rhetoric as persuasion and dialogue as teaching one to think for oneself is not, of course, quite as simple as Penner suggests, and assessments of Bakhtin's contribution to rhetoric have struggled, often uneasily, with the relationship between dialogical and rhetorical activity and with the meaning and purpose of a dialogized or dialogical rhetoric.[44] The issues are whether or not dialogue has a place in the rhetorical tradition, whether it can find such a place without simply collapsing into another version of persuasion, and—if it can find a place in the tradition—what that place, that is, what a dialogical rhetoric, might be. In this context, dialogue sometimes seems to be distinct from rhetoric or even subordinate to rhetoric, as a particular kind of rhetoric or a setting for rhetorical activity, an opportunity or occasion for persuasion.[45] Increasingly, however, Bakhtin's concept of dialogue seems to present a fundamental challenge to traditional rhetoric, his view of the utterance as an exchange between speaking subjects upsetting the traditional relationship between speaker and listener and speech, writer and reader and text, thus inviting a thorough rethinking of the ends or purposes traditionally associated with rhetoric.[46] But the implications of this challenge remain unclear. Thus Kay Halasek pointedly asks: "Bakhtin . . . implicitly calls into question the purpose of discourse. Are its goals those delineated by Cicero—to prove, charm, or sway? Or are they those of Augustine—to teach, delight, or move—or others not yet systematized or theoretically articulated?"[47] Others, turning their attention to Bakhtin's early work, pose new and troublesome questions for rhetoric, communication, and composition studies: How can we bridge the experiential abyss between ourselves and others?[48] Or should we not try? How can we bridge the abyss between ourselves and the cultural values that so often seem to be imposed upon us by disciplinary and other kinds of authoritative texts?[49] How can we surround ourselves with difference without succumbing to power and prejudice, injustice and intolerance?[50] Bakhtin's reading of the Socratic dialogue provides partial answers to some of these questions.

Dialogue and Dialogical Rhetoric

Dialogue seems at times to be distinct from rhetoric, at times subordinate to rhetoric—a particular kind or subset of rhetoric. Don H. Bialostosky looks to Bakhtin for "an art of dialogics" distinct from rhetoric, modeled after Plato's *Symposium* and directed toward the remaking of literary criticism as dialogue.[51] Bialostosky reads Bakhtinian dialogics as distinct from dialectic and rhetoric on the basis of the centuries-old tradition that associates rhetoric exclusively with persuasion: "As dialectic strives for conviction on a question and rhetoric for persuasion of an audience, dialogics strives for comprehensive responsiveness and responsibility to the consequential person-ideas of a time, culture, community, or discipline—that is, for the fullest articulation of someone's ideas with the actual and possible ideas of others."[52] Others similarly turn to Buber for a "dialogical rhetoric" distinct from traditional rhetoric and characterized as existential-ontological rather than pragmatic, attentive and responsive to others rather than persuasive and manipulative of others, and personal and communal rather than social psychological and logical.[53] They perceive this rhetoric to be grounded in living mutual relationships between oneself and others and thus to be momentary, ephemeral, and fleeting and, as a consequence, very difficult to research, except through studies of one's own and others' lives.[54]

Simon Dentith seems to subordinate dialogue to rhetoric as a particular kind or subset of rhetoric when he claims that a broad concept of rhetorical criticism can accommodate Bakhtin's dialogics.[55] Like Bialostosky, Dentith associates rhetoric with persuasion, but he is prepared to accommodate a wide range of discourse practices under the rubric of rhetoric on grounds that every utterance is "suasive" and *"interested."*[56] Thus, while he acknowledges Bakhtin's preference for "the plural and the dialogic over the singular or monologic" he nonetheless envisions a rhetorical criticism that grasps "the situatedness" of every utterance and is thus capable of both accommodating novelistic prose as Bakhtin conceives it and accurately describing it.[57] Others see a possibility of expanding, perhaps even altering, our notion of what counts as rhetorical discourse by accommodating Bakhtinian dialogics. Halasek, for example, distinguishes "polemic" rhetorical forms such as epic, encomium, apologia, and epideictic from "parodic" rhetorical forms such as symposia, diatribes, and soliloquies and associates the former with official culture and monologic rhetoric, the latter with unofficial culture and Bakhtinian dialogic rhetoric.[58] According to Halasek, parodic rhetorics broaden and enrich the tradition by introducing multiple and sometimes conflicting intentions and purposes into rhetorical texts.[59] Similarly, James Jasinski distinguishes rhetorical advocacy as personal polemic isolated from social practice from rhetorical performance as a practical discursive event situated in its social and historical context and associates the former with Bakhtinian rhetoric, the latter with Bakhtinian dialogue.[60] Jasinski thus finds Bakhtinian dialogue not in rhetorical forms but in public discursive practices—political, legal, and epideictic.[61]

Dialogue as the Occasion for Persuasion

Dialogue seems to be subordinate to rhetoric in another sense as well, when it is conceived as a setting for rhetorical activity, an opportunity or occasion for persuasion. In this sense, Bakhtinian dialogue is antithetical or even peripheral to rhetoric because it does not share rhetoric's instrumental (and persuasive) purpose. John M. Murphy sees dialogue and rhetoric as antithetical and claims that even advocates of a dialogic rhetoric such as Halasek and Jasinski actually dissociate rhetoric from dialogue, Halasek by dissociating official from unofficial culture, Jasinski by dissociating decontextualized rhetorical advocacy, which seeks only victory, from contextualized rhetorical performance, which "manages tensions, orchestrates voices, and reveals anxiety."[62] Murphy seeks to restore the instrumental purpose that seems so antithetical to Bakhtin's view of dialogue but that nonetheless lies at the very heart of the rhetorical tradition.[63] Thomas B. Farrell similarly emphasizes the instrumental purpose of rhetorical activity but sees Bakhtinian dialogue not as antithetical but rather as peripheral to rhetoric, as an opportunity or occasion for persuasion.[64] Farrell situates Bakhtinian dialogue in a long line of historical development that apparently begins with Homer and Aristotle. In Homer, conversational dialogue originated as a break in the extended poetic monologue, a break initiated by an interruptive question, a request that the poet repeat a statement that seems to be unsatisfactory or unclear.[65] It is a reminder of *"contextuality,"* a reminder, that is, that the poetic monologue is not monologue but dialogue.[66] In Aristotle, rhetoric and other modes of inquiry retain this conversational quality since each is a response to different kinds of questions.[67] Analytic responds to questions about the causes of the essential nature of things based upon unproblematic principles and materials.[68] Dialectic not only responds to questions but in turn invites another's response. Dialectic responds to questions in problematic contexts based upon generally accepted premises and framed to invite participatory answers of affirmation or denial.[69] Rhetoric responds to questions about appearances by identifying signs, probabilities, and examples on either side of an issue, thereby representing appearances with sufficient clarity to guide us toward prudent decisions and conduct.[70] Because it deals with appearances, rhetoric contests the very notion of the problematic, "even as it aims to facilitate judgment based on persuasion."[71]

In Farrell's reading, Bakhtinian dialogue is ordinary conversation, which—like Homeric conversation and Aristotelian dialectic—provokes or invites a response. Rhetoric is a persuasive response to questions or issues that arise in ordinary conversation. Rhetoric is "monologic, partisan, and directed outward to the attention of others, who then judge its quality"; conversation is "dialogic, bipartisan, and directed only to those in the immediate encounter, who may appreciate, but never fully grasp, the holistic form itself."[72] According to Farrell, rhetoric enters into conversation at occasions or "junctures" of tension, intervening with "intentional consciousness—the practical intent to shape discourse toward extrinsic goals."[73] These occasions or junctures of tension are moments of premeditation, where the content and/or direction of a conversation has been prepared in advance by at least one of the participants; disturbance, where the definition or status of a developing conversation is contested; and disputation, where the participants openly disagree about some issue outside the parameters of the conversation.[74] Rhetoric responds to these moments with positions of partisanship and advocacy directed toward practical and purposeful conduct, which may nonetheless require the cooperation of the other participant(s) in the conversation.[75] At these moments, conversation becomes rhetorical and persuasive.

Dialogue as an Exchange of Speaking Subjects

Bakhtin's concept of dialogue, however, also seems to challenge traditional rhetoric by redirecting rhetorical activity away from persuasion toward a wider range of ends or purposes. In particular, Bakhtin's notion of the utterance as an exchange between speaking subjects redirects rhetorical activity by radically altering the relationship between speaker and listener and speech, writer and reader and text—a relationship that becomes even more complicated in the light of recent attention to Bakhtin's early work.[76] Bakhtin's concept of dialogue seems similarly to challenge traditional dialectic. Gary Saul Morson and Caryl Emerson argue that Bakhtinian dialogue resembles neither Buber's I-Thou relationship nor the Hegelian and Marxist dialectics, which Bakhtin characterizes as "deeply monologic."[77] Jean-François Côté maintains, however, that Bakhtin's notion of the utterance as a unit of speech marked by a change of speaking subjects recalls Hegel's dialogue with other philosophies and reveals a fundamental affinity between Bakhtinian dialogism and Hegelian dialectic, between "our possible *perception* of an event called 'dialogue'" and our understanding of "the *essential structure of experience*" as a movement from dialogue to its abstraction in dialectic to further dialogue.[78] Michael Gardiner perceives a resemblance between Bakhtin's dialogism and Maurice Merleau-Ponty's dialectics but notes that both attempt to rethink traditional dialectic by returning to the conversational model inspired by Socrates, thus resituating dialectic in the utterances, activities, and aspirations of people who live in a world that is inconclusive and open and free.[79]

The Bakhtinian challenge to traditional rhetoric seems at times to be a simple rejection of rhetoric. Thus Morson and Emerson, for example, recall Bakhtin's claim that the reestablishment of rhetoric helps to strengthen the position of contemporary formalist critics by giving them a tool for analyzing, rather than simply rejecting, novelistic language.[80] Bialostosky explains that Bakhtin challenges the formalists' rhetoric because it seeks to silence opponents and advance its own monologic pronouncements, because it overlooks the multivoicedness inherent in all discourse, including rhetorical discourse.[81] But Morson and Emerson also point out that Bakhtin seeks not simply to reject or even to supplement rhetoric, pragmatics, and other contextual approaches to language but to fundamentally reconceive them.[82] Their exposition on Bakhtin's concept of dialogue suggests how such a reconceptualization is possible. According to Morson and Emerson, Bakhtin's concept of dialogue is grounded in his view of the utterance as unit of speech communication situated in relation to other utterances.[83] Unlike the sentence (as it is conceived in traditional linguistics), an utterance exists only in context: it is spoken by someone, in response to something, in anticipation of a response from someone else.[84] It thus exists not in isolation but only in relation to other utterances—in an exchange of utterances.[85] The utterance therefore requires the active understanding of the listener, who must grasp the utterance and prepare to respond to it, who thus participates in shaping the utterance *as* it is being made (not *after* it is made).[86] From the point of view of linguistics, two utterances spoken in succession—"Life is good." "Life is good."—are simply repetitious.[87] From the point of view of logic, they are identical.[88] From a dialogic perspective, they constitute an exchange of utterances, an expression of *agreement* between the first speaker and the second.[89] Bakhtin's view of the utterance as part of an ongoing exchange of utterances helps to explain related concepts such as *heteroglossia* and *dialogized heteroglossia*.[90] Heteroglossia is the mix and diversity of languages that represent various professions, generations, classes, geographic areas, ethnic groups, and so on.[91] As Morson and Emerson point out, however, these languages, like individual utterances, exist not in isolation but always in relationship to each other. Dialogized heteroglossia is the interanimation of languages that occurs as each language is viewed from the perspective of the other.[92] Bakhtin's view of the utterance thus informs his thinking about dialogue and about language practices generally. As Emerson and Michael Holquist point out, Bakhtin uses the Russian word *slovo* in a broad sense (not *word,* but *discourse*)—much as the Greeks used the word *logos*—as a "diffuse way of insisting on the primacy of speech, utterance, all *in praesentia* [in presence] aspects of language."[93]

These concepts challenge traditional rhetoric because they place greater emphasis upon the listener or reader as an active participant in the making of meaningful communication.[94] Indeed in the context of an exchange of utterances the very concept of listener/reader becomes suspect since the listener/reader is not simply a *listener* or *reader* but the next person in a sequence of speakers/listeners or writers/readers who participate in the exchange. Assessments of Bakhtin's contribution to rhetoric and composition studies have noted this shift in emphasis and have begun to explore its implications for rhetorical theory. In an early study of Bakhtin's "rhetoric," Charles I. Schuster observes that Bakhtin upsets the Aristotelian paradigm that has dominated rhetorical theory throughout its long history: the "rhetorical triangle" of "speaker-listener-subject."[95] Bakhtin shifts the traditional emphasis away from the speaker by replacing "subject" with "hero" and by recognizing both the hero and the listener as equal participants (with the speaker) in a complex dialogic interaction.[96] Halasek similarly observes that the traditional rhetorical triangle of "speaker, audience, and subject" fails to recognize the importance of the utterance "as part of an ongoing, complex, interactive web of discourse set within a social context," and she begins to explore the multiple roles of the listener/reader/audience within this complex web of discourse.[97] The implications of this shift for rhetorical theory are not simply a broadening of what counts as rhetorical discourse but more fundamentally and more importantly a resituating of rhetorical forms and a redirecting of rhetorical purposes within the context of ongoing dialogic interactions. John Bender and David E. Wellbery are explicit: "For Bakhtin every utterance is many utterances; every speaker is many speakers; and every seemingly rhetorical context encodes many other occasions."[98] Similarly, Frank Farmer observes: "Bakhtin understands that all our efforts to persuade, convince, move, inform, affect, contend, agree . . . are dialogically situated."[99] All of these efforts need the voices that they address and answer; they need their "other words."[100] Moreover, as Halasek points out, not only agonistic but also epideictic or ceremonial forms of rhetorical discourse are dialogically situated, with the consequence that traditional rhetorical ends or purposes change fundamentally: the ends of persuading, instructing, or proving become secondary to the ends of establishing and maintaining communities and affirming political, social, and cultural beliefs.[101]

Recent attention to Bakhtin's early work further complicates the traditional paradigm. Whereas Halasek emphasizes the ends of community building and cultural affirmation, readers of the early work observe the abyss between ourselves and others, between ourselves and our cultural beliefs and values. Emerson observes in "Author and Hero in Aesthetic Activity" Bakhtin's absolute affirmation of the radical difference, the unbridgeable gap, between self and other and the consequent need that each of us has for the other—for each of us can see the clear blue sky that provides the background to the other's suffering.[102] Each of us, that is, needs the other because that other can see what we cannot see for ourselves. Emerson believes that Bakhtin would advise us, therefore, to associate with people who are different from ourselves: "Saturate a self in otherness and surround it with difference: That is how it will find its own freely constituted way."[103] She nonetheless acknowledges the difficulty of Bakhtin's position: how can we surround ourselves with difference without risk of surrounding ourselves with people who are powerful or prejudiced, unjust or insensitive or hurtful toward others?[104] Bialostosky observes in *Toward a Philosophy of the Act* a similar gap between ourselves and our cultural beliefs and values: nothing less than "a contemporary cultural crisis in which the weight of what is already known and established threatens to preempt individual authorship altogether."[105] According to Bialostosky, the early Bakhtin believes that the world of culture seeks to impose upon living consciousnesses what he would later call "authoritative discourse": published knowledge, moral laws, aesthetic judgments, and the like.[106] Bakhtin himself seeks not an imposition of cultural values but an integration of culture and life in which uniquely situated individuals evaluate the cultural values offered to them in acts that constitute what Bakhtin would later call—in contrast to authoritative discourse—"internally persuasive discourse."[107] Contemporary writers, Bialostosky maintains, continue to "write against the backdrop of disciplines whose accumulated knowledge demands their acquiescence and threatens to silence or preempt them."[108]

DIALOGICAL RHETORIC AS
TESTING, CONTESTING, AND CREATING IDEAS

Bakhtin's reading of the Socratic dialogue suggests how he might respond to some of these challenges. Like the early Bakhtin, the Socrates of the early dialogues felt the burden of cultural values that were not his own. Like others of his time, he was heir to the Homeric oral tradition, with its cultural ideal of excellence *(aretē)*—noble birth and high social standing joined, in the warrior, to courage (sometimes *manly courage*) and skill in battle.[109] Like others, too, he was heir to the newer cultural ideal of virtue *(aretē)*—courage joined to justice and temperance (often *self-restraint*)—an ideal that nourished and sustained the Athenian democracy and that applied, in principle at least, to both men and women.[110] Unlike others, however, he believed that courage and skill in battle, exercised in an unjust cause, was no virtue at all. He opposed the Athenian pursuit of empire, which Pericles himself admitted was expedient but unjust. He questioned those who held beliefs that they apparently did not understand: Athenian generals such as Laches and Nicias, who professed courage but could not explain it; sophists such as Protagoras and Gorgias, who claimed to teach virtue and the arts of discourse but were unable to explain or defend either; Callicles, the contemporary embodiment of Periclean injustice and Periclean rhetoric; and, finally, even Pericles himself.

The Socrates that Bakhtin finds in these early dialogues is a Socrates who tests and contests and creates ideas in dialogue or discussion *(dialegesthai)*—not dialectic *(dialektikē)*—with others.[111] This Socrates is not the speaker/writer/rhetor who seeks to persuade others to accept his own account of the virtuous life—his own *logos*—but the listener/reader/respondent who renders and receives accounts with others, thus contributing to the multiplicity of meanings associated with the term and the concept of *logos* in the ferment of the fifth century BCE.[112] He is the questioner who draws forth and juxtaposes the inconsistent and conflicting beliefs of others, thus testing not only their ideas but also their persons (for the idea and the person were not yet separate), not only what they think but who they are and how they live. He is the *midwife* who brings together diverse ideas, thereby creating new ideas, new cultural hybrids. He is the participant in carnival-like debate, contesting others' ideas and decrowning their persons with the base and lowly language of the streets. He is not, as Michel Meyer points out, a person of authority but an ordinary citizen who questions persons of authority and position, the leading citizens of his time, who do not understand and cannot explain their own beliefs.[113]

Bakhtin's Socrates thus provides one kind of response to the challenge of individual differences, the seemingly unbridgeable gap between self and other. Situated contextually and extratextually, this Socrates also provides a response to the problem and the challenge of cultural differences. Socrates tests and contests not only individuals, their ideas and their persons, but also their most deeply held cultural convictions, in particular their unreflective commitments to the traditional virtue of courage, exercised in pursuit of an unjust empire, on the one hand, and the newer virtues of justice and temperance, proclaimed as the basis of civil society, on the other. Thus he brings these cultural conflicts into the light of day, asks persons of authority to reflect upon them, to accept responsibility, and to acknowledge their accountability for what they think and say and do. As re-created in the early dialogues under Plato's guiding hand, Bakhtin's Socrates is the artful practitioner of anacrisis and syncrisis and novelistic polyphony, hybridization, parody, and carnival. In the *Laches,* he tests Laches' and Nicias' ideas of courage, drawing forth (anacrisis) and juxtaposing (syncrisis) the conflicts in their ideas and in their lives, leading them to acknowledge that they do not understand their own most deeply held convictions. In the *Protagoras,* he ridicules Protagoras' speech of display and parodies his method of interpreting poetry, but he accepts Protagoras' proud commitment to the civic virtues of justice and temperance. He nonetheless believes that Protagoras' view of civic virtue is incomplete if it does not encompass the traditional virtue of courage, so with Protagoras and the other sophists he works to create the new idea of the unity of virtue—a cultural hybrid that joins courage to the other virtues. He refuses, however—or Plato refuses—to acknowledge Protagoras' contribution and forces him to acquiesce to the new ideal. In the *Gorgias,* he contests Gorgias' and Polus' and Callicles' ideas about rhetoric and justice, decrowning each of them with carnivalesque images, forcing them to acknowledge that a rhetoric without justice is no true rhetoric. Finally, he contests Pericles' unjust pursuit of empire and the rhetoric that sustains it and asserts his own belief in courage joined to civic virtue and his commitment to dialogue as the only true art of politics—the summation of his life and work as he stands at the threshold of death.

Bakhtin's Socrates thus illustrates the possibility of a dialogized or dialogical rhetoric—the possibility of restoring to the rhetorical tradition the multiplicity of voices that Bakhtin believes are always there, whether we listen to them or not. Socrates' own conclusion about dialogue, presented at the end of what may be the latest of the early dialogues—the *Gorgias*—is that rhetoric and dialogue are distinct and opposed endeavors—rhetoric a vehicle of persuasion in pursuit of an unjust empire, dialogue the only true art of politics in pursuit of justice and the other virtues. Bakhtin, however, perceives in Socrates' artfully re-created practice of dialogue the possibility of reconnecting dialogue to the rhetorical tradition, not by rhetoricizing dialogue and thus reducing it monologue but by dialogizing rhetoric: by introducing the voices of others into rhetorical discourse, by showing how these voices test and contest and create or re-create ideas tacitly and unreflectively held to be true, by asking those of us who speak and write to render ourselves accountable to others in an ongoing exchange of voices.

Bakhtin's Socrates upsets the traditional polarity between speaker and listener, writer and reader, inviting us, each in turn, to examine the ideas and the persons of others and to submit our own ideas and our persons—our *selves* and our lives—for examination by others. This process of examining by testing and contesting and creating ideas is not restricted to oral discourse. Bakhtin's concept of dialogue and his vision of a dialogized or dialogical rhetoric extends to all forms of human discourse, both oral and written.[114] Moreover, the Socratic dialogue itself is a hybrid form, oral discourse transcribed and transformed in writing. As Bakhtin's own concept of polyphony reminds us, and as Gadamer also reminds us, Plato's authorial hand—his "surplus" of knowledge and active understanding—is ever present, and sometimes intrusive, even in the early dialogues.[115] Furthermore, the oral/written hybrids characteristic of this early period of manuscript literacy reappear in contemporary electronic media, in the give-and-take exchanges in electronic mail, electronic bulletin boards, and chat spaces and in the hypertextual linking of the World Wide Web. Thus Jay David Bolter observes a parallel between the Socratic dialogue and "network" structures such as the nonlinear "antibook" and the "hypertextual essay," for example, and Kathleen E. Welch observes a similar parallel between Isocratean written speeches and contemporary forms of "electric rhetoric."[116] Socrates, the speaker who did not write, and Isocrates, the writer who did not speak, thus reappear in contemporary hybrid forms of electronic discourse, which are at once oral and written and graphic and which seem to provide new opportunities for interactivity, intersubjectivity, collaboration, and dialogue.[117] However, as I argue in my epilogue, dialogue as a Bakhtinian/Socratic testing, contesting, and creating of ideas is neither impossible nor inevitable but is merely possible and only possible in any medium if we are willing to hear and to engage in the ongoing exchange of voices in each of them.

2

The Traditional Socrates

Dialogue, Rhetoric, and Dialectic

Socrates is frequently criticized as a rationalist who nonetheless practices a fallacious logic and a devious rhetoric by which he leads others to accept conclusions that he has previously determined to be true.[1] From the perspective of the more mature dialectic and rhetoric of Plato or Aristotle, Socrates may seem to be, at best, a canny rationalist and, at worst, a devious manipulator. But the Socrates who emerges in studies of the early dialogues (including Mikhail M. Bakhtin's) was less concerned with establishing positive knowledge and persuading others to accept that knowledge, by whatever means, than he was concerned with improving his own and other people's lives by examining, together, their most fundamental beliefs.[2] These studies situate Socrates within the context of fundamental but inconsistent and conflicted values deeply rooted in Greek culture and history.[3] In this context, the Socratic art of dialogue was neither a *dialectic* nor a *rhetoric* in the traditional sense of these terms but a means of testing Socrates' own and other people's beliefs, revealing their inconsistencies, contesting false beliefs when necessary, and creating new beliefs, with others, when possible. This art of dialogue disappears as it is transformed into Plato's dialectical rhetoric and Aristotle's dialectic and rhetoric but reappears in the nineteenth century in opposition to the unified truths of philosophy and science and the persuasive purposes of traditional rhetoric.

In the rhetorical/philosophical tradition of Plato and Aristotle, Socrates is the practitioner of a dialectical/dialogical method that appears intermixed with the dialectic and rhetoric of the *Gorgias,* becomes transformed into the dialectical rhetoric of the *Phaedrus,* and disappears entirely from the ideal state of the *Republic*.[4] In this tradition, Socrates is also the originator of a rudimentary form of inductive method in search of universal definitions that becomes refined as a method of argument and persuasion in Aristotle's dialectic and his rhetoric.[5] In nineteenth-century British empirical thought, Socrates is the practitioner of a negative dialectic that helps to build the unified truths of philosophy and science and at the same time permits and requires each of us to contest those truths.[6] In more recent studies of the early dialogues, in contrast, Socrates is the practitioner of an art of dialogue that seeks not positive knowledge but a solution to the pressing ethical problem of how we should live our lives.[7] The problem arises from a fundamental conflict in cultural values—a conflict between self-regarding and other-regarding virtue, between the traditional Homeric ideal of courage and skill in battle and the newer civic ideal of justice and temperance, between the ideal of justice in Athens and the reality of injustice in the regular and systematic expansion of its empire.[8] In his creative reading of the Socratic dialogue, Bakhtin interprets dialogue not as an emerging dialectic or rhetoric but as a means of testing one's own and others' ideas, at times contesting others' ideas, at times joining with others to create new ideas.[9] From this perspective, Socrates' response to the problem of how we should live is his practice of the art of dialogue—the true political art—by which he tests his own and others' ideas, always seeking to confirm his own most fundamental belief that one cannot practice the self-regarding without the other-regarding virtues, that one cannot be courageous but unjust.

SOCRATES' LIFE AND WORK

Socrates' life and work is obscure, his life retold in fragments in quite disparate sources, his work recorded and probably transformed in the early dialogues of Plato.[10] As retold in ancient and contemporary sources, Socrates' life is set against the active political and intellectual life of his time, a period spanning roughly the last seventy years of the fifth century, following the Greeks' successful defense against Xerxes and his Persian invaders, concurrent with the development of the Periclean democracy and the growth of the Athenian empire, and ending shortly after the conclusion of the Peloponnesian War, with Athens' capitulation to Sparta and the dissolution of its democracy and its empire.[11] Both Athens and Sparta had earned lasting fame in the early stages of the defense against the Persian invasion. Athenian hoplites successfully routed the Persians at the battle at Marathon (490 BCE), with little assistance from other Greek states, including Sparta, and its heavier ships and crews outmaneuvered the Persian vessels at the naval battle at Salamis (480 BCE)—the battle in which the Persian Artemisia was said to have distinguished herself by fighting better than the men.[12] Earlier in the same year, Sparta, with a force of three-hundred hoplites, plus its allies, had withstood the entire Persian army at the pass at Thermopylae before falling to vastly superior numbers, their courage memorialized in Simonides' poem of praise, "The Greek Dead at Thermopylae."[13] Athens' success against the Persians profoundly affected its subsequent history, its successes at Marathon and at Salamis justifying the claims of its hoplites and even its poorer oarsmen (and the women who served with them) to broader participation in the Athenian democracy, its position of dominance among the Greek states justifying—to Athens at least—the creation and systematic expansion of its empire.[14] Athens' very success, however, seems to have been one of the causes of its undoing, its arrogant self-interest in the pursuit of empire leading to war in the Peloponnese and the disastrous campaign at Syracuse, which left Athens weakened before a rebuilt Spartan naval force and led ultimately to the dissolution of its democracy and its empire and the brief but violent rule of the so-called Thirty Tyrants.[15]

Socrates lived his life, conducted his discussions, and met his death against the background of these events.[16] Physically, Socrates was unattractive and even comical, "snub-nosed, with wide nostrils, protruding eyes, thick lips, . . . and a paunch."[17] He served as a hoplite in the Peloponnesian War, earning a reputation for his courage in battle and for his endurance in harsh winter conditions and becoming legendary for his courage during the retreat from the battle at Delium (424 BCE).[18] Socrates enjoyed extraordinary freedom of speech throughout the latter years of the fifth century and especially under Pericles, who was well known for his personal support and patronage of visiting sophists such as Protagoras.[19] In his exercise of this freedom, he was known as a relentless questioner, who challenged other people's pretensions and revealed inconsistencies in their beliefs and who was in this respect indistinguishable from the sophists, at least in the popular imagination.[20] He was also in Plato's later description (*Theaetetus* 148e–51d) a "midwife," who helped to give birth to the ideas of others.[21] In his infrequent forays into public life, Socrates acted strictly in accord with Athenian law or refused to act.[22] Nonetheless, he had associates among both proponents of the democracy and the Thirty Tyrants and was reputed to have influenced Alcibiades, Charmides, and Critias, who became notorious for their opposition to the democracy and to Athens itself.[23] Alcibiades, for example, was vilified in Athens for persuading the Athenian assembly to launch the disastrous expedition against Syracuse, then defecting to Sparta, leaving the expedition under the command of the popular but indecisive Nicias, whose delays at critical moments led to the destruction of the Athenian army and navy and to Nicias' own death.[24] Socrates was tried on vague charges of failing to recognize the gods and corrupting the youth of the city but according to ancient tradition may in fact have been condemned for his association with figures such as Alcibiades.[25] He was sentenced to death and executed in the year 399 BCE.[26]

Socrates' work is represented by his oral discussions, which he did not commit to writing. As recorded in Plato's early dialogues, Socrates' discussions were evidently transformed, by Plato's philosophy, perhaps, and certainly by his artistry.[27] Studies of the early dialogues have nonetheless sought to distinguish the earlier Socratic from the later Platonic dialogues and to identify their characteristic features, without resolving the issue of whether the early dialogues represent the views of the historical Socrates or the early Plato.[28] Studies of the chronology of the dialogues posit four main groups and characterize the first two groups as Socratic, the second two groups as transitional or Platonic—with some disagreement, however, about the position of the *Protagoras* and the *Gorgias* relative to each other and to the other early dialogues.[29] Terence Irwin presents roughly the current consensus, as follows: Group 1 (Early): *Apology, Crito, Laches, Charmides, Euthyphro, Hippias Minor, Ion,* and *Protagoras;* Group 2 (Early): *Lysis, Cratylus, Euthydemus, Gorgias, Hippias Major, Menexenus, Meno, Phaedo,* and *Symposium;* Group 3 (Middle): *Republic, Parmenides, Theaetetus,* and *Phaedrus;* and Group 4 (Late): *Timaeus, Critias, Sophist, Statesman, Philebus,* and *Laws.*[30] Irwin takes the two early groups to be Socratic and supposes that the *Protagoras* belongs late in the first group, the *Gorgias* relatively early in the second group.[31] Others generally concur with these groupings but disagree, especially, about the place of the *Protagoras* and the *Gorgias* in relation to the other early dialogues.[32] Charles H. Kahn offers the most radical revision when he proposes to place the *Gorgias* before and the *Protagoras* with or perhaps after *Laches, Charmides,* and *Euthyphro,* on grounds that the *Gorgias* does not share but the *Protagoras* does share close thematic connections with these three dialogues and also with the *Meno.*[33] For example, though the *Gorgias* implicitly endorses the concept of the unity of the virtues, it does not include any unmistakable reference to the thesis that virtue is knowledge.[34] The *Protagoras,* in contrast, affirms the unity of virtue on grounds that virtue is knowledge and explores the teachability, the nature, and the parts of virtue, issues that link the *Protagoras* directly with *Laches, Charmides, Euthyphro,* and *Meno.*[35] Whatever the order of these early dialogues, the *Republic* and the *Phaedrus* are almost certainly later.

These efforts to distinguish the earlier from the later dialogues are complicated, however, by evidence of Plato's ever-present and artful hand, which permits both Plato and his readers to enter into and participate in the dialogues. Charles L. Griswold Jr. and Drew A. Hyland explain Plato's use of the dialogue form as an attempt to show, through dramatic art, how philosophy emerges from nonpropositional concrete experience and popular opinion.[36] Kahn rejects the notion of a sharp break between the earlier and the later dialogues and argues that the earlier dialogues are Plato's attempt to bridge the psychological distance between his "otherworldly vision" and that of his audience through his consummate literary artistry.[37] Hans-Georg

Gadamer observes that the effect of Plato's dramatic art is to transcend the point of view of the individual participants.[38] The Socratic dialogue, the art of using words as a midwife of ideas, is directed toward the participants in the dialogue but generates a truth that is larger than both: "What emerges in its truth is the logos, which is neither mine nor yours and hence so far transcends the interlocutors' subjective opinions that even the person leading the conversation knows that he does not know."[39] This *logos* is partly the participants' creation, but it is partly Plato's and partly the readers' creation as well, hence the importance of hermeneutics as an interpretive practice.[40] Similarly, Paul Kameen notes that the Plato's dramatic art permits readers to enter into and disrupt the apparent meanings of the texts.[41] In the *Protagoras* and the *Phaedrus* in particular, Kameen observes, "Plato provides systematically an array of gaps and fissures through which a reader can enter highly ambiguous spaces in relation to the declared significance of the texts."[42] Given these difficulties, studies of the earlier dialogues have not resolved, and likely will never resolve, the issue of whether these dialogues represent the views of the historic Socrates or the early Plato, but they nonetheless hold that the earlier dialogues are—in some sense—more *Socratic,* the later dialogues more *Platonic.*[43] Thus we may speak of *Plato's Socrates, the Socrates of the early dialogues,* or (as Bakhtin does) *the Socratic dialogue,* but not simply *Socrates.*

THE PHILOSOPHICAL/RHETORICAL TRADITION: FROM DIALOGUE TO DIALECTIC AND RHETORIC

Within the philosophical/rhetorical tradition of Plato and Aristotle, Socrates was the practitioner of both the dialectical/dialogical method that Plato transforms into the dialectical rhetoric of the *Phaedrus* and the inductive method in search of universal definitions that Aristotle refines as a method of argument and persuasion in his dialectic and his rhetoric.[44] Socrates has consequently become the object of criticism in contemporary literary theory, rhetoric, and composition studies, first, for launching the quest for a rationally ordered, unitary truth that now seems fruitless and misguided and, second, for practicing a devious logic that seems more like *mere rhetoric* than either philosophy or science.[45] In contemporary interpretations of Plato's dialectic and rhetoric, Socrates is usually represented by his appearance in the *Gorgias* and the *Phaedrus,* the two dialogues most concerned with rhetoric and its relationship to dialectic.[46] In these interpretations, Socrates is the practitioner of a dialectical/dialogical method and proponent of a rhetoric directed toward a just and temperate civic life that together become the dialectic/rhetoric or dialectical rhetoric of the *Phaedrus.* He is also a resilient and Janus-like figure whose art of dialogue *(dialegesthai)* survives alongside and as part of the dialectic *(dialektikē)* and rhetoric *(rhētorikē)* of the later

Phaedrus and disappears only in the ideal state of the *Republic,* in the unity and stability of Plato's conservative view of justice.

The *Gorgias* shows Socrates practicing a dialogical/dialectical method to demonstrate the limitations of Gorgias' rhetoric and to advocate an alternative philosophical rhetoric directed toward a just and temperate civic life.[47] In George A. Kennedy's close reading of the dialogue, Socrates' dialogical/dialectical method is a mixture of dialogue and dialectic, combining elements of question-and-answer, definition and division, and testing of hypotheses and leading the respondent to greater understanding, without Socrates' knowing with certainty what the outcome will be but nonetheless with a certain feeling of inevitability.[48] Kennedy characterizes this dialogical/dialectical method as itself a kind of "rhetoric," a mix of logical argument, irony, and ethical and emotional appeals that is "not always fair."[49] Thomas M. Conley similarly characterizes the method as frequently fallacious but nonetheless compelling.[50] Richard Leo Enos, however, finds that the very act of writing the *Gorgias* transforms the dialogical/dialectical method into a rhetorical composition, "one detailed argument of proposition under the guise of a dialogue."[51] All agree that, to one degree or another, the *Gorgias* contains elements of dialectic and rhetoric that anticipate the later *Phaedrus*.

The dialogue itself is a sequence of three discussions: one with Gorgias about the nature of rhetoric (449c–61b); one with Polus about whether it is better to do wrong or to suffer wrong (461b–81b); and one with Callicles about how one should live and specifically about the role of justice in civic life (481b–505d).[52] The first two discussions illustrate the dialectic of definition and division; the third describes the true philosophical rhetoric as the art of engendering justice in the soul. In the first discussion, Socrates questions Gorgias, asking him (in search of a definition) what rhetoric is and leading him (by the method of division) to respond that rhetoric is persuasion that produces belief, rather than knowledge, about right and wrong, the just and the unjust *(dikaion, adikon)* (449c–55a).[53] Conley explains the method of division in a simple formula: "It [the topic under investigation] must be A or B or C; it is not A, nor B; so it must be C."[54] Socrates uses this method to divide A (persuasion that produces belief) from B (persuasion that produces knowledge):

> SOC. Then would you have us assume two forms of persuasion—one providing belief without knowledge, and the other sure knowledge?

> GORG. Certainly.

> SOC. Now which kind of persuasion is it that rhetoric creates in law courts or any public meeting on matters of right and wrong? The kind from which we get belief without knowledge, or that from which we get knowledge?

GORG. Obviously, I presume, Socrates, that from which we get belief.

SOC. Thus rhetoric, it seems, is a producer of persuasion for belief, not for instruction in the matter of right and wrong.

GORG. Yes. (454e–55a)

Socrates thus elicits Gorgias' admission that persuasion produces belief rather than knowledge. He is then able to lead him into self-contradiction, pressing him to acknowledge that the rhetorician must know what is just and unjust and, knowing the difference, cannot act unjustly, contrary to his belief that rhetoric is about justice and injustice indiscriminately (460a–61b).

In the second discussion, Polus questions Socrates, provoking him to respond with a comparison of rhetoric to cookery, one of a series of comparisons in an elaborate division and subdivision the true arts of the soul and body and their corresponding *arts* or knacks of flattery.[55] The true arts include legislation and justice, as arts of the soul; and gymnastics and medicine, as arts of the body. The *arts* of flattery include sophistic and rhetoric, as arts of the soul; and cosmetics and cookery, as arts of the body. These arts constitute a series of comparisons: as sophistic is a sham of legislation, so rhetoric is a sham of justice; as cosmetics is a sham of gymnastics, so cookery is a sham of medicine. Rhetoric, like cookery, is a sham, imitating justice in the way that cookery imitates medicine. R. E. Allen characterizes this series of comparisons as an early application of the method of division, "used to show identity of relation between diverse terms, as geometric proportion shows identity of ratio in diverse multitudes or magnitudes."[56]

Finally, in the third discussion, Socrates questions Callicles, the most recalcitrant of the three, and presents his own view of rhetoric as an art of justice, which Kennedy claims is the essence of the philosophical rhetoric of the *Gorgias*.[57] Callicles holds that self-interest, though unjust by convention, is just by nature and that by nature the strong should always rule over the weak (482e–84c). Socrates responds with his own view of rhetoric as the art of engendering justice. He claims that rhetoric must always be concerned with how the orator may improve the souls of other citizens: "it is this that our orator, the man of art and virtue, will have in view, . . . how justice may be engendered in the souls of his fellow-citizens, and how injustice may be removed; how temperance may be bred in them and licentiousness cut off; and how virtue as a whole may be produced and vice expelled" (504d–e).

If a justice-engendering rhetoric is the true philosophical rhetoric of the *Gorgias,* then its method of definition and division, transformed into a dialectic/rhetoric or dialectical rhetoric, is the essence of the philosophical rhetoric of the *Phaedrus*.[58] As Kennedy indicates, however, the Socratic dialectic as a method of question and answer survives, paradoxically, in the myth about the invention of writing at the end of the dialogue.[59] The *Phaedrus* has two main parts, the first a series of three speeches on love (227a–57b), the second an exposition on dialectic, rhetoric, and writing, including the myth (257b–79c).[60] The first speech, composed by Lysias and read by Phaedrus, presents love as evil and is repetitive and unfocused (230e–34c, 243a). The second speech, attributed first to a clever boy and then to Phaedrus and spoken by Socrates, similarly presents love as evil but is carefully structured, beginning with a definition of love and proceeding by division of the effects of love as advantage or harm to the beloved and a division of the latter as harm to the beloved's soul, body, and estate and to the beloved's feelings, both during and after love (237b–41d). The third speech, attributed to Stresichorus and spoken by Socrates, presents love as good and is again carefully structured, proceeding by a division of divine madness as inspiration of the prophets, madness expressed through purifications and rites, inspiration of the poets, and the madness of the lover (hence a definition of love as a kind of divine madness) and presented in a striking metaphor of the soul as a charioteer who guides a team of winged horses toward a vision of absolute and eternal justice, temperance, and knowledge (243e–57b).

The exposition on dialectic, rhetoric, and writing presents dialectic and rhetoric as closely related and even equivalent procedures—a dialectic/rhetoric or dialectical rhetoric. Dialectic is the double method illustrated in its true form in Socrates' second speech; it is both a definition, a bringing together of scattered particulars into a single idea; and a division, a separating of single ideas or things into classes of particulars or parts (264e–66b). Rhetoric is synonymous with persuasion and hence requires a knowledge of the various kinds of souls and the various kinds of speeches, so that the rhetorician will know which sort of person is persuaded by which sort of speech (269c–72b). Dialectic and rhetoric are equivalent since the same person must know both procedures and so may be called either a *dialectician* or a *rhetorician* (266b–c, 277b–c). This dialectic/rhetoric or dialectical rhetoric is a lengthy and difficult but necessary procedure since it enables the orator in the public assembly or in the law courts to distinguish the truth about what is just and good from a probability, which is a mere likeness of truth (261a–64e, 272b–74b).[61]

The myth about the invention of writing at the end of the dialogue preserves as a part of this dialectical rhetoric the Socratic art of dialogue as a dialectic of question and answer. The myth is the story of the Egyptian king Thamus and Theuth, the inventor of writing (274b–78b). Socrates speaks for Theuth, who claims to have discovered writing and who offers them to Thamus as "an elixir" *(pharmakon)* that will make Egyptians wiser and improve their memories (274e). Socrates then speaks for Thamus, who objects to writing because it will discourage the practice of memory and thereby produce forgetfulness. Socrates concurs and defends his own dialectic of question and answer: "serious discourse . . . is far nobler, when one employs the dialectical method and plants and sows in a fitting soul intelligent

words which are able to help themselves and him who planted them, which
are not fruitless, but yield seed from which there spring up in other minds
other words capable of continuing the process for ever, and which make their
possessor happy, to the farthest possible limit of human happiness"
(276e–77a). This defense of dialectic as a method of question and answer is
paradoxical, Kennedy notes, since Plato has written the dialogue in which the
defense appears and since he presents dialectic not as a method of teaching of
what one already knows but as a planting in the minds of others ideas that will
forever have a life of their own.[62]

Such a dialectic of question and answer has no place in the ideal state of
the *Republic,* however, for in this ideal state the philosopher-king who has
perfected the art of dialectic orders the virtues within the state in harmony
with the virtues within the parts of the individual soul: for the rulers, wisdom;
for the soldiers, courage; for everyone, temperance and justice—temperance,
to ensure concord between rulers and ruled, and justice, to ensure the order
that results from "doing one's own business" (427d–34c).[63] Such an ideal
state, Julia Annas observes, is by its very definition a unity in which all citizens are "at one in finding harmony between the interests of the city as a
whole and their own interests as members of their own group."[64] Its sense of
justice, Eric A. Havelock maintains, is a "symbol of unchanging stability" that
can only be explained by Plato's conservative social background.[65] Such a
state does not admit nor does it require either a dialectic of question and
answer or a rhetoric of persuasion. Harvey Yunis explains: "Political discourse in the ideal *polis* appears to be a straightforward matter: the ruling
expert issues authoritative advice, all other members of the *polis* obey."[66] Thus
Socratic discussion, the two-way discussion to which both parties contribute,
gives way to "a discourse of command."[67]

In contemporary interpretations of Aristotle, Socrates is best known as
the originator of the use of inductive method in search of universal definitions that Aristotle refines as a method of argument and persuasion in his
dialectic and in his rhetoric.[68] Contemporary interpreters take as their point
of departure Aristotle's assertion in the *Metaphysics* that Socrates may fairly
be credited with two innovations, "inductive reasoning and general definition," both of which "are associated with the starting-point of scientific
knowledge" (1078b).[69] They also note Aristotle's observation that Socrates
concerned himself with the moral virtues only but that he did not, like the
later idealists, posit a separate existence for either universals or definitions.
They conclude, therefore, that Socratic reasoning was dialectical and rhetorical, not scientific, and observe its limitations as either philosophy or science.
J. D. G. Evans claims that Socratic reasoning was dialectical, in Aristotle's
assessment, because it was concerned with both definition, the cornerstone
of syllogistic reasoning, and induction and thus introduced the two basic
forms of dialectical argument, syllogism and induction.[70] However, even as

dialectic, Socratic reasoning was inadequate because it supposed that dialectical reasoning was *necessarily* concerned with definitions, a supposition that led Plato to posit definitions of universals as separately existing Forms.[71] W. K. C. Guthrie notes that Socratic reasoning was also rhetorical since, according to Aristotle, the use of illustrative examples resembles induction.[72] Following Evans's argument, Socratic reasoning might also be considered rhetorical since it provides the cornerstone of syllogistic reasoning and since the rhetorical enthymeme resembles the syllogism.[73]

Aristotle includes Socratic reasoning in both his dialectic and his rhetoric. He explains the deficiency of the Socratic search for definitions in the *Topics*.[74] But he includes Socratic induction as a method of argument and persuasion in both the *Topics* and the *Rhetoric*.[75] The Socratic search for definitions is usually explained as a search for an answer to the question, "What is X?"—that is, a search for the real definition of a moral term.[76] Richard Robinson explains that the Socrates of the early dialogues apparently assumes that we can know nothing whatever about X until we know what X is and that we must answer this question before we attempt to answer any other questions about X.[77] Socrates' repeated failure to answer this question led the Plato of the later dialogues to posit an answer to the question in the form of Ideas or essences in general.[78] Aristotle objects to this answer, of course, but he also objects to the question itself. In the *Topics*, he claims that Socrates led Plato to get the wrong answer because he asked the wrong question. Instead of asking a "What is X?" question, such as, "What is man?" he should have asked, "Is 'the good' used in this or in that sense?"—a question that admits of affirmation or denial (158a). Aristotle does not object, however, to the dialectic of question and answer itself, and he includes a long section on questions and answers at the end of the *Topics* (155b–164b).

Socratic induction is sometimes explained as a form of reasoning from particulars to universals.[79] Robinson, however, explains it more broadly as a form of inference from one proposition or set of coordinate propositions to another proposition that is either superordinate (more universal) or coordinate to the first proposition or set of propositions.[80] In the *Topics*, Aristotle explains induction as "the progress from particulars to universals" and provides a characteristically Socratic example: "If the skilled pilot is the best pilot and the skilled charioteer the best charioteer, then, in general, the skilled man [i.e., person] is the best man in any particular sphere" (105a). Aristotle uses the example to illustrate the progress from particulars to a universal, but it can also be explained as an inference from a set of coordinate propositions (the skilled pilot is the best pilot; the skilled charioteer is the best charioteer) to a superordinate proposition (the skilled person is the best person). In a similar example from the *Protagoras*, Socrates cites particular instances that show that people who have knowledge, such as divers, horsemen, and bucklers, are more bold than those who do not, and he concludes that those who are wisest are most bold and being most bold are most courageous (349e–50c).[81] C. C. W. Taylor maintains that the shift in this argument from knowledge *(epistēmē)* to wisdom *(sophia)* is only apparently equivocal since both terms clearly refer to knowledge as technical expertise.[82] Norman Gulley, however, observes that Socrates uses these same examples in both the *Laches* and the *Protagoras* to raise the question of what kind of knowledge counts as courage and concludes in both instances that the kind of knowledge that counts is not knowledge as professional skill or technical expertise but the knowledge of good and evil.[83] Conley points out that these shifts in meaning are common in the early dialogues and, while frequently fallacious, are nonetheless compelling.[84] In the *Rhetoric,* Aristotle explains induction as an illustrative example, citing an instance of example by comparison drawn directly from Socrates: "if someone were to say that officials should not be chosen by lot (for that would be as if someone chose athletes randomly—not those able to contest, but those on whom the lot fell); or [as if] choosing by lot any one of the sailors to act as pilot rather than the one who knew how" (1393b). The example—which Robinson would explain as an inference from a set of coordinate propositions (about the athlete and the sailor) to another coordinate proposition (about the magistrate)—has no scientific validity, of course, but it may nonetheless have persuasive force.

These developments in Aristotle's dialectic and rhetoric notwithstanding, Socratic reasoning may nonetheless appear to provide the foundation for scientific inquiry since it is "associated with the starting-point of scientific knowledge" (*Metaphysics* 1078b). As Aristotle indicates in the *Topics,* dialectic is able to raise difficulties on either side of an issue and thus to determine the truth or falsity of particular points of interest to each particular science (101a). Evans argues that dialectic is external though not irrelevant to the sciences since its scope is not restricted to any particular area of study and since it, not the particular sciences, is concerned with induction.[85] Nonetheless, the link between Socratic reasoning and Aristotle's dialectic and rhetoric and between Aristotle's dialectic and the particular sciences is sufficiently clear in Aristotle's assessment. Contemporary critics have therefore not surprisingly found Socratic reasoning wanting, on the one hand, because it apparently leads to the quest for a rationally ordered, unitary truth that now seems fruitless and misguided and, on the other hand, because it succeeds in its quest only by practicing a devious logic that seems more like *mere rhetoric* than either philosophy or science. J. Hillis Miller, for example, writes of "Socratic, theoretical, or canny critics," who are likely to speak of themselves as scientists and who are "lulled by the promise of a rational ordering of literary study on the basis of solid advances in scientific knowledge about language."[86] Victor J. Vitanza writes of a Socrates who seeks unity and sameness and who only "counted to *one.*"[87] Livio Rossetti cites Socratic strategies of concealment, insinuation, persuasive definitions, examples, and analogies and compares the

Socratic "rhetorical machinery" to "successful advertising, propaganda, and other even more fearful manipulations of opinion."[88] James J. Sosnoski explains Socratic dialectic as a means of drawing students out and leading them to accept the same hegemonic cultural values that many teachers deplore, adding simply "Socrates Begone!" from the rhetoric and composition classroom.[89] Such comments can best be explained, and perhaps only explained, by the historical development of Socratic thought from the dialectical/dialogical method of the early dialogues to the dialectical rhetoric of the later Plato and to the dialectic and rhetoric of Aristotle.

THE BRITISH EMPIRICAL TRADITION: LOGIC AND SOCRATIC NEGATIVE DIALECTIC

Within the tradition of nineteenth-century British empirical thought, Socrates is both heir to the philosophical tradition that he is said to have originated and practitioner of a negative dialectic that is said to be uniquely his own. Socrates, like the sophists and in some of the same writings, was subject to widespread revival and reinterpretation in the nineteenth century, the reinterpretations usually reflecting the views of the interpreter.[90] For G. W. F. Hegel, Socrates represented the morality of the critically reflective individual in a clash with the collective moral sense of the whole people, a tragic but necessary stage in a dialectical process that leads to a higher unity in which individuality is constituted by its role in the collective.[91] For Søren Kierkegaard, Socrates represented the morality of a subjective inward truth and a subjective faith in God, expressed as irony, "the very incitement of subjectivity."[92] For Friedrich Nietzsche, Socrates was the subject of ambivalence, most memorably, however, the representative of scientific rationalism, a profound delusion destructive of art and culture (and the inspiration for Miller's remark cited in this chapter).[93] For George Grote and John Stuart Mill, Socrates was the originator of the Platonic/Aristotelian logic of induction that produces unanimity of truth and opinion and practitioner of a negative dialectic that enables each of us to contest that truth.[94]

In his *History of Greece,* Grote credits Socrates as the originator of the logic of Plato, Aristotle, and Mill and as the practitioner of a negative dialectic that was inseparable from his logic of definition and induction.[95] According to Grote, the logic initiated by Socrates was improved by Plato, developed as a comprehensive system of logic by Aristotle, and enlarged and revised by Mill "commensurate with the vast increase of knowledge and extension of positive method belonging to the present day" (234). This logic bound together "the dialectic method and the logical distribution of particulars into species and genera" (236). The dialectic initiated a discussion in search of a definition of a generic term and tested the definition by bringing it into collision with various particulars, usually revealing the generic term to be merely nominal and fallacious. This same dialectic was also an "indirect and negative proceeding" by which Socrates challenged other people's most confidently held convictions, leading them into self-contradiction and inconsistency while disclaiming any positive knowledge of his own (248). Even as a negative dialectic, however, it served the positive purpose of clearing the mind of "its mist of fancied knowledge" and "laying bare the real ignorance," thus introducing the possibility of the birth of positive knowledge (252).

Mill admired Grote's portrait of Socrates and probably drew upon it for the development of his own view of the relationship between logic and Socratic negative dialectic.[96] In his *Logic* and "On Liberty," he shows how the logic of induction builds positive knowledge on the foundation of our collective human experience and how the Socratic negative dialectic serves as a check on human experience and as an assurance of our right to contest that experience.[97] In the *Logic,* he explains deduction as a process of reasoning from a generalization to particulars, for example, from "All men are mortal" to "Socrates is a man," to "Socrates is mortal" (7:184).[98] He claims that such reasoning proves nothing since we cannot know the general principle, "All men are mortal," unless we already know the conclusion, "Socrates is mortal," and he concludes that "no reasoning from generals to particulars can, as such, prove anything: since from a general principle we cannot infer any particulars, but those which the principle itself assumes as known" (7:184). Mill explains induction as a process of reasoning from particulars to a generalization, that is, "the process by which we conclude that what is true of certain individuals of a class is true of the whole class" (7:288).[99] He claims that this process is valid: "Whenever the evidence which we derive from observation of known cases justifies us in drawing an inference respecting even one unknown case, we should on the same evidence be justified in drawing a similar inference with respect to a whole class of cases" (7:284).

Though Mill believes that this process is valid, he also recognizes that it presents a fundamental problem (often called *Hume's problem,* after the philosopher David Hume).[100] If it is true, he observes, that we can reason from a set of particulars (white swans) to a generalization (all swans are white), it is also true that we cannot do so with any certainty in the validity of the generalization since we cannot be certain that the next particular that we encounter (it might be a black swan) will resemble, in relevant respects, the set of particulars upon which we have based the generalization. Granted that we can reason from a set of particulars to a generalization on the assumption of uniformity in the course of nature, we nonetheless encounter difficulty with respect to the generalization: "The universe, so far as known to us, is so constituted, that whatever is true in any one case, is true in all cases of a certain description; the only difficulty is, to find what description" (7:306). Moreover, we encounter a similar difficulty with respect to the

assumption of uniformity in the course of nature since "this large generalization" is "itself an instance of induction" and "far from being the first
induction we make . . . is one of the last" and is therefore subject to the same
difficulty as all the others (7:307).

Given this problem in inductive reasoning, Mill sets in place of the generalization our own experience. He explains that the assumption of uniformity
in the course of nature does not hold in every instance, that nature varies, so
that while "we have always a propensity to generalize from unvarying experience," we have to be sure that if there are instances contrary to our experience, we can know them, and "this assurance, in the great majority of cases,
we cannot have, or can have only in a very moderate degree" (7:312). Never-
theless, he believes that our experience is genuine, even when it is insufficient
to establish a generalization: "That all swans are white, cannot have been a
good induction, since the conclusion has turned out erroneous. The experience, however, on which the conclusion rested, was genuine" (7:313). Mill
concludes that since we can reason from particulars (e.g., white swans) to our
experience (Swans are usually white or insofar as we have experience are
white) with only a moderate degree of assurance, we cannot reason from our
experience to other particulars (other white swans) with absolute certainty. He
nonetheless believes that we can increase our assurance that our reasoning is
valid by trusting our collective human experience and by practicing the
Socratic negative dialectic as a test of that experience.

In the *Logic,* he explains that we can increase our assurance if we trust
our collective human experience. He observes that our process of reasoning
from particulars to our experience depends not only upon our immediate
and limited experience (e.g., with white swans) but also upon our broader
experience (e.g., with the colors of animals). Why, he asks, do we not reject
the assertion that there are black swans though we would surely reject the
assertion that there are men who wear their heads beneath their shoulders?
He answers that we accept the former but reject the latter because our experience of uniformity in the course of nature varies, because that experience
tells us that "there is less constancy in the colours of animals, than in the
general structure of their anatomy" (7:319).[101] And what assurance can we
have that our reasoning, based upon this broader experience, is valid? Mill
explains that experience is its own test, "that we need experience to inform
us, in what degree, and in what cases, or sorts of cases, experience is to be
relied on" (7:319). He therefore claims that our own limited experience
must be based upon our collective human experience, upon "a general
knowledge of the prevalent character of the uniformities existing throughout nature," so that the necessary and indispensable foundation of "a scientific formula of induction" must be "a survey of the inductions . . . conducted in unscientific practice" (7:319–20). On the basis of this collective
experience, we can apparently reason with greater assurance about the vari-

ety of colors in animals or the structure of their anatomy, for example, than we can about the white swans.

In his essay "On Liberty," Mill explains that we can further increase our assurance that our reasoning is valid if we practice the Socratic negative dialectic as a test of our collective experience. Whereas in the *Logic* he had allowed that experience is its own test, he now maintains that experience alone is incorrigible but that it can be corrected through public discussion. People are capable of correcting their mistakes, he claims, by discussion and experience: "Not by experience alone. There must be discussion, to show how experience is to be interpreted. Wrong opinions and practices gradually yield to fact and argument: but facts and arguments, to produce any effect on the mind, must be brought before it" (231). He still maintains the validity of our collective human experience and claims that our well-being "may almost be measured by the number and gravity of the truths which have reached the point of being uncontested" (250). However, he also maintains that this collective experience must be tested and corrected continuously and that it can be tested and corrected only if we possess some method of ensuring its "intelligent and living apprehension" (251). He claims that the Socratic negative dialectic is just such a method:

> The Socratic dialectics, so magnificently exemplified in the dialogues of Plato, were a contrivance of this description. They were essentially a negative discussion of the great questions of philosophy and life, directed with consummate skill to the purpose of convincing any one who had merely adopted the commonplaces of received opinion, that he did not understand the subject—that he as yet attached no definite meaning to the doctrines he professed; in order that, becoming aware of his ignorance, he might be put in the way to attain a stable belief, resting on a clear apprehension both of the meaning of doctrines and of their evidence. (251)

This method of public discussion is so important that where it cannot be found to exist it must be imagined: "if opponents of all important truths do not exist, it is indispensable to imagine them, and supply them with the strongest arguments which the most skilful devil's advocate can conjure up" (245).

Mill's attempt to explain induction by joining our collective human experience to the Socratic negative dialectic revives the dialectical/dialogical method of the early Socratic dialogues. Nonetheless, his linking of the inductive and dialectical/dialogical methods creates a tension between the progress toward a rational and unified truth, on the one hand, and the openness of dialectic or dialogue, on the other. Post-colonial critic Homi K. Bhabha explores this tension as it is expressed in Mill's concept of public discussion.[102] Bhabha finds in this concept both a practice of public rhetoric as dialogue and a limitation of this practice by the rationality of the collective mind and by Britain's unified colonial vision. According to Bhabha, Mill creates "a form of *public rhetoric* able to represent different and opposing political 'contents' not as a priori preconstituted principles but as a dialogical discursive exchange."[103] This public rhetoric presumes that knowledge can only become political through such an exchange: "dissensus, alterity and otherness are the discursive conditions for the circulation and recognition of a politicized subject and a public 'truth.'"[104] Nonetheless, Mill's concept of a public rhetoric is limited in practice because it depends upon the rationality of "the 'whole truth'" and "the unreal neutral space of the Third Person . . . who witnesses the debate from an 'epistemological distance' and draws a reasonable conclusion," even as it suggests something "much more dialogical: the realization of the political idea at the ambivalent point of textual address, its emergence through a form of political projection."[105] Mill's public rhetoric is also limited in practice by Britain's unified colonial vision, a vision that Mill seems to have shared. In his work as an examiner of correspondence for the East India Company, Mill envisioned "a perfect system of recordation," a complete written record of all executive orders and acts performed in India, designed as "a strategy for policing the culturally and racially differentiated colonial space," as "a strategy of colonialist regulation," and as "a colonial substitute for democratic 'public discussion.'"[106]

The Dialogical Tradition: Testing, Contesting, and Creating Ideas

In his striking portrait in *The Post Card,* Jacques Derrida envisions a Socrates who writes and who therefore disrupts the "historical teleology" by which a letter (or a postcard) always arrives at its destination and the "common sense of the chronology" according to which Socrates always says only what Plato wants him to say.[107] Derrida describes a postcard that depicts Socrates seated and writing as Plato stands behind him apparently dictating what Socrates writes.[108] Derrida calls this Plato "authoritarian, masterly, imperious," perhaps even "wicked," because he seeks "to kill," "to eliminate," and "to neutralize" Socrates by putting his own words into Socrates' mouth and, as the postcard suggests, into his pen as well.[109] Derrida's portrait of Socrates writing suggests the possibility of revisioning the Socrates of the early dialogues as a Socrates who says (or writes) what he, not Plato, wants to say. Studies of the early dialogues have sought to recapture this Socrates as the practitioner of an art of dialogue that was not yet inextricably intertwined with the rhetorical and philosophical traditions that extend from Plato and Aristotle through George Grote and John Stuart Mill even to the present time. These studies distinguish the earlier from the middle and later dialogues and situate them in relationship to their cultural and historical setting.[110] Bakhtin's reading of the Socratic dialogue suggests how these dialogues might be rehistoricized, how Socrates might be reconfigured as a Socrates who examines and tests ideas and people but does not seek to persuade: testing his own and others' ideas in early dialogues such as the *Laches,* collectively creating ideas with others in the *Protagoras,* and testing and also contesting the ideas of others in the *Gorgias.*

In contrast to the middle and later dialogues, the early dialogues seem to be exclusively ethical, aporetic or inconclusive, and exhortative rather than persuasive. Gregory Vlastos finds ten points of difference between the early and the middle dialogues.[111] Most importantly, the Socrates of the early dialogues is concerned with ethical or moral issues and, "seeking knowledge elenctically, keeps avowing that he has none"; the Socrates of the middle dialogues is concerned with a whole range of philosophical issues, has "a grandiose metaphysical theory of 'separately existing' Forms" and "a complex, tripartite model of the soul," and "seeks demonstrative knowledge and is confident that he finds it."[112] Terry Penner similarly characterizes the early dialogues as "aporetic and without positive results," "amusing, bantering, extroverted, optimistic, and mischievous in tone," "almost exclusively ethical in content," and lacking any interest in the question of the immortality of the soul, which is so passionately embraced in later dialogues.[113] Thomas C. Brickhouse and Nicolas D. Smith explain Socrates' ethical concern, quite simply, as a concern with living rather than knowing: "Socrates does not say that untested propositions are not worth believing or that unexamined beliefs are not worth holding; he says that the unexamined *life* is not worth living."[114]

Situated in its cultural and historical setting, the ethical problem of the early dialogues seems to emerge from the conflict between competing ideals of virtuous living, more specifically, the conflict between self-regarding and other-regarding virtue, between the courage and skill required in a warrior culture and the justice and temperance required in a civil society.[115] This problem is frequently approached as a question about the relationship of the virtues: whether the individual virtues are related as part to whole, as part to part, or as one with the whole, as an identity or unity.[116] But the question, and the underlying ethical problem, remains open and unanswered, at least in the early dialogues. Irwin characterizes the problem broadly as a conflict between self-regarding and other-regarding virtue.[117] Arthur W. H. Adkins describes it as a conflict between the bravery, skill, and success of the warrior and the "quiet virtues" of justice and temperance.[118] He explains that the conduct of both the assembly and the law courts within Athens and the empire beyond its walls required good counsel or sound judgment *(euboulia),* directed toward success in politics in the same way that courage and skill were directed toward success in battle.[119] Such a concept of virtue *(aretē),* he argues, "requires courage, initiative, and the willingness to take risks to achieve a desired end . . . and hence is unlikely to be conducive to peace and justice between states or within the state."[120] The concept justified Athens' rule over its empire but also led to the dissolution of its democracy and its empire and the rule of the Thirty Tyrants, for which "the Athenian democracy paid in blood."[121]

This ethical problem surfaces in the ordinary uses of language, for example, in the use of the same term to refer to refer to either professional skill or knowledge *(epistēmē)* and wisdom *(sophia).*[122] Derrida illustrates the problem in his explication of the *Phaedrus* as "a chain of significations."[123] According to Derrida, Plato's reference to writing as *pharmakon* conveys the double meaning of both *remedy* and *poison* and suggests other meanings as well through its etymological link to Socrates, "he who does not write," he who is both *pharmakeus* (a magician or sorcerer) and *pharmakos* (magician or poisoner and also scapegoat).[124] Unlike Plato, however, who sought to fix meanings in writing (paradoxically protesting as he did so), the Socrates of the early dialogues plays upon these multiple meanings to effect a cultural transformation, leading others to understand true courage as courage in a just cause, true knowledge as the knowledge of good and evil.

Socrates, however, approaches the problem by way of exhortation rather than persuasion. That is, he seeks rather to lead others to their own solution to the problem, and simultaneously to confirm his own tentative solution to the problem, than to persuade others to accept a conclusion that he has previously determined to be true. Socrates' exhortative approach is usually referred to as the *elenchos* (refutation or cross-examination), though Socrates does not claim to have a method as such.[125] Irwin explains the *elenchos* as the process by which Socrates leads others into self-contradiction.[126] Socrates typically asks a question about the virtues, either a "What is X?" question about a particular virtue or some other question. The other person in the discussion responds with a proposition, Socrates asks further questions, and the other responds with additional propositions. Socrates then shows the other person that these additional propositions lead to a proposition that directly contradicts the original proposition, leaving the other in a state of aporia, uncertain which proposition to accept or reject. Irwin claims that the *elenchos* is exhortative *and* persuasive.[127] Penner maintains, however, that Socrates construes "rhetoric" as teaching rather than persuasion and explains teaching as bringing people to understand, for themselves, but with the help of Socratic questioning, what is and is not the case.[128] Brickhouse and Smith claim that Socrates exhorts people "to *do the right thing*," that he persuades them, perhaps, but only in the sense that he exhorts them to act as they, not as he, believes they should act.[129]

Bakhtin's reading of the Socratic dialogue suggests how the Socrates of the early dialogues might be recaptured as a Socrates who exhorts but does not seek to persuade.[130] Bakhtin claims that the Socratic dialogue is a testing not only of ideas but also of the people who represent them. Brickhouse and Smith explain that Socrates is often said to practice the "method of *elenchos*" but that he himself claims only that he "examines," "inquires," "investigates," "searches," and "questions."[131] Moreover, he examines not ideas but people: "Socrates does not say that he examines what people say or even what they believe; he says he examines *people,* . . . and as we have said, by this he means examining the ways in which they live."[132] He therefore insists that others say what they really mean, for only in this way can he be certain "that he is really testing an aspect of how they think they should live."[133] This testing of ideas and especially of people is evident in the *Laches,* in Socrates' testing of Laches and Nicias and in Plato the author's allusions to the historical persons, which remind us that people's ideas can and do shape their lives.

Bakhtin also describes the Socratic dialogue as a creating of ideas between people with the help of the Socratic midwife. Myles F. Burnyeat claims that the concept of Socrates as the midwife of ideas should be attributed to the later Plato and not to the historic Socrates.[134] He suggests that the Socrates of the early dialogues tests but does not create ideas and that the later Plato creates ideas not in interaction with others but in isolation, in a creative interaction between (his own) reason and inspiration.[135] Bakhtin, however, finds the Socratic midwife in the early dialogues in the dialogic interaction between people by which truth is born. This creating of ideas between people is evident in the *Protagoras,* which is usually read from the perspective of either Protagoras or Socrates, not both, but which seems more than any of the other early dialogues to illustrate Bakhtin's concept of dialogue as a creative interaction between people, for both Protagoras and Socrates contribute substantively to the new ideas in the dialogue, in particular the new idea that courage is inseparable from the other virtues, that the virtues are therefore one—a unity.

Finally, Bakhtin describes the Socratic dialogue as a carnivalesque debate between opposing points of view, with a ritualistic crownings and decrownings of opponents. I call this Socratic form of debate a *contesting* of ideas to capture the double meaning of the Socratic debate as both a mutual testing of oneself and others and a contesting or challenging of others' ideas and their lives. Brickhouse and Smith explain that Socrates' testing of ideas and people is a mutual testing not only of others but also of himself: Socrates claims that he has been commanded by the god to examine himself as well as others; he claims that the unexamined life is not worth living; and, since he rarely submits to questioning himself, "it must be that in the process of examining others Socrates regards himself as examining his own life, too."[136] Such a mutual testing of ideas provides the only claim to knowledge that Socrates can have: since neither he nor anyone else knows the real definitions of things, he cannot claim to have any knowledge of his own; since, however, he subjects his beliefs to repeated testing, he can claim to have that limited human knowledge supported by the "inductive evidence" of "previous elenctic examinations."[137] This mutual testing of ideas and people is evident in the *Laches* and also appears in the *Gorgias* in Socrates' testing of his own belief that courage is inseparable from the other virtues and in his willingness to submit his belief and indeed his life to the ultimate test of divine judgment, in what Bakhtin calls a *dialogue on the threshold*. The contesting or challenging of others' ideas and their lives and their ritualistic crowning/decrowning is evident in the *Gorgias,* in Socrates' successive refutations and humiliations of Gorgias, Polus, and Callicles.

3

Mikhail M. Bakhtin, Dialogical Rhetoric, and the Socratic Dialogue

Mikhail M. Bakhtin envisions a Socrates quite different from the Socrates passed down to us in the Western philosophical and rhetorical traditions. Bakhtin's Socrates is not a rhetor but a respondent, not an answerer but a questioner. As sketched in "Epic and Novel" and in *Problems of Dostoevsky's Poetics,* Bakhtin's Socrates is the practitioner of anacrisis and syncrisis, the drawing forth and juxtaposing of different ideas and different persons not for the purpose of persuading but for the purposes of testing, contesting, and creating ideas.[1] Bakhtin often seems to be openly hostile to rhetoric, but his objections are directed not so much toward the rhetorical genres themselves, which Bakhtin claims are intensely dialogized, but toward the formal analysis of these genres in linguistics, in the philosophy of language, and in rhetoric.[2] Bakhtin recognizes the possibility of representing internally persuasive discourse in the image of speaking persons and thereby subjecting this discourse to questioning, exposing its weaknesses, testing its boundaries, even experiencing it physically, but he believes that this possibility is not reducible to formal analysis.[3] Nonetheless, Bakhtin's concept of dialogue as a change— and as an exchange—of speaking subjects helps to explain how the rhetorical genres might be dialogized, that is, how they might recapture the multiplicity of voices that Bakhtin believes is always inherent in them.[4] His reading of the Socratic dialogue suggests not only how rhetoric might be reconceived as dialogue but also why a dialogized or dialogical rhetoric is so important for the rhetorical tradition.

Bakhtin's concept of dialogue as an exchange of utterances—an exchange between speaking subjects—is not simply an exchange of voices, a kind of turn-taking, but a viewing of each voice from the perspective of the other, as illustrated by his concepts of *heteroglossia* and *dialogized heteroglossia*.[5] His critique of the rhetorical genres is that they appear—in formal analysis—as a mere parceling out of voices, not as a rich double-voicedness, achieved through a reaccentuation of past voices and an anticipation of future voices.[6] His reading of the Socratic dialogue suggests how such a double-voicedness might be recaptured and restored to the rhetorical tradition.[7] This reading is sketchy in itself but is enriched by the broader context of Bakhtin's work, by his notion of polyphony as both a creating and testing of ideas, for example, and by his notion of carnival as a contesting of ideas that is also a process of social transformation and creative renewal.[8] It is enriched, too, by Bakhtin's insistence that we situate texts contextually and extratextually, that is, within the context of other texts and within the context of their historical and cultural context.[9] Reading the Socratic dialogues in this way shows us how the Socrates of the early dialogues tests ill-defined and conflicting ideas about the virtues— especially ideas about the relationship of courage to the other virtues; how he works with others to create ideas—such as the new idea of the unity of courage with the other virtues; and how he contests ideas that he believes are simply wrong—such as the Periclean ideal of an unjust empire and the unjust rhetoric that sustains it. Such a reading of the Socratic dialogue thus shows us not only how rhetoric might be reconstituted as an exchange between speaking subjects but also why such an exchange is so important for the rhetorical genres— because it asks rhetors, as it asks all of us, to render themselves accountable for what they think and say and do.

BAKHTIN'S LIFE AND WORKS

Mikhail Bakhtin lived in tumultuous times.[10] He grew up in bustling Russian border towns, reached adulthood on the eve of the revolutions of 1917, and lived through the Bolshevik revolution and the growing oppression that reached its peak under Stalin in the 1930s.[11] Born in Orel, south of Moscow, in 1895, Bakhtin grew up in Vilnius and Odessa, cosmopolitan border towns that offered an unusually heterogeneous mix of disparate languages and cultures. He studied classics and philology at St. Petersburg University, then moved to the country, first to Nevel and then to Vitebsk, in the wake of the revolutions. There he maintained an association with other intellectuals, the so-called Bakhtin circle, among them Valentin Voloshinov and Pavel Medvedev. Bakhtin shared with members of this circle a variety of interests, most especially Immanuel Kant and contemporary German philosophy and the new physics of Max Planck, Albert Einstein, and Niels Bohr. During this period, he completed several of his early works on ethics and aesthetics, including "Author and Hero in Aesthetic Activity" and *Toward a Philosophy of the Act.*[12] From 1924 to 1929, Bakhtin lived in Leningrad, supported by his wife, Elena Alexandrovna, while unemployed due to suspicions arising from his religious activities and to a bone disease, which necessitated the amputation of his right leg in 1938. During the late 1920s, he wrote a book on Fyodor Dostoevsky, originally titled *Problems of Dostoevsky's Creative Art,* published in 1929.[13] He may or may not have written several books published in others' names but sometimes attributed to him, including Voloshinov's *Freudianism* and *Marxism and the Philosophy of Language* and Medvedev's *Formal Method in Literary Scholarship.*[14] Bakhtin was arrested in 1929, probably as a result of his religious activities, and exiled in Kazakhstan, where he stayed until 1936, when he accepted a professorship at the Mordovian Pedagogical Institute in Saransk. During the 1930s and early 1940s, he completed some of his most important studies of the novel, including "Epic and Novel" and "Discourse in the Novel," and he also completed his major work on François Rabelais, submitted as his doctoral dissertation to the Gorky Institute of World Literature in Moscow in 1941 (he was later awarded the lower degree of Candidate). Forced to move from Saransk to Savelovo to escape the Great Purge of 1937, Bakhtin returned after the Second World War, his relative obscurity during the Stalinist oppression perhaps saving his life. A successful teacher in Saransk during the 1950s, Bakhtin was discovered in the early 1960s by a group of Moscow graduate students who had read his Dostoevsky book. He published a second edition of the book, *Problems of Dostoevsky's Poetics,* in 1963, and the Rabelais book, *Rabelais and His World,* in 1965. Two collections of Bakhtin's essays were published soon after his death in 1975: *Questions of Literature and Aesthetics,* in 1975 (including several essays published in English in *The Dialogic Imagination,* in 1981); and *Aesthetics of Verbal Creativity,* in 1979 (including several essays published in English in *Speech Genres and Other Late Essays,* in 1986).[15] Bakhtin's work spread throughout the West in the 1980s and was the subject of vigorous debate and reassessment in Russia in the 1990s.[16]

Bakhtin's interests in his early years shaped his thinking throughout his career. His experience in Vilnius and Odessa exposed him to a rich and complex mix of different language groups, cultures, and classes, illustrative of the mix of languages that he would later call *heteroglossia.*[17] His interest in recent developments in physics seems to have shaped his understanding of dialogism.[18] From Einstein's demonstration that "one body's motion has meaning only in relation to another body," he apparently inferred that all meaning is relational, the result of a *"dialogue"* between and among bodies—physical, political, and conceptual.[19] His religious activities as an intellectual from the orthodox tradition seem to have offered him an alternative to the Bolshevik interpretation of communism, something akin to his notions of heteroglossia or polyphony translated into social terms.[20] Inspired by the communal ideal of the early church, he envisioned a new social order characterized by "the concept of *sobornost'*, 'togetherness' or 'true sense of community,'" and a model of intellectual activity as "*sobornoe* or 'joint' creativity."[21] Influenced by Stoicist and Johannine traditions of the embodied word but turning them on their head, he viewed language as a cacophony of voices or heteroglossia that gives rise to the complex unity of the polyphonic novel.[22] Finally, Bakhtin's response to the Stalinist authoritarian rule and the Stalinist rhetoric—though recently the subject of considerable controversy—seems to have inspired a strong opposition to both official culture and monologic rhetoric.[23] Apparently as a reaction to the Stalinist hierarchization and centralization of institutions, the increasing state control and oppression, Bakhtin offered his vision of carnival, with its opposition to the official culture of church and state and its celebration of folk culture and folk laughter as the expression of freedom and "joyful relativity."[24] Apparently in opposition to the Stalinist rhetoric, with its homogenization of language and its authoritarian pronouncements, Bakhtin expressed his hostility toward monologue and his enthusiasm for openness and incompleteness, becoming rather than being, the created rather than the given, the unfinished rather than the finished.[25] Quite explicitly in opposition to monologic rhetoric generally, he offered his own concept of dialogue and his revisioning of the rhetorical tradition as Socratic dialogue.

DIALOGICAL RHETORIC AS AN
EXCHANGE OF UTTERANCES

Bakhtin's comments on rhetoric have provoked considerable controversy and little agreement about their meaning and implications for the study of rhetoric. As I indicated in chapter 1, some readers find in Bakhtin a direct and forceful challenge that holds promise of a fundamental rethinking of the rhetorical tradition.[26] Others perceive in Bakhtin an equally forceful opposition and a failure to grasp what is best and most worthy of cultivation in the rhetorical tradition.[27] I cannot hope to resolve these differences, but I believe that Gary Saul Morson, Caryl Emerson, and Don H. Bialostosky are most nearly correct when they argue that Bakhtin objects not so much to rhetoric as to the formal analysis of rhetoric as it was practiced in his time.[28] To say as much, however, is not merely to condemn formal analysis and to accept whatever kind of analysis we ourselves wish to practice but rather to attempt to understand what kind of rhetoric Bakhtin seeks to recapture when he rejects formal analysis. Situated in the context of "Discourse in the Novel," Bakhtin's comments about rhetoric suggest that he seeks not to reject but to dialogize rhetoric by recapturing the multiplicity of voices that he believes is always inherent in it, both the voices of listeners and the voices of prior speaking persons, voices that answer or otherwise respond to rhetorical discourse and voices that rhetorical discourse itself transmits and so also inevitably reaccentuates (267–69, 279–81, 336–55). Situated within the broader context of his work, these comments suggest that a dialogized rhetoric will be no mere diversity of voices but an exchange of utterances and a viewing of each of these utterances from the perspective of the others. Bakhtin's reading of the Socratic dialogue shows how such a dialogized rhetoric might be realized as a drawing forth and juxtaposing and thus a testing and contesting and creating of ideas. His concepts of polyphony and carnival show how Plato the author, too, helps—sometimes unwittingly—to create such a dialogized rhetoric by transmitting and reaccentuating in the written texts of the dialogues voices from the past that can still be heard in Socrates' time—the voices of Homer and Simonides, Thucydides and Pericles.

Bakhtin's comments on rhetoric sometimes seem to be strikingly forceful and bitter. Bakhtin asserts, for example: "In rhetoric there is the unconditionally innocent and the unconditionally guilty; there is complete victory and destruction of the opponent. In dialogue the destruction of the opponent also destroys that very dialogic sphere where the word lives."[29] Some of his most important and controversial comments about rhetoric appear, however, as a critique of rhetorical study in the fields of linguistics, the philosophy of language, and rhetoric, not as a critique of the rhetorical genres themselves. In "Discourse in the Novel," Bakhtin claims that the rhetorical genres—he is referring specifically to the Aristotelian deliberative, forensic, and epideictic genres—are intensely dialogized forms, but he complains that these genres are treated in linguistics, the philosophy of language, and even in rhetoric as the object of mere formal, logical analysis (348, 353–54). The rhetorical genres, Bakhtin says, are dialogized in two senses: they are oriented toward the listeners whose voices answer or respond to them and toward the prior speaking persons whose voices they themselves transmit and reaccentuate. The orientation toward the listener is inescapable in living dialogue: "every word is directed toward an *answer* and cannot escape the profound influence of the answering word that it anticipates" (280). This orientation toward the listener is "the basic constitutive feature of rhetorical discourse," a part of its "very internal construction," and the orientation toward the answer is similarly "open, blatant and concrete" (280). Nonetheless, Bakhtin complains, linguists and philosophers of language have missed this fundamentally important aspect of rhetorical discourse, for they have concerned themselves with the "artificial, preconditioned status of the word, a word excised from dialogue and taken for the norm" (279). Thus, though they have taken an interest in rhetorical discourse, they have considered only "the compositional forms by which the listener is taken into account, . . . precisely those aspects that are deprived of any internal dialogism, that take the listener for a person who passively understands but not for one who actively answers and reacts" (280). Bakhtin thus objects not to rhetorical discourse as such but to the limited understanding of rhetorical discourse—and specifically the formalism—in linguistics and in the philosophy of language.

The orientation of the rhetorical genres toward prior speaking persons is equally obvious and equally problematic. The tendency to assimilate other persons' discourse, Bakhtin claims, is fundamentally important to a person's ideological becoming (342). Another person's discourse is merely *"authoritative discourse"* when it provides information, directions, rules, models, and the like; it becomes *"internally persuasive discourse"* when we assimilate it and thus make it the basis of our ideological relationship with the world, the basis of our behavior (342). Internally persuasive as opposed to externally authoritative discourse is affirmed through assimilation, but it remains active within us as it struggles with other internally persuasive discourses (345–46). This struggle among internally persuasive discourses is readily represented in the image of a speaking person and is especially obvious in the realms of ethical, legal, and, of course, rhetorical discourse (347–50). In ethical and legal discourse, however, this image of the speaking person is subordinate to the special interests of these disciplines (350). In rhetorical discourse, this image of the speaking person who assimilates, transmits, and reaccentuates another's discourse is fundamentally and indisputably important, for the rhetorical genres—judicial, political, and publicist—"possess the most varied forms for transmitting another's speech, and for the most part these are intensely dialogized forms" (353–54). In judicial rhetoric, for example, the speaker accuses or defends the person on trial and so relies upon this person's words, interprets them, polemicizes them, uses them to create potential (possible but never actually uttered) discourses, and so on (353). Nonetheless, in rhetorical discourse, the image of the speaking person is usually not very deep, for it is structured on a mere diversity of voices rather than on a genuine "double-voicedness," and in most cases "the double-voicedness of rhetoric is abstract and thus lends itself to formal, purely logical analysis" (354). Thus it misses the vivid transmission and reaccentuation of other persons' discourse inherent in the rhetorical genres themselves. Bakhtin rejects such formalist treatments of the rhetorical genres because, as Morson and Emerson point out, he seeks not to supplement one formalist approach with another—for example, linguistics with rhetoric or pragmatics—but to fundamentally reconceive the whole question of language as dialogue.[30]

Bakhtin's concept of language as dialogue helps to explain how rhetoric might be reconceived dialogically and how the Socratic dialogue, in particular, might be reconceived as a dialogical response to the rhetorical tradition. At its most fundamental level, language as dialogue is best captured in Bakhtin's notion of the utterance as a unit of speech communication marked by a change of speaking subjects and—equally—by an exchange between them.[31] In "The Problem of Speech Genres," Bakhtin claims that traditional linguistics regards language from the standpoint of the speaker "as if there were only *one* speaker who does not have any *necessary* relation to *other* participants in speech communication" (67). In contrast, Bakhtin argues, live speech—real speech—is inherently, actively responsive (68–69). Thus, whereas traditional linguistics regards the *sentence*—and its component parts: phrases, words, and syllables—as the fundamental unit of analysis, Bakhtin maintains that the real unit of speech communication is the *utterance* (both oral and written), which is signaled not by any formal markers but by the change of speaking subjects (62–63, 70–71). Unlike the sentence, this unit of speech communication does not stand in isolation but in a necessary relation to other units of speech communication, as part of an ongoing exchange between them: "One does not exchange sentences any more than one exchanges words . . . or phrases. One exchanges utterances that are constructed from language units: words, phrases, and sentences" (75). Speech is thus inherently dialogic since it depends upon "others' active responsive understanding" and indeed their actual response to one's own utterance (71–72). Bakhtin's notion of the utterance has profound implications for rhetorical studies since it fundamentally alters the relationship between speaker and listener, writer and reader. As Thomas Kent observes, traditional theories of language emphasize the intentional role of the speaker or writer and deemphasize or even ignore the role of the other person in the communicative interaction, the listener's or reader's "responsive and interactive stance toward the speaker/text."[32] Bakhtin's notion of the utterance, in contrast, cannot be captured by formal analysis of the speaker, the speaker's intention, or the speaker's text and can only be captured (if it can be captured at all) in the give-and-take of dialogic interaction.[33]

Bakhtin explains, moreover, that language as dialogue is not only a change of speaking subjects or an exchange of utterances between them but also an active viewing of each utterance from the perspective of the other. Language as a change or exchange of utterances would be a mere cacophony of voices, a complex and diffuse mix of languages, which Bakhtin sometimes calls *heteroglossia*.[34] As Morson and Emerson point out, however, Bakhtin never conceives heteroglossia to be a mere mix of languages and voices but a viewing of each from the perspective of the others and an interanimation of each by the others—a *dialogized heteroglossia*.[35] Even in his early work, Bakhtin had recognized the fundamental importance of the other for our own understanding of ourselves. In "Author and Hero," Bakhtin explains my experience of another person as a process of both empathy and detachment (22–27). I may experience another person's suffering, for example, by projecting myself into the other person, but I must also return to myself if I am to render this projection meaningful (25–26). Only by returning to myself am I able to see, for example, the clear blue sky that provides the background to the other's suffering (25). Emerson observes the radical difference, the experiential abyss, between self and other proclaimed in this work but adds that only such a radical difference can assure the absolute need that each of us has for the other.[36] Elsewhere, Bakhtin similarly explains our experience of other cultures as a process of both empathy and detachment. To understand another culture, he claims, we must enter as living beings into that culture and see the world through its eyes, but we must also return to our own place within our own culture, for only in this way can we see that other culture whole: "our real exterior can be seen and understood only by other people, because they are located outside us in space and because they are *others*."[37] Such a dialogic encounter between cultures results not in a mixing and merging of cultures, however, but in the mutual enrichment of each by the other. We need other cultures, as we need other people, Bakhtin tells us, to see what we cannot see for ourselves and thus to make ourselves whole.

Bakhtin brings this insistence upon our need for other persons and other cultures to his understanding of the utterance. In "Discourse in the Novel," he explains how the relationship of individual utterances gives rise to the complex mix of languages and cultures that he calls *heteroglossia* and *dialogized heteroglossia* (271–73). The individual utterance has life only in relationship to other utterances: "The living utterance, having taken meaning and shape at a particular historical moment in a socially specific environment, cannot fail to brush up against thousands of living dialogic threads, woven by socio-ideological consciousness around the given object of an utterance; it cannot fail to become an active participant in social dialogue" (276). This living utterance is a complex mixture of forces and tendencies, including both the centripetal forces that centralize and unify a language and the centrifugal forces that decentralize and disunify: "Every utterance participates in the 'unitary language' (in its centripetal forces and tendencies) and at the same time partakes of social and historical heteroglossia (the centrifugal, stratifying forces)" (272). This mixture of utterances is not a mere mixture, however, a mere cacophony of voices, but a viewing of each of the languages and cultures of heteroglossia from the perspective of the other—a dialogized heteroglossia.[38] Bakhtin invites us to imagine two conditions in the life of an illiterate peasant: an ideal condition in which the peasant lives in several linguistic and cultural systems—the language of prayer, of song, of labor and everyday life, and of the local official culture—moving from one to another automatically and unreflectively, and a subsequent condition in which "a critical interanimation of languages" begins to occur in the consciousness of the peasant (295–96). In this latter condition, the peasant begins to realize that these several languages and cultures are both connected and contradictory to each other and also internally variegated and is therefore forced to reflect upon and to choose an orientation toward them. In such a condition, the heteroglot world in which the peasant lives has become dialogized, as the peasant begins to view each language and each culture from the perspective of the others.

Bakhtin's notion of the utterance as a change—and as an exchange—of speaking subjects, broadened and enriched by his concepts of heteroglossia and dialogized heterglossia, suggests that he might attempt to dialogize the rhetorical tradition by subjecting the rhetor to the active responsive understandings of others. His reading of the Socratic dialogue shows that he approaches this task by rereading the Socratic dialogue as an active responsive understanding that draws forth and juxtaposes and thereby tests and contests and creates ideas.

BAKHTIN AND THE SOCRATIC DIALOGUE

Bakhtin's reading of the Socratic dialogue appears in the context of his attempt to trace the lineage of Dostoevsky's polyphonic novel and the novelistic spirit generally in "Epic and Novel" (24–26) and in *Problems of Dostoevsky's Poetics* (106–37). But his reading of the Socratic dialogue is also a response and an alternative to what Bakhtin perceives to be the dogmatism and one-sided seriousness of the rhetorical tradition. In *Problems of Dostoevsky's Poetics,* Bakhtin traces the lineage of the polyphonic novel from its origin in the serio-comical genres, which include, in addition to the Socratic dialogue, the mimes of Sophron, symposium and memoir literature, pamphlets, bucolic poetry, and the Menippean satire (106–9).[39] These genres have their roots in oral folk-carnival genres and are characterized by a carnival sense of the world and by what Bakhtin frequently refers to as an atmosphere of joyful relativity. Bakhtin finds in these genres an alternative to the dogmatism and one-sided seriousness of the rhetorical tradition. He insists that the Socratic dialogue is not a rhetorical genre but a carnivalistic genre, like the other serio-comical genres in its carnival atmosphere but perhaps more serious than comical in its concern with the dialogic nature of truth and of human thinking about the truth (109–12, 132–33).[40] Although he admits that the serio-comical genres, including the Socratic dialogue, have a rhetorical element, he claims that the *"joyful relativity"* of these genres weakens "its one-sided rhetorical seriousness, its rationality, its singular meaning, its dogmatism" (107). The Socratic dialogues themselves exhibit an "authentic (not rhetorical) dialogicality" that prevents their congealing into "abstractly dogmatic (monologic) ossification" (164).

Although the genre of the Socratic dialogue was widespread in its time, Bakhtin is specifically concerned only with the earlier dialogues of Plato, including summing-up or confessional dialogues such as the *Apology,* a special type that Bakhtin calls *dialogue on the threshold.*[41] Studies of Bakhtin's writings on the classics have documented his tendency toward overgeneralization in his readings of ancient poetry, especially epic and lyric poetry.[42] This tendency extends to his reading of the earlier dialogues, which are not as distinct from the later dialogues as Bakhtin suggests. The ending of the *Gorgias* has a confessional quality that recalls the earlier *Apology,* for example, and the *Phaedrus* has a complex interplay of multiple voices that recalls the complex layering of voices in earlier dialogues such as the *Protagoras*.[43] Bakhtin, however, claims that in the early dialogues "the dialogic nature of truth is still recognized in the philosophical worldview itself, although in weakened form" (110). In the later dialogues, the monologism of the content begins to destroy the dialogue form, as it enters into the service of established, dogmatic worldviews and becomes "a simple form for expounding already found, ready-made irrefutable truth" (110). The early dialogues are characterized by a dialogic search for truth through the testing and contesting and creating of ideas. The testing of ideas and the (pro)creating of ideas through Socratic midwifery are characteristic features of the genre and are also evident in the Dostoevsky novels. The contesting of ideas is characteristic of the carnivalistic genres generally and is also evident, in a stronger form, in the Rabelais book.

Testing Ideas and Persons

The two basic devices of the Socratic dialogue, anacrisis and syncrisis, are not just rhetorical or stylistic devices but a means of testing both ideas and persons. Anacrisis is "a means for eliciting and provoking the words of one's interlocutor, forcing him [or her] to express his opinion and express it thoroughly" (110). Syncrisis is "the juxtaposition of various points of view on a specific object" (110). Together, anacrisis and syncrisis "dialogize thought, they carry it into the open, turn it into a *rejoinder,* attach it to dialogic intercourse among people" (111). In the context of the Socratic dialogue, anacrisis and syncrisis "lose their narrow, abstractly rhetorical character" and become a means of testing truth, for "the very event that is accomplished in a Socratic dialogue (or, more precisely, that is reproduced in it) is the purely ideological event of seeking and *testing* truth" (111). Socrates himself was a great master of anacrisis and syncrisis. He did not try to tell others that their opinions were right or wrong, and he did not try to persuade them to accept his opinions. Rather, he invited them to test themselves by drawing forth their opinions and by juxtaposing them to other opinions, thereby leading them to see for themselves the errors and inconsistencies in their ideas. Socrates was a master of anacrisis: "he knew how to force people to *speak,* to clothe in discourse their dim but stubbornly preconceived opinions, to illuminate them by the word and in this way to expose their falseness or incompleteness; he knew how to drag the going truths out into the light of day" (110–11). He was also, of course, a master of syncrisis: he knew not only how to force people to speak but also how to lead them into contradictions and inconsistencies, to set their conflicting opinions before them, to invite them to view each from the perspective of the other, and to decide for themselves which, if any, they should continue to hold.

The Socratic dialogue, moreover, is a testing of not only the idea but also the person, not only what people think but how they live their lives. One the one hand, people represent ideas; they are *"ideologists"* (111). On the other hand, ideas are inseparable from the people who hold them, for "the idea is organically combined with the image of a person" (111). As a consequence, the "dialogic testing of the idea is simultaneously also the testing of the person who represents it" (111–12). Julia Kristeva explains that the idea is not only inseparable from the person but *is* the person since the very notion of an idea separate from the person had not yet entered human thought: "the process separating the *word* as act, as apodeictic practice, as articulation of difference from the *image* as representation, as knowledge, and as idea was not yet complete when Socratic dialogue took form."[44] Among the Socratic dialogues, the *Laches* provides a particularly striking illustration of the simultaneous testing of ideas and persons. As I explain in chapter 4, much of the recent scholarship on the *Laches* has been concerned with the nature of the relationship between courage and the other virtues—whether courage is just a part of virtue or whether it is equivalent to the whole of virtue, the knowledge of good and evil. But a long tradition of scholarship has also recognized the relationship between Laches' and Nicias' ideas about courage and their personal lives. Nicias himself says that Socrates examines not only what people think and say but also how they have lived and how they do live their lives. Socrates examines the lives of Laches and Nicias by drawing forth and juxtaposing their beliefs about courage and the other virtues, revealing to them the inconsistencies in their beliefs, and showing them how these mistaken beliefs have led to failures in their actions and in their lives.

(Pro)Creating Ideas through Socratic Midwifery

Much of the energy, the *eventness,* of the Socratic dialogues is given to this kind of testing of ideas and persons. As Bakhtin points out, however, the Socratic dialogues not only test ideas but also create new ideas, new *truths,* through a process of dialogic interaction.[45] Bakhtin explains this process of (pro)creating new ideas as a birthing process, with Socrates' in his self-appointed role as midwife. Official monologism, he claims, "pretends to *possess a ready-made truth*" (110). Dialogue, in contrast, seeks an emergent truth through a collective search: "Truth is not born nor is it to be found inside the head of an individual person, it is born *between people* collectively searching for truth, in the process of their dialogic interaction" (110). Socrates participates in this birthing process as a "pander," who brings people together and makes them quarrel and thereby give birth to truth (110). He participates also as a "midwife" and as an "obstetric," who assists in the birth but who never claims that he himself possesses a ready-made truth (110). The other characters in the dialogues also participate in the process, their mutual testing of ideas producing "an embryonic *image of an idea,*" which they then develop in a free and creative interplay: "The ideas of Socrates, of the leading Sophists and other historical figures are not quoted here, not paraphrased, but are presented in their free and creative development against a dialogizing background of other ideas" (112).

More than any of the other early dialogues, the *Protagoras* illustrates this process of collective searching for truth. Studies of the *Protagoras* persistently defends the merits of *either* Protagoras' arguments or Socrates' arguments, not both. But the very force of these arguments on either side suggests the possibility of some merit on *both* sides. Protagoras and the other sophists contribute to the development of the art of dialogue by negotiating with Socrates the guidelines for its use and application. Both Protagoras and Socrates contribute to the practice of the art by offering substantive arguments to the discussion. Protagoras presents an elaborate defense of the quiet or other-regarding virtues, including justice, as the basis of civic life. Socrates accepts this argument but develops it further by showing Protagoras that the virtues are related, both reciprocally and as a unity, so that one cannot have any one of them without having all of them. When Protagoras suggests that courage, at least, is distinct from the other virtues, Socrates leads him from his own premises to the conclusion that courage requires a knowledge of good and evil and so is like the other virtues, so that one cannot be, for example, courageous but unjust. Socrates' (and Protagoras') conclusion produces a joint account of the unity of virtue that joins the traditional ideal of courage to the newer civic virtues of justice and temperance. Later in this chapter, I suggest that even the parodies of Protagoras' views help to further the development of the argument of the dialogue, broadly considered—if they are read not as mere destruction through ridicule of Protagoras' views but as a re-creation of these views that respects all of the voices and all of the intentions that we can hear in them. In chapter 5, I present my argument for the *Protagoras* as a collective search for truth in greater detail.

Contesting Ideas in Carnivalesque Debate

The Socratic dialogues not only test and create but also contest ideas in the sense that they mutually test one's own and others' ideas in carnivalesque debate. They also contest ideas in the sense that they oppose and attempt to refute other persons' ideas and thus transform them into new ideas or new truths. As described in *Problems of Dostoevsky's Poetics* and in "Epic and Novel," the Socratic dialogue is a carnivalesque genre and as such is characterized by contrast and opposition, originating in folk-carnival debate but exhibiting the joyful relativity that Bakhtin associates with carnival rather than with the single-minded seriousness that he associates with rhetoric.[46] Carnival, Bakhtin emphasizes, is not a literary phenomenon but a ritualistic pageant, in which all participate: "Carnival is a pageant without footlights and without a division into performers and spectators. In carnival everyone is an active participant, everyone communes in the carnival act. Carnival is not contemplated and, strictly speaking, not even performed; its participants *live* in it, they live by its laws as long as those laws are in effect; that is, they live a *carnivalistic life*" (*Problems* 122). Carnival is characterized by contrast and opposition: debates between polar opposites, mixtures of the serious and lofty with the comic and the base, combinations of thoughts and images—all permeated with an atmosphere of change and joyful relativity.

The Socratic dialogue illustrates these contrasts and oppositions. Its carnivalistic base lies in the folk-carnival debates between life and death, darkness and light, winter and summer—"debates which did not permit thought to stop and congeal in one-sided seriousness or in a stupid fetish for definition or singleness of meaning" characteristic (according to Bakhtin) of rhetorical dialogue (132). Its discovery of the dialogical nature of truth presumes a carnivalistic familiarization of the relations among people and of attitudes toward thought itself, a mixing of the serious with the comical, the lofty with the base, the thought with the image, exhibited in rituals of crowning/decrowning, Socratic laughter, and Socratic degradations. The ritual of the mock crowning/decrowning of the carnival king is the primary carnivalistic act, illustrative of the shifts and changes of order that characterize the carnival: "Crowning/decrowning is a dualistic ambivalent ritual, expressing the inevitability and at the same time the creative power of the shift-and-renewal, the *joyful relativity* of all structure and order, of all authority and all (hierarchical) position" (124). Socratic laughter is reduced laughter, often expressed as irony. As such, it is indirect; "it does not ring out" (178 n. 4). It grasps a phenomenon in the process of change, transition, and creative renewal; it prevents change from becoming absolutized or congealing in "one-sided seriousness" (164). Socratic degradations are "an entire system of metaphors and comparisons borrowed from the lower spheres of life—from tradespeople, from everyday life, etc."—designed to bring the world closer so that it can be investigated fearlessly and freely ("Epic and Novel" 25). These mixtures of lofty ideas with base images—Bakhtin calls them "unrestrained mésalliances of thoughts and images"—are common in the early dialogues (*Problems* 132).

Although all of the early dialogues illustrate these contrasts to some degree, the *Gorgias* is the most strikingly carnivalistic. The *Gorgias* is structured as a series of contests or debates between justice and injustice, Socrates representing justice, Gorgias, Polus, and Callicles injustice in various forms: the power of rhetoric to persuade, whether justly or unjustly; the power of the orator or the tyrant to do what he wishes; the power of the person of courage and practical wisdom to pursue pleasure and self-interest without regard for others. These debates are conducted as ritual crownings/decrownings, Gorgias, Polus, and Callicles each in turn claiming authority and Socrates contesting and seeking to refute them, undermining their authority with carnivalistic laughter and degradation. Gorgias claims that he teaches rhetoric and if necessary will also teach justice, and Polus and Callicles claim that they can defend his position better than he can because they will not permit themselves to be shamed into professing to believe in justice. Socrates defeats and symbolically decrowns them with his lowly comparison of rhetoric to cookery, with his ironic claim that to do injustice is worse than to suffer it, and with his base comparison of the person of courage and intelligence to the lowly and shameful catamite. The *Gorgias* shows how Socrates engages his art of dialogue to contest and refute others' ideas and also to test his own ideas, revealing inconsistencies in others' beliefs and thus establishing, to his own satisfaction at least, the consistency of his own belief that the truly courageous person is also a just and temperate person. Later in this chapter, I argue that the *Gorgias* also shows how Socrates engages his art of dialogue to contest ideas in the sense that he opposes and attempts to refute the linguistic and cultural ideals of contemporary Athens and to transform these ideals into his own ideal of the just and virtuous life. In chapter 6, I present these arguments in greater detail.

Dialogue on the Threshold

The early Socratic dialogues also include some extraordinary instances in which a plot situation operates alongside anacrisis as a means of drawing forth ideas and persons—or ideas/persons. Bakhtin explains that such an extraordinary plot situation is "one which would cleanse the word of all of life's automatism and object-ness, which would force a person to reveal the deepest layers of his [or her] personality and thought" (*Problems* 111). He observes situations of this kind in the *Apology* and in the *Phaedo,* and he explains the *Apology* as a summing-up or confession of a person "standing *on the threshold*" (of death), hence the name of this special type of dialogue, the "dialogue on the threshold" (111). The *Gorgias* concludes with allusions to Socrates' trial and death and with a similar summing-up or confession of Socrates' life—a dialogue on the threshold. The conclusion of the *Gorgias* is frequently read as a withdrawal from political life and as an acknowledgment of Socrates' failure to persuade Callicles to accept the life of virtue. But it has also been read as a reaffirmation of Socrates' own life and as a moment of recognition of death not as the end but as the beginning of life. Later in this chapter, I argue that Socrates' challenge to Callicles to accept the life of virtue is also a challenge to the official language and culture of contemporary Athens—the rhetoric of Pericles and the sophists, on the one hand, and the political culture of injustice and the pursuit of empire, on the other. From this perspective, the conclusion of the *Gorgias* is not only a summing-up of Socrates' life but also an invitation to Callicles and to Athenians generally to prepare for their own confessions—their own dialogues on the threshold. I return to this theme at the end of chapter 6.

THE SOCRATIC DIALOGUE AS *NOVELISTIC*

Bakhtin reads the Socratic dialogue as a primitive or preliminary form that led to the novel but that was not in itself *novelistic*. He claims that ancient forms such as the Socratic dialogue and the Menippean satire were primitive in comparison to Dostoevsky's novels and could at best prepare certain generic conditions necessary for the emergence of polyphony, the defining characteristic of the novels (*Problems* 122).[47] He also links the Socratic dialogue with the carnival forms of antiquity that freed critical philosophy from its "one-sided rhetorical seriousness" and led to the monumental achievement of Rabelais, whose works constitute the greatest literary expression of folk humor (*Rabelais* 3–4, 121). Nonetheless, Bakhtin probably overemphasizes the memoir quality of the Socratic dialogue, its character as "reminiscences of actual conversations that Socrates had conducted, transcriptions of remembered conversations framed by a brief story" (*Problems* 109; "Epic and Novel" 24). The Socratic dialogue, while neither polyphonic nor *novelistic* in a strict sense, is surely more than mere recorded conversation or even carefully composed dialogue. As Morson and Emerson point out, novelistic dialogue is not to be found in "the 'compositionally expressed dialogues' among the characters" but "in the hybridized, double-voiced, dialogized heteroglossia of the author's own voice."[48] The Socratic dialogue exhibits these features of novelistic discourse. It is a polyphonic creating and testing of ideas in which the author participates along with the characters and the readers and in which novelistic devices such as parody and hybridization contribute to the creative development of the ideas. It is also a carnivalesque testing and contesting of ideas for the purpose of both opposing official languages and cultures and also, in the process, transforming and perhaps even redeeming them.

Polyphony as a Creating and Testing of Ideas

As described in *Problems of Dostoevsky's Poetics,* Bakhtin's notion of polyphony is a process of creating and testing ideas, a process that engages the author and the readers as well as the characters in the polyphonic novel. Indeed the author seems to be so much a part of the creative process that one contemporary critic has suggested that Bakhtin's notion of polyphony situates novelistic creativity within the mind of the author alone.[49] Natasha Alexandrovna Reed argues that the polyphonic novel as Bakhtin conceives it is entirely a conversation within the author's own mind, a dialogue of self without other.[50] Reed claims that Bakhtin emphasizes the intentional aspect of language while ignoring the genesis of intentions and de-emphasizing the conflictual aspect of interacting utterances.[51] As a consequence, his notion of polyphony is restricted to the limited domain of "the mental activity and intentions ('desires') of prose writers," and the prose writer is restricted to simply writing down conversations among ideas in his or her own mind.[52] Bakhtin's notion of polyphony, in this view, is not so much theory of dialogue as a theory of romantic self-expression that substitutes the mental conversations that one conducts with oneself for dialogues between individuals, treats one's own ideas as equivalent to real, objectively existing others, and expels the real other both from Dostoevsky's novels and from his own theory of dialogue, thus creating a dialogue of self without other.[53] Emerson suggests, however, that Reed's reading of Bakhtinian polyphony as authorial creativity might be extended to his notion of polyphony as a testing of ideas, with similar results, for just as Bakhtin's notion of polyphony would seem to exclude real people, so also his notion of the testing of unfinalized ideas seems also to exclude real people, whose completed deeds would be subject to real verdicts, sentences, and punishments and who could themselves be acquitted or locked up or even shot.[54] Emerson maintains, however, that such a reading of Bakhtinian polyphony depends upon one's acceptance of the "simple, trapped perspective of the created hero," with whom the ordinary reader is most likely to identify.[55] From the perspective of the author or the critic, Bakhtinian polyphony might equally well be read as an exercise in relativity, in the sense, of course, that we shift our perspective from that of the hero to that of the author but also in the sense that we grasp the relativity—not relativism—of ethical decision making, which denies the existence of any single unitary standard of judgment and which requires of each of us our own "singular, tiny, local dialogic gestures, which may or may not be registered and elicit a response" and which require "a great deal of tolerance and patient work."[56] Much the same point could be made about the Socratic dialogue, were it not the case that Plato so often seeks to enter into the dialogue and to do our work for us.

At first notice, Bakhtin's assessment of the Socratic dialogue would appear to be an inversion of his notion of polyphony, for the Socratic dialogue as history or memoir seems to leave no opportunity for authorial creativity. Bakhtin perhaps overemphasizes the memoir quality of the Socratic dialogue to reinforce his contrast between the early and the later dialogues of Plato, in which the author's voice takes over entirely in "the service of the established, dogmatic worldviews of various philosophical schools and religious doctrines," to which the other characters in the dialogues merely give their assent (*Problems,* 110). Bakhtin's concept of polyphony, however, helps to situate the Socratic dialogue at a point of development somewhere between the simple history or memoir of Socrates' conversations (which Bakhtin claims it is) and the more authoritative and dogmatic monologue (which Bakhtin claims the later dialogues come to be). In particular, his concept of polyphony helps to explain how Plato the author (in the character of Socrates) participates with the other characters in the creation of the truths of the dialogues, and his concept of the surplus of meaning helps to explain how Plato the author not only participates in dialogues with the other characters but also frequently makes his own authorial presence felt in the Socratic *conversations,* even in the early dialogues.

Morson and Emerson argue that Bakhtin's concept of polyphony is "in essence a theory of creativity" and that two characteristics—a dialogic sense of truth and the new position of the author—are constitutive of polyphony.[57] In *Problems of Dostoevsky's Poetics,* Bakhtin explains the dialogic sense of truth as a creating and testing of ideas and persons, and he explains the new position of the author of the polyphonic novel as the position of an equal participant in a dialogic relationship with the characters and the reader, one who retains no surplus of meaning except the minimum of pragmatic meaning required to move the narrative forward.[58] Bakhtin's reading of the Socratic dialogue suggests that it shares with the polyphonic novel the first of these characteristics. His elaboration of the concept of polyphony suggests that the Socratic dialogue only partially and imperfectly shares with the polyphonic novel the second of these characteristics, for Plato the author clearly possesses a surplus of meaning inaccessible even to Socrates, the *character* who most closely approximates Plato's own views.

With respect to the first characteristic, the dialogic sense of truth, Bakhtin explains that Dostoevsky understands the dialogic nature of human thought as a creating and testing of ideas and the persons who are the carriers of those ideas.[59] Bakhtin claims that in the polyphonic novel the idea lives and gives birth to new ideas only in its dialogic relationship to other ideas: "The idea begins to live, that is, to take shape, to develop, to find and renew its verbal expression, to give birth to new ideas, only when it enters into genuine dialogic relationships with other ideas, with the ideas of *others*" (88). So also the idea in its dialogic relationship with other ideas is "tested, verified, confirmed or repudiated by them," and likewise the person who carries the idea is set in a dialogic relationship with other people and is made to collide with them "for the purpose of *testing* the idea and the man [i.e., person] of the idea, that is, for testing the 'man in man'" (89, 105). Bakhtin's reading of the Socratic dialogue as a testing of ideas and persons suggests that it shares this characteristic of the polyphonic novel.

With respect to the second characteristic, the new position of the author, Bakhtin claims that Dostoevsky as author of the polyphonic novel participates in the creation of the truth of the novel as equal with the characters and the reader and thus possesses no surplus of meaning except that surplus required by the pragmatics of the developing narrative.[60] As a consequence, the author occupies a new position in relation to the characters and exercises a new creative process productive of a complex unity of creative events.[61] The authorial position is "a *fully realized and thoroughly consistent dialogic position,*" in which the author speaks with, not about, a character as someone who is actually present (63–64). The characters participate as equals in this ongoing dialogue, not as objects of the author's consciousness but as "*free* people, capable of standing *alongside,*" agreeing or disagreeing with, even rebelling against, their creator (6). The reader, too, participates in the dialogue and indeed must participate since the dialogic interaction "provides no support for the viewer who would objectify an entire event according to some ordinary monologic category (thematically, lyrically or cognitively)—and this consequently makes the viewer also a participant" (18). As an equal participant in this dialogue with the characters and the reader, the author does not possess any surplus of meaning that is inaccessible to the characters, except that surplus required by the pragmatics of the narrative.[62] However, the author does share with the characters the surplus of the good listener—which Morson and Emerson call "the *addressive* surplus."[63] The author "never retains any essential 'surplus' of *meaning,* but only that indispensable minimum of pragmatic, purely *information-bearing* 'surplus' necessary to carry forward the story" (73). Nonetheless, the author, along with the characters, does retain the surplus of the good listener—"an active (not a duplicating) understanding, a willingness to listen"—which, however, "is never used as an ambush, as a chance to sneak up and attack from behind."[64] Only by relinquishing an excess or surplus of meaning can the author create unfinalized and unfinalizable characters who engage in open-ended rather than "finalized and objectivized" or "rhetorically performed" dialogue (73).

This new position of the author in relation to the characters and the reader requires a new creative process and produces a complex unity of creative events. The new creative process requires that the author engage in dialogue with the characters as though they were actually present and capable of responding "in the *real present*" and not as they would appear in a "stenographer's report of a *finished* dialogue," from which the author has already withdrawn and over which the author now presides as a higher authority (63). This creative dialogue with the characters (and also with the reader) produces a complex unity of live events, which Bakhtin is able to explain only by analogy with the concept of relativity in physics.[65] The idea, the truth, that is born in the polyphonic novel is not a formation created in a person's head but a *"live event"* created in "dialogic communion *between* consciousnesses" (88). It requires "a plurality of consciousnesses, one that cannot in principle be fitted into the bounds of a single consciousness, one that is, so to speak, by its very nature *full of event potential* and is born at a point of contact among various consciousnesses" (81). Such an idea, such a unified truth, combines several autonomous consciousnesses into "a higher unity, a unity, so to speak, of the second order," analogous to "the complex unity of an Einsteinian universe" (16). Bakhtin's reading of the Socratic dialogue as a collective searching for truth suggests that it, too, shares this characteristic of the polyphonic novel. However, even the early dialogues show evidence of Plato's hand, his exercise of his authorial surplus of meaning: allusions to the characters' fates and the outcome of historical events, for example, and efforts to force closure, to finalize the characters and finish the dialogue—evidence that these early dialogues are neither mere histories or memoirs nor true polyphonic novels (or even true polyphonic dialogues) but the beginnings of Platonic monologue.

Plato the author is surely, therefore, something more than a mere recorder or even composer of the conversations of Socrates. Even if we read the dialogues quite literally as recorded conversations, we will see signs of Plato's hand—his essential surplus of meaning—in his allusions, in the *Laches,* to the lives of Laches and Nicias and to their unfortunate deaths and, in the *Gorgias,* to the likelihood of Socrates' being dragged into court and put to death. Moreover, if we read the dialogues not only as recorded conversations or even as philosophy but also as dramatic art, we will see in them the artful juxtapositions of the contrasting points of view of Laches and Nicias, Socrates' (or more likely Plato's) crafty parody of Protagoras' practice of interpreting poetry, and the crescendo effect of Socrates' successive conversations with Gorgias, Polus, and Callicles, each of whom articulates a view of injustice more callous and shameless than the one who preceded him. As I hope to demonstrate, we will also see in the *Protagoras* an artfully creative interplay of ideas that leads to the emergence of a new cultural ideal of the unity of virtue, though we will also see evidence of Plato's hand—his *addressive surplus*—in his attempt to finalize the unfinalizable meaning of the dialogue by refusing to acknowledge Protagoras' substantial contributions to the development of the ideas in the dialogue and by forcing Protagoras to acquiesce to the Socratic ideal.

Hybridization, Parody, and the Creative Development of Ideas

In "Discourse in the Novel," Bakhtin describes several devices that contribute to the creative development of the ideas in the novel: "hybridizations," "the dialogized interrelation of languages," and "pure dialogues" (358). These devices, he says, are theoretically separable but are in fact inextricably woven together in the artistic image of languages in the novel. They appear in the Socratic dialogue and help to explain features of the *Protagoras,* in particular, that appear to be incidental but in fact are integral to the development of the main idea in the dialogue, the Socratic concept of the unity of virtue. In the novel, pure dialogue appears only superficially in the dialogues and monologues of the characters; it is, more fundamentally, an open and endless encounter of linguistic and cultural forces (364–66). Pure dialogue is a dialogue of both languages and social forces "perceived not only in their static co-existence, but also as a dialogue of different times, epochs and days, a dialogue that is forever dying, living, being born" (365). In the novel, pure dialogue is interwoven with hybridization and the dialogized interrelation of languages in the form of stylization and parody.

Like pure dialogue, hybridization is both linguistic and cultural (358–62, 366).[66] Hybridization "is a mixture of two social languages within the limits of a single utterance, an encounter, within the arena of an utterance, between two different linguistic consciousnesses, separated from one another by an epoch, by social differentiation or by some other factor" (358). Hybridization may be either intentional or unintentional. Unintentional hybridization is "a mixing of various 'languages' co-existing within the boundaries of a single dialect, a single national language, a single branch, a single group of different branches or different groups of such branches, in the historical as well as paleontological past of languages" (358–59). Intentional hybridization, such as the artistic image of a language re-created in the novel, is not only a mixing of various languages but is more importantly a "collision between differing points of views on the world" that produces "a *semantic* hybrid; not semantic and logical in the abstract (as in rhetoric), but rather a *semantics that is concrete and social*" (360). Intentional, novelistic hybridization is thus productive of new linguistic and cultural possibilities, for just as the mixing of heteroglot languages forms a complex unity of self with other, so also the mixing of differing worldviews forms novel cultural hybrids.

In hybridization, this mixing of languages and cultures occurs within a single utterance, in which one language is rendered in light of another, which remains outside the utterance (362). In the interrelation ("interillumination") of languages, in contrast, two languages—two "individualized linguistic consciousnesses"—are both present in the same utterance, as they are present, for example, in stylization and parody (362–64). In *Problems of Dostoevsky's Poetics,* Bakhtin explains this kind of utterance as double-voiced discourse—dialogue in its restricted sense as distinct from monologue.[67] Dialogue as double-voiced discourse encompasses a second voice within an utterance, the author making use of the second voice for his or her own purposes, "inserting a new semantic intention into a discourse which already has, and which retains, an intention of its own" (189).[68] Double-voiced discourse includes several types, among them stylization, parody, *skaz* or narrated story, and hidden polemic.[69] Of these several types, parody most closely resembles stylization but differs from it because the parody or representing discourse introduces a semantic intention that is directly at odds with the intention of the parodied or represented discourse. Stylization "forces another person's referential (artistically referential) intention to serve its own purposes, that is, its new intentions"; it does not collide with the thought or style of the other, however, "but rather follows after it in the same direction, merely making that direction conventional" (189, 193). In doing so, it renders the discourse of the other conditional; it "casts a slight shadow of objectification over it" (189). Morson and Emerson explain that the stylist tests the discourse of the other and agrees with it (implying that he or she might also disagree with it), thus incorporating it into a dialogue.[70] Parody, in contrast, introduces into the discourse of the other "a semantic intention that is directly opposed to the original one"; it clashes with the other's discourse and forces it to serve directly opposing aims, creating "an arena of battle between two voices" (193).

Morson emphasizes the oppositional quality of Bakhtinian parody when he identifies its three essential characteristics: it must evoke another utterance, its target or object; it must be antithetical to its target; and it must clearly establish the higher semantic authority intended by its author.[71] Bakhtin is careful to point out, however, that in opposing the discourse of the other parody re-creates rather than destroys that discourse. In "Discourse in the Novel," he explains parody as a kind of stylization—"a parodic stylization"—presumably because it strives to achieve a delicate balance between opposing (the parodic element) and respecting (the stylizing element) the other's discourse (364). A parodic stylization sets the intention of the parody or representing discourse at odds with the intentions of the parodied or represented discourse. However, it does not destroy but rather re-creates the parodied discourse "as an authentic whole, giving it its due as a language possessing its own internal logic and one capable of revealing its own world inextricably bound up with the parodied language" (364). A parodic stylization is thus unlike rhetorical parody, which is simply "a gross and superficial destruction of the other's language" (364).

The *Protagoras* includes elements of parody of Protagoras' thought and style, often viewed as mere ridicule of Protagoras' position, presumably for the purpose of destroying it. In Bakhtin's rich understanding of parody, however, these elements encompass—and respect—both the parody and the parodied, the representing and the represented, discourses. Thus they preserve rather than destroy the authenticity of the represented discourse; they re-create its language and its world in its wholeness and integrity. Moreover, these elements, embedded within the larger context of the dialogue, live in a dialogical relationship with the other elements in the dialogue and with other dialogues. Thus they take on a life of their own beyond the immediate context of the parody. For example, the brief parody of Protagorean relativism, alleging the relational character of the good among animals and plants, reveals the world of the represented discourse as it recalls Protagoras' serious assertion of the relativity of one's frame of reference, which Socrates counters with his hedonistic art of measurement later in the dialogue, but which reasserts itself in Socrates' objections to hedonism in the *Gorgias,* on precisely the same grounds of the relativity of one's frame of reference. Again, the parody of Protagoras' method of critically analyzing poetry reveals the world of both of the represented discourses: both the poet Simonides' apparent rethinking of the traditional virtue of courage in its relationship to justice and to the other virtues and Protagoras' own rethinking of poetry as an object to be not only analyzed but also altered. The parody reveals the world of both of the represented discourses, recalling the problem of the cultural conflict between the virtues that Socrates will address in the remainder of the dialogue and recalling as well the potential of Protagoras' own method of analyzing poetry to address this problem—if only Socrates were to take him seriously. These parodic elements thus encompass both the parody and the target of the parody, both the representing and the represented discourses taking on a life of their own, speaking back to and influencing the development of the discussion within the *Protagoras* and beyond it in other dialogues. These parodic elements, moreover, are interwoven with elements of cultural hybridization. The parody of Protagorean relativism introduces the problem of the relational character of the good, which Socrates addresses with his art of measurement later in the dialogue, and the parody reasserts itself in the *Gorgias* as a problem of the relativity of the good for someone, which Socrates addresses with his art of dialogue. The parody of Protagoras' method of critically analyzing poetry reintroduces the problem of the cultural conflict between courage and the other virtues, a problem that Socrates resolves by transforming Protagoras' view of civic virtue into a new idea of the unity of virtue—a cultural hybrid that joins Homeric courage to Protagorean justice and temperance. Socrates thereby silences Protagoras, but he does not and cannot finalize him, for Protagoras' voice continues to speak out from behind the parody, well beyond the immediate context of the dialogue.

Carnival as a Contesting of Languages and Cultures

In *Rabelais and His World,* Bakhtin describes carnival as a contesting and opposing of official languages and cultures, not a mere testing but an intense struggle between one language and culture and another that provokes the mutual accommodation and transformation rather than the destruction of either by the other. Carnival is itself the most vigorously contested idea in all of Bakhtin's work, its optimism about human solidarity and community and the redemptive and transformative power of language seeming to clash with the reality of state control and repression of the individual and the dogmatism of official monologic rhetoric. As characterized in the Rabelais book, carnival is both a contesting and opposing of official languages and cultures and a mutual accommodation between official and carnivalesque languages that has the power and potential to revitalize and transform both. As represented by the *Gorgias,* the Socratic dialogue is carnivalesque in both senses. On the one hand, the *Gorgias* shows how Socrates uses his art of dialogue to contest and oppose the power of sophistic rhetoric and the dominant political culture of Athens and how the city exercises its power to repress and silence him. On the other hand, it shows how Socrates envisions his art as a means of transforming both the lives of individuals and the rhetoric and culture of Athens itself.

Bakhtin's notion of carnival has been challenged by contemporary theorists in both Russia and the West as a means of control of individuals by collective and institutional entities but also credited with a redemptive and transformative power over these same entities.[72] Russian theorists note parallels between Bakhtin's characterization of carnival and the political oppression the Stalinist state. Mikhail K. Ryklin maintains, for example, that Bakhtin discovered in Rabelais a convenient site for reenacting and overcoming the trauma of the Russian intelligentsia during the Stalinist era.[73] Ryklin takes the Moscow metro stations of the Stalinist years to be emblematic of the trauma brought upon the masses by the Stalinist Terror, their pictorial imagery displaying the "collective corporeality" that turns violence into spectacle, thus "bringing the nonindividuality of the masses to its logical conclusion."[74] He suggests that Bakhtin found in the Rabelais book a "self-therapeutic text" that enabled him to invert the logic of terror by imagining a collectivity capable of endlessly transforming itself both physically and rhetorically.[75] Alexandar Mihailovic finds a parallel between the Stalinist show trials of the 1930s and Bakhtin's carnivalesque language of praise and blame.[76] He explains the show trials as a binary opposition between the luminous ideals of the true heroes of socialism and the "dirt and vegetative infestation" of the enemies of the people.[77] As a parallel, he cites Bakhtin's characterization of the marketplace word in the second chapter of the Rabelais book as "an amalgam of praise and verbal abuse, public humiliation and exaltation," strongly reminiscent of the purges and their attendant rhetoric.[78] Unlike Ryklin, however, Mihailovic reads Bakhtinian carnival from the perspective of the Stoicist and Johannine embodied word and thus as an attempt to redeem the public square as the site not of conflict between the individual and the state or, worse, the absorption of the individual by the state but rather as a true merging and joining of the individual with the universe at large.[79]

From a quite different perspective, theorists in the West read carnival as a mechanism of social control and oppression of the individual but also note its redemptive and transformative power. Terry Eagleton, for example, notes that carnival "is a *licensed* affair in every sense" and thus is "as disturbing and relatively ineffectual as a revolutionary work of art."[80] Peter Stallybrass and Allon White concur that carnival is "simply a form of social control of the low by the high and therefore serves the interests of that very official culture which it apparently opposes."[81] They add, however, that carnival may have revolutionary potential if it challenges not only linguistic codes but also the sites or domains from which those codes emanate: "Only a challenge to the hierarchy of *sites* of discourse, which usually comes from groups and classes 'situated' by the dominant in low or marginal positions, carries the promise of politically transformative power."[82]

In the Rabelais book, Bakhtin sometimes characterizes carnival as a contest or direct opposition between official and carnivalesque languages, for example, as an opposition between the persuasive discourse of the church and the carnivaleque language of the marketplace or between the apparent timelessness and fixedness of medieval Latin and the changing languages of the vernacular. At other times, he characterizes carnival as a contest or an intense struggle between official and carnivalesque languages and cultures that is both oppositional and mutually accommodative and transformative and is thus generative of new linguistic possibilities. Thus he constructs a creative tension between contestation and opposition, on the one hand, and mutual accommodation, change, and renewal, on the other. Morson and Emerson find a strong sense of binary opposition in the Rabelias book, especially as compared to the Dostoevsky book: an opposition between the carnival world as open and incomplete and the official world as closed and complete; between carnival debasement and mockery and official seriousness; between the convexities and orifices of the grotesque body and the smooth, impenetrable surface of the body; between the shouted and unprintable language of the marketplace ("the 'public-square word'") and the authoritative language of church and state.[83] Such binary oppositions, they claim, are contrary to the rich mixture of languages, intentions, and worldviews in Bakhtin's concepts of dialogue, heteroglossia, and polyphony.[84] Mihailovic, however, finds a strong sense of unity and wholeness in the Rabelais book and a continuity and coherence between the Rabelais book and Bakhtin's earlier work.[85] Mihailovic argues that Bakhtin's concept of discourse embraces diversity within unity, linguistic contestation, and mutual accommodation within the context of historical processes of change and the birth of new linguistic consciousnesses.[86] Viewing carnival from the broader perspective that embraces both official and carnivalesque languages and cultures, he finds redemptive and transformative power in these processes of historical change and renewal.

Bakhtin's characterization of the carnival reflects this creative tension. Viewing carnival as separate from official culture, Bakhtin emphasizes the opposition between the two cultures. He claims that the official culture as represented by official feasts "asserted all that was stable, unchanging, perennial; the existing hierarchy, the existing religious, political, and moral values, norms, and prohibitions" (9). The official culture and official feasts were "the triumph of a truth already established, the predominant truth that was put forward as eternal and indisputable" (9). In contrast, carnival and marketplace festivals were "the second life of the people, who for a time entered the utopian realm of community, freedom, equality, and abundance" (9). Carnival celebrated the "temporary liberation from the prevailing truth and from the established order" and the "suspension of all hierarchical rank, privileges, norms, and prohibitions" (10). Viewing carnival as inclusive of official culture, however, Bakhtin suggests the possibility of universal participation in carnivalesque revival and renewal:

> Carnival is not a spectacle seen by the people; they live in it, and everyone participates because its very idea embraces all the people. While carnival lasts, there is no other life outside it. During carnival time life is subject only to its laws, that is, the laws of its own freedom. It has a universal spirit; it is a special condition of the entire world, of the world's revival and renewal, in which all take part. Such is the essence of carnival, vividly felt by all its participants. (7)

Carnival as a universal spirit thus seems in principle to be inclusive of official culture, and, as Simon Dentith observes, it apparently did in Rabelais' time include not only the *people* in a narrow sense but people from all ranks and classes, who presumably shared its spirit of change and renewal.[87]

Bakhtin's characterization of carnivalesque languages similarly reflects a creative tension between contestation and opposition, on the one hand, and inclusiveness, mutual accommodation, and creative renewal, on the other. In his description of the language of the marketplace, for example, Bakhtin emphasizes the opposition between official and marketplace languages. But in his description of the struggle between official and vernacular languages, he emphasizes the mutual accommodation between and among these languages and the potential for linguistic change and renewal. The language of the marketplace contests and opposes official languages such as the persuasive language of the medieval church. Marketplace language is a language of contrast and ambivalence, of renewal and destruction, birth and death, praise and blame, the sacred and the profane, heaven and earth. It is, most evidently, the language of urine and excrement, of debasement and destruction, but also, as the language of the lower body, the language of the genitals and the reproductive capacity, of fertility and birth. It is the language of praise and blame, the exalted and the lowly, heaven and earth, captured neatly in the author's praise of his book in the prologue to the second book:

> Then find me a book in any language, in any branch of art and science that possesses such virtues, properties and prerogatives. Find it, I say, and I will buy you a pint of tripes! No, gentlemen, no, none such exists. My book is peerless, incomparable, nonpareil, and—I

> maintain it in the teeth of hellfire—unique! If anyone contradicts me,
> let him be herewith denounced as a false prophet, a champion of pre-
> destination, a poisoner, and a seducer of the people. (162)[88]

This language of praise and blame, Bakhtin writes, "is a parody and travesty of the ecclesiastical method of persuasion" (167). Behind the praise lie the Gospel and the church's exclusive truth. Behind the blame, the abuses, and the curses lie the church's intolerance and intimidation and its methods of establishing truth and conviction, "which are inseparable from fear, violence, morose and narrow-minded seriousness and intolerance" (167–68). Such a language the language of the marketplace can only contest and oppose.

The official and vernacular languages of Rabelais' time, in contrast, show evidence of mutual accommodation, transformation, and creative renewal. Mihailovic explains the tensions and indeed the intense struggle between and among these languages as an "almost Darwinian contestation" but argues that this contestation led to mutual adaptation, adjustment, and perhaps even reconciliation.[89] Bakhtin observes tensions, for example, between the progressive language of the humanists and the "gay word of the people," between the Latin and vernacular languages, and between the rhetorical speeches and "the popular-festive, elemental imagery" of Rabelais' novel—Rabelais' own "last word"—but he also sees these languages as reciprocally related (452–54, 465–73). The revival of Cicero's Latin in its classic purity, for example, transformed it into a dead language but also revealed the ugliness and limitations of medieval Latin and thus hastened its demise as well. The vernacular languages replaced Latin but retained elements of official speech derived from it and also introduced elements from other vernaculars, Italian making its way into French, for example. Moreover, these transformations in official and vernacular languages also reflected deeper cultural transformations, the eternal, unchanging world of the medieval Latin giving way to the local, provincial vernaculars with their sense of situatedness in time and space. The language and culture of the Renaissance was born, Bakhtin argues, of just such a series of transformations: "The primitive and naïve coexistence of languages and dialects had come to an end; the new consciousness was born not in a perfected and fixed linguistic system but at the intersection of many languages and at the point of their most intense interorientation and struggle" (471). This struggle was not only linguistic but also cultural:

> Languages are philosophies—not abstract but concrete, social philosophies, penetrated by a system of values inseparable from living practice and class struggle. This is why every object, every concept, every point of view, as well as every intonation found their place at this intersection of linguistic philosophies and was drawn into an intense ideological struggle. (471)

Through this struggle, a new language and a new culture was born.

In the *Gorgias,* the most carnivalesque of the early dialogues, Socrates contests and opposes the official language and culture of Athens for the purpose of transforming it, not destroying it. The official language of Athens was the rhetoric of Pericles and the sophists, and its official culture was the political culture of injustice in the pursuit of empire. Socrates contests Gorgias' rhetoric because it represents an official language that fails to distinguish between just and unjust arguments, and he contests Callicles' politics because it represents the official political culture of courage and practical wisdom without regard for justice that Athens has cultivated for the purpose of maintaining and expanding its empire. However, he does not merely contest and oppose the official language and culture of Athens but seeks to create through his art of dialogue a new linguistic and cultural consciousness that joins the cultural ideal of courage in battle upheld in the Homeric epics with the newer civic ideal of justice and temperance. He believes that Athenians simultaneously maintain these two conflicting sets of cultural values, that they are unable to see the conflicts and inconsistencies in their own beliefs, that Periclean and sophistic rhetoric promotes the political culture of injustice and self-interest, and that only his art of dialogue can demonstrate to others, as it has demonstrated to Socrates himself, that they do not know what they think they know, that they are as ignorant of virtue as he believes himself to be.

READING TEXTS CONTEXTUALLY AND EXTRATEXTUALLY

Bakhtin's thinking about dialogue provided the inspiration for Kristeva's concept of intertextuality, which has been widely influential though also frequently criticized for its alleged departures from the spirit of Bakhtin's thought.[90] Though the term *intertextuality* has been widely adopted, Kristeva's concept of the text in relation to other texts and to their contexts probably owes more to Jacques Derrida and to French and American post-structuralists than it does to Bakhtin.[91] These two lines of thought develop in opposite directions, however, both largely unsympathetic to Bakhtin. On the one hand, post-structuralists multiply contexts indefinitely, viewing textual/contextual relationships as boundless and meaning thus as ultimately indeterminate.[92] On the other hand, Kristeva eliminates context entirely, viewing texts in relationship to other texts but abstracting them from their historical and human contexts.[93] Bakhtin, in contrast to both, insists upon the historical reality of extratextual context, which situates authors, texts, and listeners (or readers) in real (and thus necessarily limited) historical time and space. In his late essays published in *Speech Genres,* he situates texts both contextually (in relation to other texts) and extratextually (in relation to their historical reality, as personified in the voices of others). Situated in different contextual and extratextual relationships, texts such as the early Platonic dialogues will have different meanings, the *Gorgias,* for example, having a different significance for the history of rhetoric depending upon whether we read or listen to it in relation to the *Phaedrus* or the *Protagoras* and whether we read these texts in relation to Homer and Simonides or to the later Plato and to Aristotle (neither reading, of course, being more historically accurate than the other).

Following but transforming Bakhtin's original insights, Kristeva explains intertextuality as a relationship of texts to other texts. In *Desire in Language,* citing Bakhtin's influence, she defines intertextuality in opposition to intersubjectivity: "any text is constructed as a mosaic of quotations; any text is the absorption and transformation of another"; thus "*intertextuality* replaces that of intersubjectivity, and poetic language is read as at least *double*."[94] Later, in *Revolution in Poetic Language,* observing the frequent use of the concept of intertextuality as mere source criticism, she reemphasizes her definition of the concept as a relationship of texts or signifying systems:

> The term *inter-textuality* denotes this transposition of one (or several) sign system(s) into another; but since this term has often been understood in the banal sense of "study of sources," we prefer the term *transposition* because it specifies that the passage from one signifying system to another demands a new articulation of the thetic— of enunciative and denotative positionality. If one grants that every signifying practice is a field of transpositions of various signifying systems (an inter-textuality), one then understands that its "place" of enunciation and its denoted "object" are never single, complete, and identical to themselves, but always plural, shattered, capable of being tabulated.[95]

Kristeva's definition of intertextuality has the effect of depersonalizing and dehistoricizing textual relationships. As Dentith observes, "Kristeva effectively deracinates the signifying process, tearing it out of the dialogic encounter which is its only imaginable context for Bakhtin."[96] As a result, intertextuality becomes a property of texts, of writing itself, not a possible way of negotiating meaning between real, historically situated speakers and listeners, writers and readers.

Throughout his work, and quite explicitly in his late essays, Bakhtin situates meaning not in depersonalized, dehistoricized texts but in texts conceived as utterances, as exchanges between speaking subjects, set in the context of other texts and in the context of their extratextual historical reality—not a reified thing-like external reality but a reality personified in the voices of real people. In "The Problem of Speech Genres," Bakhtin explains how utterances, both oral and textual, are situated in the context of other utterances by means of speech genres (60, 62–63).[97] Utterances do not live in isolation, Bakhtin insists, but in relation to other utterances, to other speakers, and to other views of the world: "The speaker is not the biblical Adam, dealing only with virgin and still unnamed objects, giving them names for the first time" (93–94). The speaker (or writer) therefore must situate each utterance in the context of the diverse social relations between speakers, sets of values and perceptions, possible actions or purposes, various styles and languages, and the like—a task that would be almost hopelessly difficult were it not for the prior existence of relatively stable types of utterances called *speech genres* (60).[98] The various speech genres may be rigid or trite, flexible or creative, but they have entered the language through a long process of testing and modification and so provide a rich repertoire of choices, for both speakers and writers (65, 78–79). These speech genres, as typical forms of individual utterances, are themselves impersonal, but in use in live spoken and written communication, they are "always individual and contextual in nature" (88).

In "Toward a Methodology for the Human Sciences," Bakhtin explains how texts are situated in relation both to other texts and to their extratextual historical context, personified in the voices of others. Though he frequently uses literary scholarship as his exemplar for the human sciences, he clearly intends his methodology to encompass the human sciences generally as opposed to the exact sciences. The exact sciences, he claims, constitute a monologic form of knowledge: "the intellect contemplates a *thing* and expounds upon it" (161). The human sciences ("sciences of the spirit"), in contrast, seek to understand the living word: the text as situated in time, in relationship to other texts and to extratextual reality, and in relationship to their authors and listeners (161). Texts are situated in historical time, "in my own context, in a contemporary context, and in a future one" (161). They are situated in relationship to other texts: "The text lives only by coming into contact with another text (with context). Only at the point of this contact between texts does a light flash, illuminating both the posterior and anterior, joining a given text to a dialogue" (162). They are also situated in relationship to external reality, not the thing-like reality that is the subject of biography, sociological causal analysis, or depersonalized history, but historical and personified reality as it shapes artistic vision and artistic thought (162). This historical and personified reality is always invested in the words of other people: the words of the mother, for example, in relation to the words of others and to one's own words; words as visions, insights, and revelations; words as intoned in orders, demands, precepts, prohibitions, promises, and the like (163–64). Finally, texts are situated in relationship to authors and listeners (or readers or viewers) and in relationship to listeners not as ideals (e.g., the literary scholar) but as empirical realities or as images in the soul of the author (165). In each instance, texts are situated in relationship to the voices of real people speaking, not in relationship to an external thing-like reality.

If we read (or listen to) the earlier dialogues of Plato in relationship to each other rather than in relationship to the later dialogues, we will hear in them, as Bakhtin hears in them, the voices of Socrates and the sophists rather than the voice of the mature Plato. We will hear these voices debating the merits of their respective methods of public discussion: Socrates' art of dialogue, Protagoras' methods of debate and instruction through poetic interpretation, and Gorgias' rhetoric. Moreover, if we listen to the voices that Socrates and the young Plato must have listened to, then we will hear Homer and Simonides, Laches and Nicias, Protagoras and Gorgias, perhaps even Thucydides, but not Phaedrus and Thrasymachus, the mature Plato, or the later Aristotle (which is not to say that we could not listen to these later voices from our own contemporary perspective, if we chose to do so, as we often do). If we observe, furthermore, that Plato the author cannot resist introducing his own voice—his own surplus of meaning—into the dialogues, then we will hear his voice as well. Indeed, we must hear his voice if we are to grasp the allusions to Laches' and Nicias' defeat and death in the Peloponnesian War in the *Laches* or if we are to understand the parody in Protagoras' comments on the relativity of the good or Socrates' interpretation of Simonides' poem in the *Protagoras* or if we are to hear the echoes of Athenian policy in Callicles' speeches or catch the allusions to Socrates' trial and execution in the *Gorgias*. We can make other choices, of course, but if we listen with Bakhtin, these are some of the many voices that we will hear.

4

Cultural Conflict and the Testing of Persons and Ideas in the *Laches*

In *Problems of Dostoevsky's Poetics,* Mikhail M. Bakhtin suggests that a reading of the texts of the Socratic dialogues will reveal a free and creative interplay of ideas and persons against a dialogizing background of other ideas.[1] In his late essays, he argues that a reading of texts of this kind will require attention to their contextual and extratextual meanings, that is, their meanings as texts in relationship to their extratextual historical reality (their historical context as expressed in the voices of other people) and also in relationship to other texts.[2] Studies of the early dialogues most concerned with public discussion usually approach them from the perspective of Plato's later philosophical or dialectical rhetoric.[3] Thus they read the *Gorgias* from the perspective of the *Phaedrus,* the earlier *Gorgias* illustrating the false rhetoric of the sophist Gorgias, the later *Phaedrus* illustrating the true dialectical rhetoric of Plato's Socrates.[4] Similarly, they read the *Protagoras* as a counterpart to the *Gorgias,* both dialogues illustrating the confrontation between the sophists' rhetorical display, on the one hand, and the philosopher's dialectical rhetoric, on the other.[5] Bakhtin, however, invites an alternative reading of the Socratic dialogue as a free and creative interplay of the ideas of Socrates and the sophists against the dialogizing background of other ideas—as an interplay of ideas within the texts, between the texts in their contextual relationships to each other, and within the texts as situated in their extratextual historical context. Thus situated, the Socratic dialogues resonate with the voices of other people—of Homer and Simonides, Pericles and (perhaps for Plato) Thucydides.[6] They also stand in multiple contextual relationships to each other, and they reveal multiple textual relationships of ideas—a testing of ideas one

67

against another, a creative interplay of ideas by which new ideas are born, and a contesting of ideas in carnivalesque debate—evidence of the author's active participation and also his occasional intervention in the creative process, through the exercise of his "surplus" of meaning and understanding.[7] If we approach the dialogues from this perspective, we will see how they reenact the cultural conflict among the virtues in late fifth-century Athens, and we will see how Socrates responds to this problem by *dialogizing* the thoughts and the lives of others, their methods of debate and persuasion, their cultural beliefs and their rhetorical practices (though from different textual and con-textual and extratextual perspectives, of course, we might also see them dif-ferently). From this perspective, we will see Socrates engaging his art of dia-logue *(dialegesthai)* as a way of revealing to others the cultural conflicts in their accounts of their ideas and themselves—in the *logos* that represents both what they say and how they live.[8] We will see him discussing his art with the sophists Protagoras and Gorgias, developing its guidelines, defending it against their methods of debate and persuasion, and concluding that the only true art of politics is his own art of dialogue. Finally, we will see him chal-lenging the cultural ideals and the rhetorical practices of Periclean Athens and reaffirming an alternative cultural ideal of the unity of virtue by his own life and death, in the dialogue on the threshold at the end of the *Gorgias*.

The cultural conflict about the virtues has its roots in the warrior culture depicted in Homer's epics.[9] Put simply, it is a conflict between the excellence *(aretē)* of the good person—noble birth, high social standing, and, in the war-rior, courage *(andreia),* skill, and, of course, success—and the virtue *(aretē)* or virtues—in particular, justice *(dikaiosunē)* and temperance or self-restraint *(sōphrosunē)*—required in a civil society.[10] The conflict evident in the Homeric epics became especially acute in late fifth-century Athens, which continued to adhere to the traditional ideal of courage, skill, and self-interest in the administration of its affairs even as it disavowed any justice in its relationship with other states, its ideal justifying equally well both the administration of the Athenian empire and the rule of the Thirty Tyrants.[11] This conflict shapes and motivates the discussions in the Socratic dialogues, especially in the *Laches,* which depicts Socrates' search for a definition of courage *(andreia),* and in the two dialogues directly concerned with methods of public discussion, the *Protagoras* and the *Gorgias,* which explore the rela-tionship of courage to justice and temperance and the rest of virtue *(aretē).*[12] The conflict presents an immediate and pressing social problem, for the Homeric ideal seems to justify the person of courage and skill who is unjust to others but who claims to remain virtuous nonetheless, and the sophists' methods of display, poetic interpretation, and persuasion seem—to Socrates—to promote rather than challenge this ideal. Socrates attempts to address these problems by *dialogizing* contemporary cultural beliefs and dis-cursive practices: testing the cultural beliefs of the most important people of his time, working to create a new cultural ideal that joins the traditional virtue of courage to the newer civic virtues of justice and temperance, and contesting the cultural ideals and the rhetorical practices that support what he believes to be an unjust empire.

In the *Laches,* Socrates tests the ideas and the persons of Laches and Nicias by drawing forth and juxtaposing their definitions of courage and juxtaposing them also to his own explanation of courage as one with the other virtues. Laches offers a Spartan account *(logos)* of courage *(andreia)* as endurance motivated by shame and respect for law but is unable to associate courage with reason, justice, and civic responsibility.[13] Nicias offers an Athenian account of courage as intelligence and skill in warfare but clings to a traditional legalistic piety that prevents him from grasping the Socratic view that courage as the knowledge of good and evil must somehow be related to civic justice, temperance, and piety.[14] Both Laches and Nicias are trapped by traditional cultural beliefs that they do not comprehend, unable to distinguish courage itself from courage in its relationship to the other virtues, unable to hear the voices of Homer and Simonides that might have helped them to understand true courage as courage in a just cause.

In the *Protagoras,* Socrates joins with Protagoras and the other sophists to create guidelines for conducting joint discussions and to create a new idea and a new cultural ideal, a cultural hybrid that joins courage to the other virtues. Protagoras upholds the civic virtues of justice and temperance but separates courage from the other virtues on grounds that some persons are exceptionally courageous but unjust. Socrates accepts Protagoras' claims about the civic virtues and then develops, with Protagoras and the other sophists, a joint account *(logos)* of the virtues that shows that they are related, both each to the others and each as part of a single whole, so that a person cannot be courageous but unjust. In the process, Protagoras parodies his own view of the relativity of the good, and Socrates parodies his method of interpreting Simonides' poetry, but the voices of Protagoras and Simonides speak out from behind the parodies, thus reasserting Protagoras' position and requiring that Plato exercise his surplus of meaning to force the dialogue to its inevitable conclusion.

Finally, in the *Gorgias,* Socrates contests Gorgias' notion of rhetoric because it produces belief, not knowledge, about justice and injustice. He contests Polus' belief in the power of rhetoric to promote injustice because he is convinced that injustice is the greatest of evils and that rhetoric is useless, except as a means of bringing the unjust person to justice. He contests Callicles' belief that the person of excellence or virtue *(aretē)* is the person of courage *(andreia)* and intelligence *(phronēsis)* and simultaneously tests his own account *(logos)* of courage as one with the civic virtues of justice and temperance.[15] Last, he contests Pericles' politics of empire and his rhetorical practice because he believes that neither Pericles' politics nor his rhetoric but only his own art of dialogue can improve people's lives by making them more just. Thus he decrowns the great Athenians of the past and present, using carnivalesque images to show them that their lofty ideals are nothing more than the stuff of pastry chefs and catamites. He hints at redemption for himself and Athens, however, with his confession of his own life and with his challenge to Callicles and to his contemporaries to prepare themselves for their own confession of their lives before their divine judges—their own dialogues on the threshold. Thus he upholds his claim that he alone practices the true art of politics: the art of dialogue.

CULTURAL CONFLICT FROM HOMER TO SOCRATES

Situated in its extratextual context, the Socratic dialogues reflect the cultural conflict about the virtues that was persistent in Greek thought from Homer to Plato. In these early dialogues, however, this conflict was not only intellectual but also personal, for at this time the idea and the person were still combined, so that the dialogical testing of the idea was simultaneously a testing of the person in a free and creative interplay with other persons. Julia Kristeva explains that at the time that the Socratic dialogues took form the person was still one with the idea because the process of separating the word as act from the image as knowledge, as idea, had not yet been completed.[16] This identification of the person with the idea was a powerful force for the preservation of traditional cultural values, values that were, however, conflicted even as they were preserved in cultural memory. Eric A. Havelock's studies of early Greek culture demonstrate the role of poetry and of Homer's epics in particular in the preservation of cultural values and the inevitable identification of the idea with the person in this process of preservation.[17] According to Havelock, Greek culture through the early fifth century was still primarily an oral culture, and so necessarily its principal means for the preservation and transmission of cultural values was the collective social memory of successive generations embodied in the only verbal technology capable of ensuring the fixedness of transmission from person to person and from generation to generation: "the rhythmic word organized cunningly in verbal and metrical patterns which were unique enough to retain their shape"—what we now call *poetry*.[18] Because it was recited and memorized, not read, poetry became a part of each person's living memory, through a process of "total personal involvement and therefore of emotional identification with the substance of the poetised statement" and a consequent "total loss of objectivity."[19] In this process, those who recited and listened to Homer's epics did not merely *observe* but *became* Achilles or Agamemnon, Odysseus or Penelope. So we need not wonder that Plato at the end of the *Republic* is so determined to exclude poetry from higher education—for reflective thought, philosophy, required the separation of the knower from the known and the recognition of the known as an object separate from oneself.[20]

But this process of separation had not yet been completed at the time that the Socratic dialogues took form, and so for Socrates the testing of the idea was also and necessarily a testing of the person who held it. Socrates perceived such a testing to be necessary because the cultural values preserved in the living memory of each person were in conflict with themselves. This conflict in cultural values from Homer to Plato has been described as a conflict between self-regarding virtues such as courage and knowledge or professional skill *(epistēmē)* and other-regarding or "quieter" virtues such as justice and temperance.[21] Traditional standards, since Homer, had associated the excellence *(aretē)* of the good *(agathos)* and noble and brave *(esthlos)* person most strongly with those qualities necessary to a warrior culture, both in war and in peace: noble birth, high social standing, courage and skill in battle, and, above all, success, without regard for good intentions. Such standards proved to be problematic, of course, in practice, since they offered no protection against persons of courage, skill, and high social standing who preyed upon others in their own self-interest or who sought to preserve and protect their own social standing and possessions from others who might prey upon them. The problem of *aretē* thus becomes, for Plato, a problem of linking a sense of justice to traditional standards of excellence. According to Arthur W. H. Adkins, "Plato's chief problem in ethics is the problem which has existed in Greek values from Homer onwards: namely, that of affixing *dikaiosune* [justice], and the quiet virtues generally, to the group of values based on *arete* so firmly as to make future severance impossible."[22] In the *Republic,* Plato solves this problem by linking the virtues to each other in a strict class system that assigns a specific role to each virtue in the proper functioning of both the state and the individual tripartite soul.[23] He thus preserves his conservative political convictions by stating them in abstract propositions permanently affixed in writing. In the *Phaedrus,* Plato assigns the virtues to a world of abstract Forms residing in the region above the heavens.[24] For the Socrates of the early dialogues, the problem of *aretē* is complicated by its situatedness within the persons and the ideas of those with whom he conducted his discussions. Thus for Socrates the problem is to draw forth from other persons a recognition of the cultural conflicts within themselves, to test his own and others' beliefs about the virtues, and to determine how to use these beliefs as a guide to right action in practical decisions about complex moral issues. Such a problem is best engaged (if not resolved) by continually testing his own and others' persons and ideas through dialogue, not through statements or pronouncements of abstract principles about the virtues. As I suggest in my Epilogue, this testing of persons and ideas persists even in the later *Phaedrus.*

CULTURAL CONFLICT IN THE HOMERIC EPICS

Homer's epics illustrate the cultural conflict between and among the virtues that was a part of the living memory of each person from Homer to Plato. The epics uphold a standard of the good *(agathos)* and noble and brave *(esthlos)* person, the person of excellence *(aretē)*, of courage and skill both in war and in peace. They also reveal the limitations of this standard. The *Iliad* tells the story of the Greeks' siege of Troy to take Helen from Paris and to return her to her husband Menelaus.[25] In the tenth year and near the end of the siege at Troy, Achilles and Agamemnon quarrel over women taken as booty in a raid on a neighboring town. Agamemnon has been allotted a woman, Chryseis, as his prize but is forced to return her to her father to put an end to a plague that her father has brought upon his army. He therefore takes another woman, Briseis, from Achilles to compensate himself for his loss (1.8 ff.). Achilles, in anger, withdraws himself and his men from the fighting, and the Greeks fare badly as a result of the loss of their greatest hero (1.488 ff.; 2–8). Realizing his mistake, Agamemnon offers to return Briseis to Achilles, with additional gifts and honors (9.9 ff.). Achilles refuses his offer, and in his absence from the fighting the Greeks are beaten back to their ships and one of their ships set afire (9.307 ff.; 10–15; 16.112–29). To save them, Achilles' friend Patroclus dons Achilles' armor, throws himself into the fighting, frightening and turning back the Trojans, but is himself killed and stripped of his armor by Hector, greatest of the Trojan heroes (16–17). Recognizing the destruction caused by his anger, Achilles returns to battle, leads the Greeks as they drive the Trojans back into their city, kills Hector, and drags his body by the heels through the dust (18–22). The Greeks bury Patroclus' body ceremoniously, and Achilles, in pity, returns Hector's body to his father for burial (23–24).

In a narrow sense, the cultural conflict in the *Iliad* is a conflict between one good person and another over the just distribution of the rewards due to the victors in battle—a conflict of self against self. Havelock explains the conflict in this narrow sense and explains also the system of procedural justice by which it is resolved.[26] According to Havelock, both Achilles and Agamemnon have reasonable claims.[27] Both are good men, good and brave fighters *(agathoi)*, men of excellence and valor *(aretē)* (1.131; 1.275; 3.179; 11.761–62; 11.782–83; 19.155). Both have high social standing, material possessions, and physical strength, and both are successful in battle, victory being their greatest honor, defeat their greatest shame.[28] By custom, Achilles has a right to the *property* (including human *property*) that has been awarded to him as his share of the booty, and Agamemnon has a right to compensation for his loss suffered as a result of his decision to return *property* that has been awarded to him (1.53 ff.).[29] The Greek company has, however, no conceptual sense of justice *(dikaiosunē)* but only general rules and procedures by which to resolve such differences.[30] They therefore meet in assembly, where they present their arguments, offer proposals, make decisions, and formalize commitments and agreements (2.50 ff.; 9.9 ff.; 19.40 ff.; 23.534 ff.).[31] Each in turn holds a scepter as symbol of the right to speak (2.100–109; 2.278–83; 9.37–39; 9.96–99; 23.566–69).[32] George A. Kennedy shows that their speeches have many of the technical and stylistic qualities later codified in formal rhetorics.[33] G. Mitchell Reyes maintains, moreover, that the speeches include persuasive appeals grounded in justice, conceived, however, not as an abstract principle but as a set of communal traditions.[34] These techniques and traditions provide rules and procedures for adjudicating conflicts between and among *good* persons, but they provide merely a prototypical procedural justice *(dikē),* not a broad concept or principle of justice.[35] Thus they provide no protection for society against good persons, especially good persons who are also good speakers, who might in self-interest do harm to others.

In a broader sense, the cultural conflict in the *Iliad* is a conflict between the immediate self-interests of good persons and the interests of both Greeks and Trojans in the long term—a conflict of self against others. This conflict is revealed in the unfolding course of events in the story and in differences of perspective between Greeks and Trojans. Initially, neither Achilles nor Agamemnon demonstrates any awareness of the interests of others. Each pursues his own self-interest in what he perceives to be the just distribution of the *prizes* taken in battle. Neither recognizes (nor does Havelock acknowledge) the interests of the women taken and exchanged as though they were mere *property* or *possessions*. Neither recognizes the harm that they are doing to the Greek company until long after the harm has been done. Agamemnon almost immediately recognizes the potential for harm to the Greek company (2.374–80), but only after they have suffered serious reverses does he seek a reconciliation with Achilles, blaming Delusion for his madness and for the evil in his heart (9.114 ff.; 19.85 ff.).[36] Achilles purposely brings devastation upon the Greeks by his absence from the fighting, but only after the death of Patroclus does he accept Agamemnon's offer of reconciliation, blaming Strife for his anger (18.97 ff.).[37] Hector, in contrast, does seem aware of the interests of others. From the Greeks' perspective, Hector is a man of valor *(aretē),* but he is also bold or daring *(tharsaleos)* for facing Achilles (22.268–69).[38] From the Trojans' and Hector's own perspective, however, Hector is not cowardly or even bold but rather noble and brave *(esthlos),* best and bravest *(aristos)* of the Trojans, for defending his family, knowing, as he does, that eventually he will be killed in battle and that his wife will become the *property* of another man (6.444; 6.460).

This conflict between self and others, which we would recognize as a conflict between the justice due to oneself and the justice due to others, is inexplicable within the framework of the *Iliad* in terms of the only standard that the poem offers: the standard of the good *(agathos)* person, the person of excellence and valor *(aretē).* The story as it unfolds before us illustrates the problem of *aretē,* the harm done to others by purportedly good persons. The quarrel between Achilles and Agamemnon encompasses both the women seized and bartered as *property* and the entire Greek company. The quarrel between Menelaus and Paris encompasses both the Greeks and the Trojans and leads to the destruction and indeed the complete obliteration of Troy. The standard of *aretē* offers no explanation and no way out of the difficulty. However, its characteristic usage suggests the possibility of linking *aretē* to the interests of others and thus to some rudimentary and as yet unarticulated sense of justice, a possibility that Socrates will exploit in the early dialogues. The standard in its simplest form is contrasted with cowardice, as illustrated, for example, by the poet's vivid portrait of forces waiting in ambush (13.275–94). In the case of Hector, the standard is contrasted not only with cowardice but also with boldness or daring—the word *tharsaleos* being applied in general to anyone who faces a superior force and in particular (and sometimes scornfully) to one's opponent (5.602; 16.493; 21.430; 21.589). From the perspective of the Greeks, Hector seems to be bold or daring for facing an opponent better than himself. From the perspective of the Trojans, however, he seems brave and noble for defending his home and family. From this same perspective, successive generations of listeners, too, must have perceived Hector's bravery to be linked to his concern for others—his family—especially if we recall that for this brief moment the reciter and the listener not only *observed* but actually *became* Hector, his wife, and the baby boy that he tosses in his arms (6.466 ff.).

Like the conflict in the *Iliad,* the cultural conflict in the *Odyssey* is a conflict of self against self and of self against other. The *Odyssey* recounts the wanderings of Odysseus on his return from the siege at Troy and of the treachery that awaits him upon his arrival in Ithaca.[39] At the beginning of the story and near the end of Odysseus' ten years of wandering, his wife Penelope and their son Telemachus are besieged by suitors to Penelope (1.44 ff.). Penelope cleverly keeps the suitors waiting for her for three years while she makes a shroud for Odysseus' father, weaving the threads by day and then unweaving them at night (2.84 ff.). Telemachus then travels from Ithaca to the Greek mainland in search of his father, leaving behind the suitors, who plot to ambush and kill him upon his return (2.129 ff.). Meanwhile, Odysseus, on his return from Troy, has lost his ships, his men, and all of his possessions and has been forceably detained on the island of the nymph Calypso (4.547 ff.). Eventually released by Calypso, he sets sail on a raft, suffers wreckage by storm, and swims ashore at Sheria, home of the Phaeacians (5). The Phaeacians receive him kindly, listen to the tale of his wanderings, and return him to Ithaca with generous gifts of clothing and gold (6–13). Upon his arrival, he hides his new possessions, disguises himself as a beggar, but reveals himself to Telemachus, who has escaped the suitors' ambush and arrived home safely (14–16). A beggar in his own household, mistreated by the suitors, Odysseus plots with Telemachus to catch the suitors unarmed and to kill them and, after some delay, does so successfully (17–22). At last, Odysseus reveals himself to Penelope and recounts his wanderings and his hardships (23). The suitors' families subsequently attack Odysseus and Telemachus and are themselves about to be killed when the goddess Athene stops the fighting and effects a truce (24).

In a narrow sense, the cultural conflict in the *Odyssey* is a domestic conflict between self-interested parties, Telemachus and the suitors, over Odysseus' wife Penelope—a conflict of self against self. In a broader sense, it is also a conflict between the self-interested suitors and the interests of Odysseus, his family, and his kingdom—a conflict of self against other. Havelock argues that the domestic conflict is irresolvable by procedural justice because one of the parties, the suitors to Penelope, inflicts such wrongs upon the other that any procedural adjustment becomes impossible.[40] He therefore seeks procedural "justice" in the potential "interpolis" or "intercity" conflict—the conflict between Odysseus and others in distant places, a conflict that reflects the interests of maritime communities in peacetime.[41] This potential conflict is averted by the hospitality shown to Odysseus, the "stranger-guest," by other peoples, such as the Phaeacians, and by members of his own household, when he appears before them as a beggar.[42] The domestic conflict, however, precisely because it is irresolvable by any procedural mechanism, also impacts others. As in the *Iliad*, each of the parties to the conflict has a reasonable claim, the suitors asking that Penelope decide among them, Telemachus that they feast in their own homes and at their own expense rather than his (1.365–80; 2.84–145).[43] They therefore meet in assembly *(agora)* in an attempt to settle their differences (2.1–259).[44] The suitors, however, threaten to kill Odysseus, breaking up the assembly (2.246–51), and later plot to kill Telemachus (2.660–72). Their threats and plots eventually destroy the suitors, however, and would also have destroyed their families, were it not for the intervention of the goddess.

As in the *Iliad*, the cultural conflict is inexplicable in terms of the standard of the good *(agathos)* person, the person of excellence *(aretē)*. Odysseus is noble and brave *(esthlos)*, Telemachus aspires to be, and Penelope, likewise, is noble and good and faithful *(esthlē)* (e.g., 1.115; 2.71; 2.117; 3.78). The suitors, similarly, remain the best and noblest and bravest *(aristoi)* and noble and brave *(esthloi)* men, despite harm that they do to themselves and others (e.g., 4.629; 4.778; 17.381; 22.204). The standard of *agathos* and *aretē* cannot differentiate between the two groups and thus offers no way of explaining or resolving the conflict. As in the *Iliad*, however, characteristic patterns of language and behavior suggest the possibility of distinguishing the good person who protects others—home and family—from the purportedly good person who is merely bold or daring. In the *Odyssey*, however, these patterns of usage are heavy with irony, created by the shifting perspectives of the poem. The suitors call Odysseus and Telemachus bold and daring *(tharsaleos)* because they seem defenseless, Odysseus in his disguise as a beggar, Telemachus as a young man and only son of Odysseus (1.381–82; 1.385; 17.449; 18.389–90; 18.410–11; 20.268–69).[45] More emphatically than in the *Iliad,* the word *tharsaleos* is used scornfully of others, with the suggestion that one perceives oneself to be the better person. In the *Odyssey,* however, the suggestion is ironic since the situation is not what it seems to be. Odysseus and Telemachus might well call the suitors *tharsaleos.* The suitors may call Odysseus and Telemachus *tharsaleos* only because they perceive neither the larger interests of family and kingdom nor the quality of men that they oppose. Within the shifting perspectives of the poem, generations of listeners, who understood the situation and could grasp the irony, must have perceived a difference between good persons who protect their homes and families and the purportedly good persons who oppose them and who are therefore merely bold or daring. Socrates plays upon these meanings as he tests his own and others' ideas in both the *Laches* and the *Protagoras.*

ANACRISIS AND SYNCRISIS: TESTING PERSONS AND IDEAS

The cultural conflict in the Homeric epics is a conflict between the purportedly good *(agathos)* person, the person of excellence and valor *(aretē),* and the justice that this person owes to others. In a narrow sense, it is a conflict between the competing claims of self-interested good persons; as such, it can be resolved through some mechanism of adjudication: the procedural justice of the *Iliad* or the blood feud of the *Odyssey.* In a broader sense, it is a conflict between the good person's immediate self-interest and the interests of others in the long term. Achilles and Agamemnon do not look beyond their own self-interest until after they have done great harm to the Greek company, and yet they remain *good* men. The suitors never look beyond their own self-interest, and yet they die *good* men. The standards of *agathos* and *aretē* offers no solution to this problem. As best, we may perhaps glimpse a possible resolution to the problem in the distinction between *aretē,* the courage or valor of the good person who defends home and family, and *tharsaleos,* the boldness or daring of the lesser person who opposes him or her. But such usage is not clear or consistent in the Homeric epics. The later Plato, as I have indicated, solves the problem of *aretē* by defining a specific role for each virtue within a strict class system and affixing it in writing. The earlier Socrates engages his art of dialogue to exploit the distinctions between courage/boldness and courage/cowardice to link courage to the knowledge of good and evil and thus to justice and the other quiet virtues, self-regarding to other-regarding virtue.

In several of the early and some of the later dialogues, Socrates tests his own and others' knowledge of the virtues, seeking but not finding a definition of each of them.[46] In early dialogues, he seeks definitions of courage *(Laches),* temperance or self-restraint *(Charmides),* and piety or holiness *(Euthyphro).*[47] In later dialogues, he seeks definitions of justice (the first book of the *Republic,* sometimes included among the early dialogues) and wisdom *(Theaetetus).*[48] In the *Laches* and the *Charmides,* he initiates a discussion of courage and temperance in relation to knowledge *(epistēmē)* or wisdom *(sophia)* and specifically the knowledge of good and evil. The *Charmides* seeks a definition of temperance and explores the possibility of explaining it as a kind of "science of sciences" or knowledge of the good.[49] The *Laches* seeks a definition of courage and suggests that it might be equivalent to knowledge of good and evil and hence to virtue itself.[50] A long tradition of scholarship on the *Laches* has emphasized the relationship of the persons of the two principal characters, Laches and Nicias, to the exposition of ideas in the dialogue.[51] Michael J. O'Brien argues, for example, that Laches and Nicias, the man of action and the man of words, offer definitions of courage that match their personalities and together represent the conception of courage that Plato would have us infer from the dialogue.[52] According to O'Brien, Laches' definition of courage as a kind of steadfastness of soul complements Nicias' definition of courage as the knowledge of good and evil.[53] Together, these two definitions point to a conception of courage as something like "intelligent steadfastness," a conception that closely approximates what Plato would have us believe is a completely satisfactory definition of courage.[54] Such a reading requires that Laches and Nicias are able to give clear if incomplete accounts of courage and thus can contribute to the development of the definition of courage that Plato's Socrates apparently wants us to hold. Walter T. Schmid, in contrast, argues that both Laches and Nicias are trapped by traditional notions of courage and unable to grasp the views that they put forward as their own.[55] Both share the Homeric view of excellence *(aretē)* as the courage and skill of the warrior, transformed, however, in both Sparta and Athens into the new ideal of the citizen-soldier.[56] According to Schmid, Laches holds the Spartan view of courage as endurance motivated by shame and respect for law and so is unable to distinguish the prudently courageous from the foolishly courageous person, courage itself from mere boldness or daring, unable in consequence to associate courage with reason, justice, and civic responsibility.[57] Nicias holds the Athenian (sophistic and Periclean) view of courage as intelligence and skill in warfare and comes to accept the Socratic view of courage as the knowledge of good and evil but clings at the same time to a traditional legalistic form of piety that prevents him from grasping, just as Laches is unable to grasp, the Socratic view that courage as the knowledge of good and evil must somehow be related to civic justice, civic temperance, and civic piety.[58] Situated thus in its extratextual context, the *Laches* shows why the Socrates of the early dialogues tests persons and ideas, why he questions Laches and Nicias, and why in questioning them he is questioning the life and mind of Athens itself.[59] Situated in its contextual relationship to the *Protagoras* and the *Gorgias,* the *Laches*

shows why Socrates in these later dialogues continues to search for a credible
and compelling solution to the problem of the relationship of the virtues, in particular the relationship of courage to the quieter virtues of justice and temperance. Both Laches and Nicias hold to traditional notions of excellence *(aretē)*
and, like Athens itself, seem unable to associate the courage and skill of the warrior with justice and the other civic virtues. Socrates engages them in dialogue
to test their commonplace cultural understandings, to reveal to them the cultural
conflicts in their accounts of courage and in themselves, hoping thereby to lead
them to a more just and temperate life.

Laches and Nicias as Historical Persons

The extratextual context of the dialogues helps to explain the cultural conflict in
the persons of Laches and Nicias and in the life of Athens itself. Writing with
the surplus of meaning afforded by historical hindsight, Plato was able to situate the *Laches* within the context of Athens' quest for empire and the war that
ended it: the Peloponnesian War (431–404 BCE) that set Athens and its empire
against Sparta and its allies, cost Laches and Nicias their lives, and brought
Athens defeat, the loss of its empire, and the dissolution of its democracy during the reign of the Thirty Tyrants.[60] Athens had pursued its empire without
regard for justice toward other states, motivated in part by economics, in part by
its sense of its own superiority, and not least by its conviction that the strong
always by right rule over the weak.[61] The Laches and Nicias of Plato's dialogue
hold to traditional notions of courage at a time when Athens had disclaimed any
concern for justice in its relationship with other states. Thus they are doubly
conflicted: they do not understand courage itself, and they do not understand
courage in relationship to other virtues. As a result, their actions and their affir-
mations of courage become hollow and empty. As re-created in Thucydides'
History of the Peloponnesian War, the Laches and Nicias of history are best
remembered for their actions in the decisive battles that cost them their lives.[62]
Laches is a less prominent figure than Nicias, appearing briefly in Book 5 as one
of the two generals who led Athens and her allies to defeat at the Battle of Mantinea (418 BCE)—according to Thucydides one of the greatest battles ever
fought between Greek states (5.74.1). At the outset of the battle, in response to
the Spartans' invasion of Mantinea, the Athenians and their allies, under the
command of Laches and Nicostratus, established a strong defensive position,
steep and difficult to approach, on a hill overlooking a plain (5.61; 5.64–65).
The Spartans advanced to within a javelin's cast of them, then strategically
withdrew. Astonished by their withdrawal, the Athenians and their allies blamed
their generals for permitting the Spartans to escape. The generals, initially
bewildered, subsequently led their army down the hill and onto the plain below.
The next day, the Spartans again advanced upon them, routed them, and would

likely have destroyed them were it not for a glitch in their formation that allowed the Athenians to escape (5.66–73). Both generals, however, were killed in the fighting (5.74). The situation in the battle is similar to the situation described in the *Laches* (193a–d), where Socrates elicits from Laches his belief that the person who endures in the weaker position is more courageous, but more foolish, than the person who endures in the stronger position—a belief directly at odds with Laches' belief that courage is a good and noble quality.[63] With his surplus of historical hindsight, Plato the author seems to be suggesting, through Socrates, that Laches' limited and conflicted understanding of courage may have led him to abandon the stronger (militarily and morally) defensive position in favor of the weaker (militarily and morally) offensive position and thus may have cost Athens the victory and Laches his life.

Nicias is a more prominent figure in Thucydides' *History,* not least because he led Athens to defeat in its assault upon Syracuse (415–413 BCE)—a total defeat for Athens and, according to Thucydides, the most brilliant success and most calamitous defeat in all of Greek history (7.87.5).[64] Nicias became the leader of the Athenian forces but managed the assault badly, acting slowly and cautiously when decisive action was needed, eventually finding his army and himself trapped by land and hoping to make their escape by sea (6.8–105; 7.1–49). At just the moment when they planned to embark, however, an eclipse of the moon occurred, causing Nicias to consult his soothsayers and on their advice to delay his departure for thrice nine days (7.50). Meanwhile, the Syracusans, learning of the Athenians' delay and hoping to prevent their departure, attacked them by sea, capturing their ships or running them ashore (7.51–71). Attempting to escape by land, the Athenian army was pursued by the Syracusans and totally defeated: many, including Nicias, were killed, and many were enslaved in stone quarries (7.72–86). Again, the situation in this battle is similar to the situation described in the *Laches* (198d–99e), where Socrates, attempting to link courage to the knowledge of good evil—past, present, and future— elicits Nicias' assent to the proposition that generalship takes precedence over prophecy, generalship having a better understanding of military operations, both what is happening in the present and what is likely to happen in the future.[65] Once more, Plato the author seems to be suggesting, through Socrates, that Nicias' limited and conflicted understanding of courage, his legalistic piety disassociated from the practicalities of military operations, may have cost Athens the victory and Nicias his life and, as a consequence, may even have contributed to the loss of the empire and to the dissolution of the democracy.

Within the broader context of Athenian policy, Nicias' participation in the fatal assault upon Syracuse is also illustrative of the deeper cultural problem of the relationship of courage to justice and to the other civic virtues. As depicted in Thucydides' *History,* Athens from the early days of its empire to the last days of the war had maintained a policy of power in the pursuit of self-interest and openly acknowledged the injustice of such a policy.[66] Athens had established its alliances with other Greek states as a defense against a recurrence of the Persian invasion.[67] It maintained these same alliances as a tyrant ruling over an empire.[68] In his Funeral Oration (2.35–42), Pericles praises the virtue and valor *(arete)* of both the men who gave their lives and the women they widowed during the first year of the war (2.35.1; 2.45.2).[69] In sharp contrast, in his speech during the Great Plague (2.60–64), Pericles boldly proclaims Athenian self-interest and injustice in the maintenance of its empire: "for by this time the empire you hold is a tyranny, which it may seem wrong *(adikon,* unjust) to have assumed, but which certainly it is dangerous to let go" (2.63.2–3).[70] Similarly, the Athenians, defending themselves against charges of aggression against the Corinthians (1.73–78), assert that their victories against the Persians at Marathon and Salamis proved to be the salvation of all of Greece, that their own honor, fear, and self-interest require that they now preserve their empire, and that the weak must always submit to the strong, without any plea for justice *(dikaios logos)* (1.76.2). Again, in their confrontation with the people of Melos, re-created in Thucydides' now famous "Melian Dialogue" (5.85–113), the Athenians reject any plea for justice and simply demand that the Melians submit to them since they all know that among practical people the standard of justice is always the power of the strong to do what they will and the plight of the weak to accept what they must (5.89; 5.97–98). In what is in fact an antidialogue, the Athenians simply demand capitulation, the Melians refuse, and in consequence the Athenians destroy them, killing their men and enslaving their women and children (5.116).

Nicias' presents similar arguments. For example, in his speech to the Athenian assembly prior to the assault upon Syracuse, he attempts to dissuade the assembly from launching the assault by arguments based upon the practicalities of power relationships between states (and Alcibiades persuades them to launch the assault by arguments of the same kind) (6.9–14; 6.16–18). In their speeches to their armies before the last disastrous encounter at sea, Nicias and the Syracusan general Gylippus envision the battle as a conflict between courage and justice (7.61–64; 7.66–68). Nicias explains the technical details of the engagement, emphasizes the plight of the Athenians, and calls upon the skill *(episteme)* and courage *(eupsychia)* of his forces (7.64.2). Gylippus, in contrast, invokes the justice of the Syracusans' cause, their right of retaliation upon an aggressor, and the certainty of their enslavement by the Athenians in the event of their defeat (7.68.1). Then Nicias, in the last moments before the battle, invokes traditional *arete*—citing the valorous deeds of his forces' illustrious ancestors—in the context, however, of a barrage of words that by this time have become conventional and hollow, saying, "whatever else men would be likely to say at so critical a moment, when they do not guard themselves against uttering what might to some seem trite and commonplace . . . in the dismay of the moment, thinking that these sentiments will be useful" (7.69.2–3). Whether or not he knew Thucydides' *History,* Plato knew well the tragic outcomes of the battle and the war. In the *Laches,* with the surplus of meaning afforded by historical hindsight, he seems to suggest that Athens' and Nicias' hollow commitment to traditional virtue, courage devoid of justice, had contributed to Athens' defeat and to Nicias' own death.

The Problem of the Virtues in Contemporary Scholarship

Thus situated in its extratextual context, the *Laches* shows why the problem of the relationship of the virtues is so important. Neither Laches nor Nicias nor Athens itself understands courage as a virtue in relationship to the other virtues. The consequences of their failures of understanding are apparent in the lives of Laches and Nicias and in the outcome of the battles at Mantinea and Syracuse and indeed of the war itself. Thus situated, the *Laches* also shows how Socrates attempts to resolve the problem and how Plato the author assists him by artfully juxtaposing the characters and their respective accounts of courage and by exercising his surplus of meaning to remind his readers of their tragic defeat and death. Socrates engages his art of dialogue by drawing forth (anacrisis) and juxtaposing (syncrisis) Laches' and Nicias' (and Athens') conflicted accounts of courage, inviting them to view each from the perspective of the other and also from the perspective of Socrates' own understanding of courage as the knowledge of good and evil and thus as one with the other virtues. Studies of the problem of the virtues in the early dialogues are divided on the issue of how the virtues are related—whether the several virtues are parts of a whole or a single unified whole, an identity or unity.[71] The parts/whole interpretation maintains that the individual moral virtues are related to wisdom as parts to whole, the identity/unity interpretation that all of the virtues together constitute a single entity that is equivalent to the knowledge of good and evil.[72] The *Laches* seems to suggest both possibilities, and indeed the issue frames the entire discussion of the virtues, beginning with Socrates' and the others' agreement that they inquire not about the whole but about a part of virtue, that is, courage (190c–d), and ending with Nicias' claim that courage is equivalent to the knowledge of good and evil and thus to the whole of virtue (199d–e), a claim at odds with their initial agreement. Proponents of the parts/whole interpretation maintain that Socrates himself agrees that courage is just a part of virtue, that he concludes that Nicias must give up his claim that courage is equivalent to the whole of virtue rather than their initial agreement, and that their interpretation is supported by their readings of other dialogues, especially the *Meno*.[73] Proponents of the identity/unity interpretation maintain that Socrates accepts Nicias' argument in support of his claim that courage is equivalent to the whole of virtue, that they need not retain their initial agreement that courage is a part of virtue rather than Nicias' claim that it is the whole of virtue, and that their interpretation is supported by their reading of other dialogues, in particular the *Charmides* and the *Protagoras*.[74]

The issue of the relationship of the virtues in the *Laches* seems irresolvable on the basis of the textual evidence alone, but it can be approached by way of the extratextual and contextual meanings of the dialogue, which suggest that some interpretations might be better than others. The extratextual context of the dialogue suggests that Socrates seeks to address the problem of the relationship of the virtues to each other and in particular the problem of the relationship of courage to the quieter virtues of justice and temperance. The contextual relationship of the *Laches* to later dialogues such as the *Protagoras* and the *Gorgias* suggests that Socrates attempts to solve the problem by linking courage to the other virtues as either parts to whole or as an identity or unity. The parts/whole interpretation maintains that justice, temperance, and the other moral virtues are related to each other as parts of wisdom, so that a person who has any one of them also has each of the others.[75] The identity/unity interpretation maintains that each of the virtues is equivalent to each of the others, so that, once again, a person who has any one necessarily has all the others.[76] Either interpretation would help to explain how Socrates solves the problem. Daniel T. Devereaux, however, takes the parts/whole interpretation to mean that the virtues are directly related only to wisdom and indirectly related, through wisdom, to each of the other virtues, with the consequence that one might be, for example, courageous but not just.[77] Such a relationship would not solve the problem and, as Devereaux admits, is not consistent with the account of the virtues in the *Protagoras*. Nor is it consistent with the account of the virtues in the *Gorgias,* which sets aside the larger issue of the relationship of all of the virtues and directly addresses the relationship of courage to justice and temperance in particular.[78] The contextual relationship of the *Laches* to the other dialogues suggests, moreover, that Socrates' solution to the problem of the virtues is not only intellectual or ideational but also personal. Nicias claims that Socrates examines not only people's ideas but also their lives and so helps them to see both how they have lived and how they ought to live (*Laches* 187e–188c), a claim supported by the *Gorgias* and also by the *Apology*. So the extratextual and contextual meanings of the *Laches* are doubly significant: they help us to sort out competing interpretations of the dialogue (though they cannot resolve the fundamental issue of the how the virtues are related), and they help us to see why these interpretations matter in people's lives.

Laches, Nicias, and the Problem of Traditional Virtue

The problem of the relationship of the virtues in fifth-century Athens was thus not merely an abstract philosophical or ethical problem but a cultural conflict of immediate and pressing significance. The extratextual context of the

Laches suggests that the problem had its roots in traditional notions of excellence *(aretē)* as courage and skill in battle that had persisted from Homer to the later fifth century. The interplay of ideas in the *Laches* reveals the failure of Laches and Nicias, both in their accounts of courage and in their lives, to provide a satisfactory solution to the problem. Plato's Socrates facilitates this interplay of ideas by testing Laches and Nicias, asking each of them to render an account *(logos)* of courage, drawing forth and juxtaposing the conflicts within their accounts, and juxtaposing these accounts both to each other and to Socrates' own account of courage in its relationship to the other virtues. This artful drawing forth and juxtaposing of the dramatic characters and their arguments reveals the limitations of both Laches' behavioral account and Nicias' moral account of courage, each in relation to the other and in relation to Socrates' account of courage as one with justice and temperance and thus with virtue itself. Plato's allusions to Laches and Nicias in their historical persons recall the many voices of Thucydides' *History* and so recall as well the limitations in the lives of the two characters, the failures of understanding that were also Athens' own failures of understanding, failures that proved so costly to each of them. Finally, the very subject of the dialogue must have recalled for Socrates' listeners and Plato's readers the voices of Homer and Simonides singing the praises of persons of courage—voices that might have helped them, though they apparently did not help Laches and Nicias, to understand courage as one with the other virtues, true courage as courage in a just cause.

The *Laches* has four main parts, plus a brief beginning and ending. In the beginning (178a–81d), Lysimachus and Melesias approach Laches and Nicias with the question of how they might educate their sons so that they will become good men. In the first part of the dialogue (181d–84c), Nicias and Laches present their views on the merits and the limits of the study of fighting in armor. In the next part (184c–89d), Socrates shifts the direction of their inquiry from means to ends, from the study of fighting in armor to the care of the soul, and he offers to question Laches and Nicias, thereby (so Nicias correctly surmises) testing both what they think and how they live. In the last two parts (189d–99e), Socrates and the others agree that care of the soul requires a knowledge of virtue and that courage is a part of virtue, and so Socrates tests Laches' (189d–94b) and Nicias' (194b–99e) knowledge of courage, demonstrating to each of them that he does not know what he thinks he knows and leading Nicias to admit that his explanation of courage as the knowledge of all good and evil equates courage with the whole of virtue, contrary to their initial agreement that courage is but a part of virtue. In the end (199e–201c), each of the participants admits that he knows nothing about courage, and Socrates suggests that they therefore look to their own education as well as that of the two boys.

The beginning and the first part of the dialogue present the problem of traditional virtue. Lysimachus and the others seek the kind of study that will make their sons good men, and they begin their search by assessing the study of the professional skills of the soldier, which in its highest form constitutes true valor *(aretē)*. The next three parts of the dialogue show how Socrates attempts to resolve the problem, engaging his art of dialogue to draw forth and juxtapose Laches' and Nicias' conflicted accounts of courage both to each other and to Socrates' own account of courage in its relationship to the other virtues. The juxtaposition of Laches' and Nicias' limited understandings of courage has suggested to some readers, most notably O'Brien, that *together* their definitions constitute the definition of courage that Socrates—and Plato—wants us to hold.[79] As I have indicated, however, I believe that Schmid is more nearly correct when he suggests that neither Laches nor Nicias understands courage as Socrates would have us understand it since neither understands courage in relationship to justice and the other civic virtues.[80] Whether Socrates supposes courage to be related to the other virtues as part to whole or as a single unified whole, he clearly believes that true courage depends not only upon the behavior or the skills of the warrior but upon a kind of moral knowledge, a knowledge of good and evil, a knowledge that encompasses all of the virtues, in particular the civic virtues of justice and temperance. Beyond the simple introduction of his own belief in juxtaposition to the beliefs of Laches and Nicias, however, Socrates does not test his belief in the *Laches,* nor does he test himself. The ending of the dialogue is therefore aporetic, for Socrates concludes, as he must, that none of the participants has the knowledge that together they seek.

At the beginning of the dialogue (178a–81d), Lysimachus and Melesias introduce the problem of traditional virtue. With Laches and Nicias, they have just observed a display of fighting in armor, and Lysimachus asks the two generals for their opinion on the value of this kind of training or other training that they believe will help to ensure that their two sons will become the best men *(aristoi)* (178a–80a). Laches defers to Socrates, who has also been observing the display, since both he and Nicias are aware of Socrates' interest in intellectual pursuits and since he also knows and respects Socrates for his conduct during the retreat from the battle at Delium (424 BCE) (180b–81b). Socrates, however, defers in turn to Laches and Nicias as older and more experienced though he also offers to add what he can to the discussion (181d). In the first part of the dialogue (181d–84c), therefore, Laches and Nicias present their opinions on the value of the study of fighting in armor. Thus they illustrate the problem that Socrates will have to address, the association of traditional excellence or virtue with the behavior and skills of the warrior, equally accessible to the bold or the courageous or even the unjust person. Nicias favors the study of fighting in armor because knowledge *(epistēmē)* of this kind promotes physical fitness, provides preparation for military duty, proves beneficial in actual battle, provides an introduction to the whole art of generalship, makes a person much more bold *(tharraleōteros)* and much more courageous *(andreioteros),* and helps him or her to develop a more smart and more terrifying appearance (181d–82d).[81] As Schmid points out, Nicias holds the characteristically Athenian view that knowledge construed as technical skill can help to make a person more fit for warfare and can even help to improve the person's character, making him or her more bold and courageous.[82] However, Nicias also believes that knowledge or skill of this kind is valuable because it serves the interests of the individual, not because it serves any useful civic purpose.[83] He does not distinguish the bold or daring from the courageous person, and he does not associate courage with civic justice or civic temperance. He seems to believe that the bold and courageous and skillful person is the best person, regardless of the purpose of his actions or the justice of her cause (and yet he was apparently anything but bold and courageous at Syracuse—so Plato the author reminds us—where in moments of crisis his legalistic piety and hollow commitment to traditional virtue cost Athens the victory and Nicias his life). Laches opposes the study of fighting in armor because he believes that the Spartans, whose only concern is warfare, have no interest in it, because those who teach it do not seem to profit from it and indeed sometimes appear to be unusually foolish, and because it would seem to make the cowardly person *(deilos)* more rash and therefore more conspicuous and the courageous person *(andreios)* more pretentious and therefore more subject to slander and laughter, unless such a person were truly superior to others in valor *(aretē)* (182d–84c). Laches holds the characteristically Spartan view that a person's behavior, motivated by shame and by a respect for law, not knowledge or skill, makes the person fit for warfare.[84] Unlike Nicias, Laches believes that a sense of shame and a respect for law will motivate a person to serve public rather than personal, civic rather than individual interests.[85] Laches cannot explain, however, what a person should do when his or her own sense of shame conflicts with civic interests (as it apparently did at Mantinea—so Plato again reminds us—where Laches allowed his army to shame him into relinquishing his superior defensive position and thus to shame him also into defeat and death).[86] Thus he is no more able than Nicias is able to distinguish the bold from the courageous person or to associate courage with the purpose of one's actions or the justice of one's cause.

The Testing of Laches and Nicias

Socrates, in contrast, seeks the kind of knowledge that constitutes and distinguishes true courage. Consequently, in the second part of the dialogue (184c–89d), he shifts the inquiry from skill at fighting in armor to knowledge of what is good for one's character or soul, from behavior and skill to moral knowledge, and he offers to question Laches and Nicias to determine whether either they or anyone among their acquaintances possesses this knowledge.

Socrates' questions, however, as Nicias correctly surmises, are not so much a means of seeking knowledge as a means of testing others' accounts of themselves—both what they say and how they live—thus demonstrating to them that they do not have the knowledge that they claim to have. Given the difference of opinion between Laches and Nicias, Lysimachus invites Socrates to join the discussion and cast the decisive vote (184c–d). Socrates protests that knowledge cannot be established by majority vote and that, in any case, skill at fighting in armor is not the kind of knowledge toward which they ought to direct their inquiry (184d–85e). He argues by analogy. Just as Lysimachus would seek an athletic trainer to prepare his son for an athletic contest, so also he should seek not a majority opinion but an expert opinion on the subject of the current discussion. And just as they would seek an expert on eyes for advice about eye drops or an expert on horses for advice on bridling horses, so with respect to the current discussion they should seek an expert on the treatment of the character or soul *(psuchē)* rather than an expert on fighting in armor, that is, an expert on the end toward which their inquiry is directed rather than the means (185e).

Socrates, however, claims no such knowledge of his own, so he offers to question Laches and Nicias, who have greater means, who are older, who have openly declared their opinions, and who therefore may be presumed to possess this knowledge (186a–87b). Nicias, having observed Socrates on other occasions, forewarns the others that Socrates will test not only their knowledge but also their lives, past, present, and future (187d–88c). He tells them that he has observed Socrates drawing others into discussion *(dialegesthai)* and then, regardless of the topic, leading them into an account *(logos)* of how they live, and how they have lived, not stopping until he has tested them thoroughly—tested them in the strong sense of cross-examining them, questioning them by torture and by the rack *(basanizein)* (187e, 188b). Nicias anticipates that he and the others will get the same treatment, that the discussion will be not about the boys but about themselves, but he nonetheless agrees to be questioned because he understands that Socrates reminds them of wrongdoing in the past only for the purpose of helping them to lead better lives in the future (188c). Laches also agrees to be questioned because he loves a discussion with a person whose words and deeds harmonize "in the Dorian mode" and because he believes that Socrates, though he knows not his words but only his deeds, will prove to be such a person (188c–89c).

In the third and fourth parts of the dialogue (189d–99e), therefore, Socrates questions and thereby tests Laches and Nicias, juxtaposing within each of them his own conflicted accounts of courage, juxtaposing these conflicted accounts to each other, and juxtaposing these in turn to his own account of courage in relationship to the other virtues. He shows Laches that his adherence to the traditional notion of courage as the steadfastness and endurance of the soldier—a behavioral quality—conflicts with his belief that courage is a noble thing and that it does not permit him to distinguish courage from mere boldness or daring (189d–94b). He shows Nicias that his unreflective commitment to courage as a kind of wisdom leads him to accept a notion of courage closer to Socrates' own, courage as the knowledge of good and evil—a moral quality—but that it does not enable him to distinguish the wisdom of the solider from the wisdom of the doctor or seer, the courage of humans from the apparent courage (mere boldness) of animals, or courage itself from the other virtues (194b–99e).

Socrates suggests at the outset that he and Laches inquire not into the whole of virtue *(aretē),* which might be too much for them, but into that part of virtue that skill in fighting in armor is supposed to promote, namely courage *(andreia),* and he invites Laches to offer a definition of courage (190c–d). Laches responds with two definitions of courage, both of which emphasize behavioral qualities of the soldier. Laches first claims that courage is the willingness of the solider to face the enemy and not run away—a kind of steadfastness that ensures that the soldier will stand and fight (190e). Socrates responds with three counterexamples, each of which shows that behavioral qualities alone cannot define courage (191a–c). The Scythians and similarly Aeneas' horses fight as much while fleeing as while pursuing, he claims, and so also the Spartans at Plataea (479 BCE) fled from the Persians at first and then, when the Persians' ranks were broken, turned and routed them. Laches points out that both the Scythians and Aeneas are horsemen and fight as such but that he is speaking of foot soldiers. He acknowledges, however, that Socrates is right about the Spartans. Schmid claims that the Spartans showed anything but a firm resolve and a willingness to stand and fight at that battle at Plataea and suggests that the battle at Thermopylae would have been a better example of Spartan resolve.[87] Schmid is perhaps right about the Spartans, but Socrates' point would have remained the same in either case: the willingness to stand and fight—the behavioral quality—does not in itself distinguish courage from the other virtues or from mere boldness or daring. Socrates is looking for something more fundamental, something common to all instances of courage, whether on the battlefield or in any difficult circumstance, such as danger at sea or illness or poverty or public life (191c–92b). He suggests that if they were looking for a definition of quickness, for example, whether in running or harping, speaking or learning, they would say that quickness is the faculty that gets a great deal done in a little time. He invites Laches to offer a similar definition of courage. He is, of course, testing and challenging Laches, attempting to determine whether Laches does or does not understand the beliefs that he professes to hold and whether he does or does not understand the consequences of those beliefs.

Laches next argues that courage is endurance of the soul, a behavioral quality still but a behavioral quality deeply rooted in the Greek and the human spirit.[88] Laches thus approaches Socrates' notion of courage as a quality of the character or soul rather than as a behavioral quality. Socrates, however, demonstrates to Laches that he does not understand his own definition—that his definition of courage is at odds with itself.[89] Socrates elicits from Laches his belief that courage conceived as endurance, when joined with wisdom, is a noble thing, and then he elicits from him the contrary belief that a person who endures without wisdom, that is, without the knowledge and skill of the soldier, is more courageous, but also more foolish, than one who endures with wisdom, so that courage seems to be a foolish thing. Laches would be able to resolve the apparent contradiction if he could see that courage conceived as endurance is wise if and when it is based upon knowledge of what constitutes just and temperate action, not when and not because it is based upon knowledge of what is or is not technically or militarily feasible or advisable, that is, if he could distinguish courage in a just cause—for example, the courage of the Spartans at Thermopylae or Plataea—from mere boldness or daring.[90] But he cannot. Socrates tests him by drawing forth and juxtaposing his conflicting beliefs, forcing him to admit that he does not know what he thinks he knows.

Laches claims that courage as a quality of the character or soul is best described as endurance (192b). Socrates responds that not all endurance is courage since courage joined with wisdom is noble but endurance joined with folly is harmful, so that only wise endurance is courageous, and Laches agrees (192c–d). Socrates then seeks to show Laches that endurance with knowledge of what is technically feasible or advisable requires less courage than endurance without such knowledge, so that foolish, not wise, endurance, seems to be courageous, contrary to Laches' initial belief (192e–93d). Socrates offers a series of examples. He asks Laches whether a person who endures in war with knowledge and advantage of superior forces and position would be more or less courageous than a person in the opposing army, and Laches says that the person in the opposing army would be more courageous, though more foolish, than the person with knowledge of superior forces and position. Similarly, Laches agrees that a person who endures in a cavalry fight with knowledge of horsemanship is less courageous than the person who endures without it, and likewise the person who endures with a skill in slinging or shooting or the person who is adept at diving into wells is less courageous than the person without such knowledge or skill. He nonetheless concedes that persons who endure without knowledge and skill, though seemingly more courageous, are also more foolish, than persons who endure with knowledge and skill. Socrates reminds him, however, that he had initially claimed that foolish boldness *(tolma)* and endurance are harmful, that courage is noble, and so leads him to acknowledge that his conclusion—that foolish endurance is courage—is at odds with his initial belief (193d).

Socrates traps Laches in self-contradiction by drawing forth and juxtaposing his inconsistent and conflicting beliefs. Laches might have escaped the self-contradiction if he had recalled that the Spartans at Thermopylae or

Plataea or the Athenians at Marathon were universally admired for their courage, even though they faced vastly superior Persian forces, because they risked and they gave their lives in defense of their city, their homes, and their families. He might even have recalled that within the shifting perspectives of Homer's poems, even the ill-fated Hector and the apparently defenseless Odysseus and the actually defenseless but clever Penelope were perceived to be *esthlos* and *esthlē,* good and noble and brave persons, because they too, despite superior opposing forces, defended city, home, and family. If he had recalled these historical events or if he had preserved these cultural memories, if he had listened to the voice of Homer or to the voice of Simonides, singing the praises of the Spartans at Thermopylae, then he might have objected to Socrates' identification of wisdom with professional knowledge and skill, his reduction of foolish courage to mere boldness or daring. But he did not.

Writing with a surplus of historical hindsight, Plato the author permits the Laches of the dialogue to comment ironically on the historical Laches when he argues that the person who has knowledge and advantage of superior forces and position is less courageous than the one who does not have such knowledge. As I have indicated, the historical Laches (as portrayed by Thucydides) seems to have been shamed into relinquishing his superior defensive position at Mantinea, shamed into defeat and death. Schmid argues that the Laches of Plato's dialogue recognizes that courage requires a Spartan steadfastness and "strength of soul" but that he does not understand these qualities in relation to a guiding intelligence that can direct bold action toward just and reasonable and noble goals.[91] Schmid finds in Laches' notion of courage a fundamental tension between a self-regarding prudence *(phronēsis)* directed toward honor for oneself and an other-regarding prudence directed toward victory for one's city.[92] He believes that the Laches of Plato's dialogue resembles the historical Laches, the Laches who was unable to stand firm against his own soldiers— unable to distinguish the lesser prudence and nobility that moved him to seek honor for himself from the greater prudence that should have moved him to seek victory for his city.[93] Schmid's reading reveals the limits of Laches' understanding of courage, his inability to perceive its moral quality. At best, Laches can understand courage as a behavioral quality (steadfastness or endurance) in pursuit of a strategic goal (victory for his city). He cannot understand courage as a moral quality related, for example, to justice or temperance. The juxtaposition of Laches' and Nicias' accounts of courage emphasizes the limits of his understanding.

Unlike Laches, Nicias does seem to recognize a moral dimension to courage when he defines courage as a kind of wisdom—the knowledge of all good and evil, past, present, and future (194d, 199b–c). Nicias, however, is merely repeating what he has heard Socrates say on other occasions. Socrates demonstrates to him, therefore, just as he has demonstrated to Laches, that he does not understand his own definition of courage. At the outset of their inquiry, Socrates had suggested that they seek not the whole of virtue but only that part of virtue called *courage,* and the others had agreed (190c–d). Now, with assistance from Laches, Socrates tests Nicias and catches him in self-contradiction, drawing forth and juxtaposing his conflicting beliefs, showing him that he is unable to explain courage as a kind of wisdom because he apparently believes that courage is equivalent to the knowledge of all good and evil and thus to the whole of virtue, so that courage and wisdom and the other virtues are one, an identity or unity, contrary to their initial belief that courage is but a part of virtue.[94] Nicias could escape the self-contradiction if he simply agreed either that courage is one with the other virtues or that courage is somehow related to the other parts of virtue, so that one could not possess any one virtue without also possessing the others, that is, if he accepted either the parts/whole or the identity/unity interpretation of the virtues. But Nicias does not understand his own definition well enough to grasp either interpretation, his repetition of Socrates' words apparently having no more meaning for him than his practice of traditional forms of piety or his invocations of conventional notions of *aretē.*

Nicias initially asserts that courage is a kind of wisdom, for he has often heard Socrates say that a person, if wise *(sophos),* is good, if not, then bad (194c–e). He claims that wisdom is specifically a knowledge of what is to be dreaded or dared, either in war or in anything else.[95] Laches accuses Nicias of babbling nonsense and points out that people such as doctors and farmers know what is to be dreaded or dared in their own crafts but are not for that reason courageous (195a–c). Nicias hints at the moral dimension to courage when he observes that doctors know only what is healthy or unhealthy for their patients, not whether it is better, for any given person, to be healthy or sick, to live or die (195c–d). Laches objects that Nicias seems to believe that seers are courageous since only they know for whom it is better to be alive or dead (195e). Nicias, however, observes, that seers know only what will happen—whether a person will meet death or disease or loss of property or victory or defeat; they do not know (any more than doctors or farmers know) what is better for any given person (195e–96a). Nicias' apparent belief that it might be better to die than to live, better even to suffer defeat than to achieve victory, reveals a moral quality, the possibility of suffering defeat and death in a just cause, such as the defense of home, family, and city—as the Spartans did at Thermopylae, for example. Nicias' belief is consistent with Socrates' belief, expressed later in the dialogue and in the *Protagoras,* in the *Gorgias,* and in other dialogues, that courage is somehow related to other virtues, such as justice and temperance, and so seems to support either the parts/whole or the identity/unity interpretation of the virtues or both. Schmid suggests, however, that Nicias grasps only Socrates' words, not his meaning, and indeed Nicias seems unable to explain his own definition of courage, to explain, that is, what kind of wisdom constitutes courage, how wisdom and courage are related, and how, as a consequence, courage might be related to the other virtues.[96]

Socrates raises two difficulties for Nicias, each inviting him to explain courage as a kind of wisdom. Socrates first invites Nicias to distinguish the courage of humans from the apparent courage of animals, and Nicias replies by distinguishing courage from boldness. Socrates claims that Nicias' belief (that courage is knowledge of what is to be dreaded or dared) seems either to deny that animals can be courageous or to attribute to animals greater wisdom than is possessed by many humans (196c–97a). Nicias replies by distinguishing courage *(andreia)* from mere boldness *(tolma),* arguing that only a relatively few humans are courageous, that many men, women, children, and animals seem to be courageous but in fact are merely rash and bold and fearless (197a–c). Nicias' distinction between courage and boldness might have led him to perceive the possibility of distinguishing courage as a kind of wisdom related to the other virtues, courage as knowledge of the rightness of one's actions or the justice of one's cause, the kind of courage that permits one to face defeat and death. Nicias might have said that courage as knowledge of what is to be dreaded or dared is a courage so related to the other virtues that the courageous person must also be just and temperate and pious—which is just what Socrates suggests later in the dialogue. Nicias, however, does not understand his own definition of courage well enough either to explain or to defend it. Socrates nonetheless expresses his confidence in Nicias' sophistic wisdom, acquired from his friend Damon, an associate of Prodicus, and so presses their inquiry (197d–e).

Socrates next shows Nicias that his belief that courage is knowledge of what is to be dreaded or dared conflicts with his initial belief that courage is but a part of virtue. He reminds Nicias that they had agreed at the outset of the inquiry that courage is only one part of virtue, the virtues including justice, temperance, and other similar qualities as well as courage (197e–98b). He then tests Nicias' definition of courage directly. He asks Nicias whether what is dreaded is what we fear and what we fear is past, present, and future evil and whether what is dared is what we feel is safe and what we feel is safe is past, present, and future good, and Nicias agrees (198b–99a). Socrates claims that courage as a knowledge of what is to be dreaded or dared thus necessarily comprehends knowledge of all good and evil, past, present, and future and that the person who possesses knowledge of all good and evil is the person who possesses all of virtue, not only courage but also justice, temperance, and piety (199a–e). So the courageous person is the virtuous person, and courage is equivalent to the whole of virtue, contrary to their initial belief that courage is but a part of virtue. Socrates thus draws forth and juxtaposes Nicias' conflicting beliefs, catching him in self-contradiction. Nicias could escape the self-contradiction if he simply agreed that courage is equivalent to the whole of virtue or if he argued that courage, though a part of virtue, is so related to the other virtues that one cannot be courageous but unjust or intemperate or impious, that is, if he explained that what is to be dreaded is what is unjust or intemperate or impious and what is to be dared is what is just or temperate or pious. But he seems not to understand his own account of courage well enough to draw either conclusion.

With his surplus of historical hindsight, Plato the author permits the Nicias of the dialogue to comment ironically upon the historical Nicias when he claims that the seer knows only what will happen—whether one will live or die, achieve victory or suffer defeat—not whether it is better to endure the one or the other. Unlike the Nicias of the dialogue, the historical Nicias (as depicted in Thucydides) turns to the seers at a moment of crisis to determine the better course of action and on the seers' advice delays his departure from Syracuse and as a consequence suffers defeat and death. Schmid argues, however, that the Nicias of the dialogue and the Nicias of Thucydides' *History* are more similar than they appear at first notice, the Nicias of history appearing to possess at least moderate military skill until, broken by the weight of responsibility, he reverts to a legalistic piety, the Nicias of Plato's dialogue appearing as a progressive general closely associated with Athenian and sophistic wisdom until, broken by Socrates' relentless questioning, he accepts Socrates' apparent identification of the person who possesses all of virtue with the pious and law-abiding citizen, the person who behaves rightly toward others and toward the gods.[97] The Nicias of the dialogue and the Nicias of history are similar in another respect as well, the Nicias of history performing traditional acts of piety and invoking conventional but meaningless notions of *aretē* in support of an unjust policy of imperialism, the Nicias of the dialogue repeating what appear to be genuinely Socratic but (to him) meaningless notions of courage and wisdom with no understanding of their relationship to justice and to the rest of virtue.[98]

The juxtaposition of Laches' and Nicias' accounts of courage suggests the limitations of both. Laches understands courage as a behavioral quality required of a soldier in war but fails to understand its moral dimension. Nicias understands courage as a moral quality, the knowledge of good and evil, but fails to understand its relationship to justice and to the rest of virtue and its application to either the policies or the practicalities of war. Socrates suggests that courage might be understood as the knowledge of good and evil and thus as one with the other virtues, but his suggestion is at odds with his earlier suggestion, to which all have agreed, that courage is merely a part of virtue. Presumably, Socrates and the others could agree to accept the conclusion that courage is one with the other virtues, but they have not tested this belief. At the end of the dialogue (199e–201c), therefore, they are left with two conflicting accounts of courage and thus are in a state of aporia or uncertainty. Confronted with the self-contradiction in his beliefs, Nicias agrees that he and Socrates have failed to discover what courage really is, and Laches scornfully recalls his hope that Nicias' sophistic wisdom would have enabled him to succeed where he and Socrates had failed (199e–200a). Nicias promises to consult with Damon, the associate of Prodicus, and then to enlighten and instruct Laches, but Laches advises Lysimachus and Melesias to dismiss them both and to consult with Socrates (200a–c). Nicias agrees, and Socrates suggests that they all work together to arrange for their own and their children's education, and so the dialogue ends (200c–201c). Schmid observes that Laches seems more willing than Nicias to learn from Socrates and suggests that the ending of the dialogue reveals the limitations of sophistic wisdom and promise of a philosophical method.[99] If we read the *Laches* from the perspective of Plato's later dialogues, then we might be inclined to agree with this assessment. From this perspective, we might find in Nicias' unreflective restatement of Socrates' ideas the beginnings of the separation of the person from the idea, the knower from the known, that Havelock finds in the later Plato.[100] We might also find in the search for a definition of courage the beginnings of the philosophical method of dialectic or the inductive method in search of universal definitions that generations of readers from Aristotle to the present have found in the earlier dialogues.[101]

If, however, we read the *Laches* from Bakhtin's perspective on the earlier dialogues, then we might be inclined to assess it quite differently. We might suppose, for example, that Nicias is unable to learn from Socrates because he is unwilling—knowing that Socrates will test him, so to speak, by torture and the rack—to say what he really thinks. So Nicias merely repeats words that he has often heard Socrates speak, just as (in his historical person) he performs traditional acts of piety and invokes conventional notions of *aretē,* without understanding any of them. Thus he permits Socrates to test his ideas but not himself. Moreover, if we read the *Laches* in its extratextual context and in its contextual relationship to other early dialogues such as the *Protagoras* and the *Gorgias,* then we might find not the beginnings of a philosophical method but an attempt to address the as-yet-unresolved problem of the relationship of courage to the other virtues that had persisted from the time of Homer to the time of Plato. From this perspective, we might see in Socrates' suggestion that Laches, Nicias, and the rest of their company work together in their search for a solution to the problem a promise not of Plato's philosophical method of dialectic but of Socrates' dialogical art of questioning others for the purpose of testing their accounts of the virtues and of themselves and also for the purpose of bringing them together to create new ideas when he finds that he can—as he does in the *Protagoras*—and to contest old ideas when he feels that he must—as he does in the *Gorgias*.

5

Truth as Dialogic

Creating a Cultural Hybrid in the *Protagoras*

The *Laches* shows how Socrates tests the persons and the ideas of Laches and Nicias, asking each of them to render an account of courage and so to render an account of his life as well. Socrates shows them the conflicts in each of their accounts (and in each of their lives) and the limitations of each of these accounts from the perspective of the other and from the perspective of Socrates' own account of courage in its relationship to the other virtues. The *Protagoras* and the *Gorgias* show how Socrates engages the most prominent sophists of his time, defending his method of dialogue against the sophists' methods of display, poetic interpretation, and persuasion, working with Protagoras and with the other sophists to develop guidelines for their discussion and to create a joint account of the unity of virtue and engaging Gorgias, Polus, and Callicles both to contest their accounts of rhetoric and justice and to test his own account of dialogue as the art of engendering justice, temperance, and the other virtues and thus as the only true art of politics.

Traditional readings of the *Protagoras* tend to view the dialogue as oppositional, setting Protagoras and Socrates against each other and supporting one or the other's arguments and his methods, not both. Eugenio Benitez, for example, claims that Protagoras is disinterested in ethical argumentation, is concerned merely with advancing individual ends, and is capable of little more than grandiloquent display.[1] Socrates, in contrast, is committed to ethical argumentation, is motivated by a desire for excellence, and is dedicated to the pursuit of consensus and mutual discovery through cooperative inquiry.[2] Norman Gulley and others observe the striking weaknesses in Socrates' arguments, especially notable in the *Protagoras*.[3] W. K. C. Guthrie nonetheless attempts to defend Socrates, suggesting that his exchange with Protagoras simply carries his arguments "to the furthest point at which a Sophist can accept them."[4] Edward Schiappa, however, while observing that Plato is assuredly on Socrates' side, nonetheless concludes that the Socrates of the *Protagoras* is simply "obnoxious."[5] Mikhail M. Bakhtin's characterization of the truth-creating potential of the Socratic dialogue invites an alternative reading of the dialogues—and the *Protagoras* in particular—as a joint creation rather than as a simple opposition of ideas. In *Problems of Dostoevsky's Poetics,* Bakhtin recalls Plato's characterization of Socrates as a "midwife" who helps to give birth to new ideas, new "truths."[6] In "Discourse in the Novel," he explains these new ideas as novel linguistic and cultural hybrids.[7] The *Protagoras,* more than other early dialogues, illustrates this creating or *birthing* of new ideas, new hybrids. Traditional readings of the *Protagoras,* though tending to support one side or the other, nonetheless document the contributions of *both* Socrates and the sophists to the development of the method of inquiry and to the exposition of the ideas in the dialogue. Both Socrates and the sophists also contribute to the outcome of the inquiry—a joint account *(logos)* of the unity of virtue—a cultural hybrid that joins the traditional virtue of courage to wisdom and so also (implicitly) to the other civic virtues.

Read—as Bakhtin suggests—in its extratextual historical context and in its contextual relationship to other early dialogues, the *Protagoras* seems to revisit the problem of the relationship of the virtues: both the philosophical problem of the relationships of part/whole and identity/unity and the cultural problem of the relationship of courage to the other virtues. Studies of the problem of the virtues in the *Protagoras* find support for both the parts/whole and the identity/unity interpretations.[8] From an extratextual and contextual perspective, however, the more immediate and pressing problem in the *Protagoras* is not the philosophical problem of the nature of the relationship of the virtues but the cultural problem of the relationship of courage to the other virtues, in particular, a problem raised but not resolved in the *Laches.* From this perspective, the problem of the virtues is not so much to demonstrate *how* the virtues are related but *that* they are related, so that one cannot have any one of them without also having the others, so that, for example, one cannot be courageous but unjust—the problem illustrated so strikingly in the persons of Polus and Callicles in the *Gorgias.* The *Protagoras* seems to provide a solution to the problem through a creative interplay of ideas between Socrates and the sophists, which gives birth to a new idea—a cultural hybrid that joins self-regarding to other-regarding virtue. Both Socrates and the sophists contribute to the development of this hybrid, and Plato the author contributes as well through the juxtaposition and interplay of complementary arguments, through the apparently coincidental parodies of Protagoras' arguments and methods, and through the exercise of his surplus of understanding, his willingness to listen—only, however, for the purpose of permitting Socrates to attack Protagoras, to force him to acquiesce, to silence and thus to finalize him. Socrates, Protagoras, and the other sophists work together to develop the guidelines for rendering an account *(logos).*[9] Thus they lead us to believe that the account itself might be a cooperative venture or joint *logos.* Both Socrates and Protagoras contribute to the development of Socrates' account of the unity of virtue, to which Protagoras, though grudgingly, gives his assent. Unlike Laches and Nicias, the Protagoras of the dialogue upholds the quiet virtues of justice, temperance, and holiness as necessary in a civil society.[10] However, he disassociates courage from the other virtues on grounds that some persons are exceptionally courageous but unjust.[11] Socrates challenges Protagoras' methods of debate and poetic interpretation but he does not challenge Protagoras' claims about the civic virtues. Rather, he accepts these claims and then works with Protagoras to produce an account of the virtues that shows how they are related, both each to the others (a relationship of reciprocity) and each as part of a single whole (a relationship of identity or unity).[12] In the process, he offers an argument for hedonism that is itself a significant contribution to ethical theory.[13]

From this extratextual and contextual perspective, the *Protagoras* echoes with other voices as well, voices that also contribute to the development of Socrates' account of the relationship of the virtues. Protagoras cuts off Socrates' account of the reciprocity of the virtues, which posits a single good through which all of the virtues are related, by pointing out that the good is relational, in the sense that the good is always good in relation to *something.*[14] Protagoras' comments on the relational character of the good, though perhaps a parody, nonetheless convey a serious point.[15] As Bakhtin observes, parody does not simply destroy its object or target but rather re-creates it, permitting it to reveal its own world, speaking out, as it were, from behind the parody.[16] Protagoras' claim about the good as relational to *something* introduces a problem that is momentarily resolved by Socrates' argument for hedonism at the end of the *Protagoras.* But it also recalls the claim of the more celebrated Protagoras, the Protagoras whom we know from the *Theaetetus,* the Protagoras who speaks out from behind the parody, the Protagoras who claims that the things of this world are relative not only to *something* but also for *someone*—a claim that Socrates himself raises in his objections to Callicles' hedonism in the *Gorgias.*[17] Later in the dialogue, Protagoras interrupts Socrates' questioning with his invitation to Socrates to interpret some lines in a poem by Simonides. Socrates' interpretation of these lines is an evident parody of Protagoras' method of interpreting poetry.[18] It also serves, however, to reintroduce the central problem of the dialogue, the problem of traditional virtue and specifically the problem of the relationship of justice to the other virtues. For Socrates' (and Plato's) immediate audience, Simonides was renowned as the poet of heroic virtue *(aretē)* and courage *(andreia).*[19] In the lines that Protagoras invites Socrates to interpret,

however, he specifically raises the problem of the good person in relationship
to justice. Socrates ridicules Protagoras' method of interpreting poetry, but
both Protagoras' choice of subject matter and his method invite us to hear the
voices behind the parody—the voice of Simonides reintroducing the problem
of the good person and perhaps also the voice of Protagoras himself offering
his own interpretation of the poem and his own definition of the good person—the person who knows justice, the benefit of cities. Socrates and Protagoras return to the problem in the last part of the dialogue and produce their
joint account of the unity of virtue. This account is uttered, however, in
Socrates' voice alone, with Protagoras' grudging and silent assent—forced,
apparently, by Plato's exercise of his "essential 'surplus' of *meaning*."[20]

PROTAGORAS VERSUS SOCRATES?

Traditional readings of the *Protagoras* recognize the individual contributions
of both Socrates and the sophists to the development of the methods and the
ideas in the dialogue.[21] Eric A. Havelock contrasts Socrates' and the sophists'
methods of discussion, crediting the latter with the development of a theory
of communication as the negotiation of opinion implicit in the practice of the
Athenian parliamentary assembly.[22] According to Havelock, the Socrates of
Plato's dialogue is dogmatic, one-sided, and unfair, the practitioner of "an
interrogation," not a dialogue, governed by rules designed to control the
respondent, not the questioner.[23] The sophists, on the other hand, developed a
theory of dialogue "as a negotiation of opinion leading to agreed decisions"
and practiced neither interrogation nor "unscrupulous persuasion" but dialogue, indeed "a whole series of dialogues . . . in which negotiation of opinion finally produces a common product."[24] Schiappa documents Protagoras'
contributions to the development of the method of poetic interpretation and
the idea of participatory democracy.[25] According to Schiappa, Protagoras
developed the practice of critically analyzing the epic poets, making *mythos*
an object of analysis, not merely a tradition to be transmitted from generation
to generation but "a text that could be analyzed, criticized, and altered."[26] He
apparently developed his own *mythos* in his Great Speech in the *Protagoras*.[27]
The Great Speech contributes to the development of the idea of participatory
democracy by offering three potentially democratizing theses: the teachability of virtue, which suggests that a person can become virtuous not only
through birth or inheritance but also through education; a reconceptualization
of punishment as education rather than as retribution or vengeance for harmful acts (a corollary to the concept of the teachability of virtue); and a rudimentary theory of discourse aimed at participation by the many in the conduct
of civic affairs—a participation limited in practice, however, by the exclusion
of women, foreigners, and slaves.[28]

Socrates, too, contributes significantly to the development of the methods and the ideas in the *Protagoras*.[29] In contrast to Havelock, Benitez claims that Protagoras is disinterested in ethical argumentation and practices methods of display and debate aimed at approval and victory over an opponent while Socrates is committed to ethical argumentation and practices methods of dialectical exposition and dialogue directed toward the search for truth through cooperative inquiry.[30] Similarly, Terence Irwin claims that whereas Protagoras is concerned merely with winning the argument, Socrates wants to examine the merits of the arguments on both sides to determine what positions these arguments really commit a person to hold.[31] Socrates also contributes arguments in support of his ideas about the relationship of the virtues and about hedonism. Gregory Vlastos claims that the Socrates of the *Protagoras,* like the Socrates of the *Laches,* upholds the "Biconditionality Thesis" about the virtues, according to which justice and the other moral virtues are species or parts of wisdom (a relationship of parts to whole).[32] Vlastos believes that Socrates distinguishes the "Biconditionality Thesis" from the "Similarity Thesis," according to which the virtues are parts of a whole in the same way that bits of gold are parts of a gold bar, and from the "Unity Thesis," according to which the virtues are identical, each with each (a relationship of identity or unity)—both of which theses he rejects.[33] Irwin claims that Socrates upholds both the "Reciprocity Thesis," according to which the virtues "imply each other, and are therefore inseparable" (a relationship of part to part), and the "Unity Thesis," according to which the virtues "are really names of one and the same thing" and so are identical (a relationship of identity or unity).[34] Irwin and others note that Socrates provides support for his thesis about the unity of virtue in the form of an elaborate argument for hedonism, which explains how the virtues might be conceived as one, the pursuit of the greatest pleasure over the whole of one's life—that is, the good.[35]

Cooperative Discussion: Creating a Cultural Hybrid

Socrates' and the sophists' individual contributions to the methods and the ideas in the *Protagoras* suggest a simple opposition, no doubt reinforced by Plato's admiration for Socrates and his suspicion and even hostility toward the sophists, particularly overt in dialogues such as the *Gorgias* and the *Sophist*.[36] Bakhtin's claim for the truth-creating potential of the Socratic dialogue nonetheless suggests the possibility of reading the *Protagoras* as a joint creation rather than as a simple opposition of ideas, a possibility supported by the degree of respect shown for Protagoras in the course of the dialogue, by the contributions of both Socrates and the sophists to the methods and the ideas in the dialogue, and, not least, by the commitment on both sides to cooperative discussion in search of a mutually acceptable account of the virtues—a joint *logos*.

As I have indicated, the *Protagoras* seems to revisit the complex philosophical and ethical problem of the relationship of the virtues—the as-yet-unresolved problem of whether the virtues are related as part to whole or as an identity or unity. The *Protagoras,* however, has a particularly strong contextual relationship to the *Laches* and to the *Gorgias,* for each of these dialogues addresses the problem of the relationship of the virtues as a cultural problem of the relationship of courage, in particular, to the quieter virtues of justice and temperance, and each of these dialogues shows how Socrates engages his art of dialogue, though in quite different ways, as a response to this problem. Situated in its extratextual context and in its contextual relationship to the *Laches* and the *Gorgias,* the *Protagoras* seems to address not only the philosophical and ethical problem of the relationship of the virtues but also and more importantly the problem of the cultural conflict between the traditional virtue of courage and the newer civic virtues of justice and temperance, between the self-regarding virtues aimed at one's own success and the other-regarding virtues directed toward the good of the community.[37] The interplay of ideas in the *Protagoras* suggests that the problem of the relationship of the virtues is resolved in Socrates' and the sophists' joint account of the unity of virtue, which merges these two conflicting ideals of the virtuous life.

Socrates, Protagoras, and the other sophists all contribute to the development of this joint account. Protagoras contributes arguments in support of his claim that justice, temperance, and holiness—the quiet virtues—are essential to a civil society. Socrates contributes arguments in support of his claims for both the reciprocity and the unity of the virtues. Socrates and the sophists together develop guidelines for their discussion—rules for rendering and receiving an account. Protagoras contributes an objection to Socrates' account of the reciprocity of the virtues in the form of an account of the relational character of the good, an account that echoes throughout the *Protagoras* and beyond. Protagoras might also have contributed a method of critically analyzing poetry and so rethinking the traditional concept of virtue, as represented by Simonides, for example—if only Socrates had been willing to take him seriously. Schiappa rightly observes that Plato the author is unmistakably on Socrates' side, in the *Protagoras* as in the other dialogues with the sophists.[38] Thus Havelock claims, for example, that Socrates unfairly compels Protagoras to engage in discussion according to his rules, and G. B. Kerferd claims that Socrates forces closure at the end of the dialogue by leading Protagoras by illusion and mystification to acceptance of his own concept of knowledge as the definition or verbal specification of a singular universal, a concept of knowledge that Protagoras "simply does not accept."[39] Bakhtin surely overstates his case, therefore, when he characterizes the Socratic dialogue as a mere transcription of remembered conversations.[40] But Bakhtin also explains the Socratic dialogue as a creative interplay between Socrates and the sophists, a creative interplay that is enhanced by Plato the author's careful juxtaposition of the complementary arguments of *both* Socrates and the sophists, a creative interplay that is, however, abruptly terminated by his exercise of a surplus of understanding that forces the dialogue to its inevitable conclusion.

Protagoras and the Problem of Traditional Virtue

The *Protagoras* seems to be most directly and immediately concerned with the question of whether or not virtue can be taught. This question, however, is simply an occasion and an opportunity for Socrates to address the more important underlying problem of the cultural conflict between courage and the other virtues. Protagoras initially maintains that virtue can be taught, Socrates that it cannot. By the end of the dialogue, Protagoras and Socrates have apparently reversed their positions, Protagoras maintaining that virtue cannot be taught, Socrates that it can. As J. C. B. Gosling and C. C. W. Taylor point out, however, this reversal depends upon a fundamental change in the concept of virtue, from Protagoras' account of virtue as habituation or social conditioning to Socrates' account of virtue as knowledge and specifically as the knowledge of good and evil.[41] This change in the concept of virtue seems to provide a solution to the problem of the cultural conflict between courage and the other virtues, for if virtue is knowledge, then all of virtue is one, a unity, and courage is both inseparable from, and one with, the other virtues. This change in the concept of virtue also seems to provide an answer to the question of whether or not virtue can be taught, for if virtue is knowledge, then it can be taught. Such a concept of virtue apparently requires an art of measurement by which we may assess relative goods, but it does not explain how we are to acquire this knowledge, the art of measurement being left for discussion at a later time. The dialogue therefore rightly ends in aporia, for while it suggests a solution to the problem of the cultural conflict between courage and the other virtues in the form of the claim that the virtues are one with the knowledge of good and evil, it does not explain how we might acquire this knowledge. Plato returns to the problem of knowledge and its relationship to virtue in the *Meno* and provides a detailed description of the art of measurement in the *Statesman*.[42] The Socrates of the *Gorgias* and the *Apology,* however, disclaims any such knowledge of virtue, excepting only the knowledge that he acquires through his practice of the art of dialogue.

The *Protagoras* can be divided, somewhat unconventionally, into four main parts, plus an introduction and conclusion.[43] In the introduction (309a–20c), Protagoras claims to teach virtue, by which he means successful management of one's own affairs and the affairs of one's city. In the first part (320c–28d), Protagoras presents his Great Speech on the teaching of virtue and affirms the civic virtues of justice, temperance, and holiness. In the second part (328d–34c), he includes courage and wisdom among the virtues but notes that a person may be courageous but unjust or just but unwise. In response, Socrates seeks to demonstrate to Protagoras that each of the individual virtues is reciprocally related to, and therefore inseparable from, each of the others. Protagoras, however, cuts short his account with his claim about the relational character of the good. In the third part (334c–48c), Socrates and the sophists work together to establish guidelines for their discussion, and Protagoras takes his turn at questioning Socrates, asking him to interpret the lines in Simonides' poem. In the fourth part (348c–60e), Socrates again questions Protagoras and seeks to demonstrate to him the relationship of the virtues as one with the knowledge of good and evil, a relationship of identity or unity. Socrates offers support for his claim about the unity of virtue in the form of an elaborate argument for hedonism. In the conclusion (360e–62a), Socrates notes that he and Protagoras have apparently switched positions, and the dialogue ends in aporia. Such a division is unconventional because it suggests a close relationship between and among the various parts of the dialogue, including the third part, the discussion of Simonides' poem, which often seems to be merely an entertaining digression or interlude.[44]

The introduction to the dialogue (309a–20c) presents the problem of traditional virtue in the form of Protagoras' claim to teach good judgment in one's own affairs and in the affairs of one's city. Socrates ventures to the home of Callias, a wealthy patron, where he meets with the sophists Protagoras, Hippias of Elis, and Prodicus of Ceos and followers such as Alcibiades and Critias (314c–16a).[45] Socrates recommends his young companion Hippocrates to Protagoras, who associates himself with the sophistic art also practiced by Homer, Hesiod, and Simonides and who claims to teach good judgment *(euboulia)* in both one's own affairs and the affairs of one's city, both how best to order one's own home and how to influence pubic affairs in speech and action (316b–17c, 318d–19a).[46] Socrates praises the political art *(politikē technē)* of making good citizens and the virtue *(aretē)* of good citizenship but expresses doubt that such a virtue is teachable and challenges Protagoras to defend his claim (319a–20b). Schiappa argues that Protagoras' claim to teach good judgment in the management of household and civic affairs provides grounds for discursive participation by many in understanding, debating, and deciding public issues and thus contributes to the development of an implicit theory of *logos* as "sound discourse."[47] Irwin nonetheless finds Protagoras' claim to be fundamentally troublesome not so much because virtue is or is not teachable but because Protagoras has not shown (nor has Socrates shown) that teaching the virtues aimed at one's own success requires that one also teach the virtues that make a good citizen.[48] Stated thus plainly, and without elaboration, Protagoras' claim to teach good judgment requires only that he teach those skills that serve one's own advantage or the city's prosperity and stabil-ity.[49] As Arthur W. H. Adkins points out, "it seems unnecessary that *euboulia* should imply anything more than an eye to the main chance."[50] Such a stan-dard, and such a set of skills, serves equally well a Pericles or a Callicles, the management of a city or an empire, a democratic or a tyrannical rule.

Protagoras on Civic Virtue

Protagoras responds to Socrates' challenge in his Great Speech (320c–28d), in which he claims not only to teach virtue but to teach those virtues that make a good citizen, specifically the virtues of justice, temperance, and holiness. Protagoras' speech is an important contribution to the theory of participatory democracy and a substantive contribution to the development of the argument in the dialogue as well.[51] Protagoras, however, curiously omits courage and wisdom (except as a kind of practical skill—wisdom in the arts) from his list of the virtues required in a civil society.[52] Socrates will challenge him on pre-cisely this ground since the omission of courage leaves open the possibility that a person might be, as Protagoras himself suggests, courageous but unjust—exactly the kind of person that Callicles claims himself to be. In his Great Speech, Protagoras argues that everyone possesses a share of political virtue, that therefore everyone has a right to participate in discussions about the affairs of the city, and that these virtues can be taught. Protagoras begins the speech with an account of the myth of creation, according to which the gods created mortal kinds and gave to each of them different abilities, to some strength, to others speed, and so on (320c–21b). To humans, the gods gave wisdom in the arts, plus fire, so that they could put to use their wisdom in daily life (321b–22a). Thus humans were able to worship the gods, to speak, and to provide for their basic needs (322a). But they did not have the art of politics, so when they gathered together in cities, they did wrong to each other (322a–c). The gods therefore gave to humans right *(dikē)* and respect *(aidōs)* and gave them to all equally (322c–d).[53] Thus, Protagoras argues, when Athe-nians consult about the art of politics, they accept advice from all, for all have a share of justice *(dikaiosunē),* temperance or self-restraint *(sōphrosunē),* and the rest of civic virtue *(politikē aretē)* (322d–23c). Nonetheless, Athenians do not believe that this virtue is either natural or spontaneous but believe rather that it can be and is being taught (323c–24a).

Protagoras turns to contemporary practices of punishment and education to demonstrate that political virtue is being taught. Athenians do not punish wrongdoing with a view to the wrongdoing itself, he argues, for to do so would be merely irrational and bestial vengeance (324a–b). Rather, they punish with a view to the future, so that neither the wrongdoer nor those who observe his punishment will do wrong again (324b). They punish for deterrence, so they apparently believe that virtue can be taught (324b–c). Likewise, they educate to ensure that all citizens have a share in the one thing required to make a city— virtue *(aretē)*, that is, justice *(dikaiosunē)*, temperance *(sōphrosunē)*, and holiness *(hosiotēs)* (324d–25a). In childhood, nurse and mother and tutor and father strive to teach their children what is just and noble and holy (325c–d). Next, teachers give them poetry and music: poetry to read and memorize and imitate and music to encourage the reading of more poetry, the works of the songmakers (325d–26b). Finally, the city, too, contributes, compelling people to learn its laws and to live by them as a pattern or example (326c–d). If, despite these efforts, good parents sometimes have worthless children, then the fault is not the parents' failure to teach but the children's lack of natural ability (326e–27c). Because everyone teaches virtue, just as everyone teaches Greek, Protagoras observes, Socrates has mistakenly concluded that no one does (327e).

Schiappa claims that Protagoras' argument for the teachability of virtue, his reconceptualization of punishment, and his theory of discourse all contribute to the development of participatory democracy.[54] Protagoras' argument for the teachability of virtue shows how a person might become virtuous through education rather than through birth or inheritance only and how some persons, by this means, might become more virtuous than others.[55] Protagoras' argument thus extends the possibility of participation in civic affairs to far greater numbers of people.[56] Protagoras' reconceptualization of punishment as education redirects punishment from retribution motivated by vengeance toward deterrence and reform of criminal behavior and thus provides further support for Protagoras' claim for the teachability of virtue.[57] Finally, Protagoras' theory of discourse as participation by the many in the conduct of civic affairs provides a reasoned defense of participatory democracy—broad in principle, however severely restricted in practice.[58]

These substantial contributions to the theory of participatory democracy notwithstanding, Protagoras' Great Speech nonetheless presents several difficulties, only one of which is satisfactorily addressed in the *Protagoras*. First, Protagoras' earlier claim that he teaches good judgment in the management of household and civic affairs seems at odds with his later claim that he teaches the civic virtues of justice, temperance, and holiness. As Irwin explains, Protagoras claims to teach, on the one hand, skills and abilities that promote the success of the individual and, on the other hand, virtues that promote good citizenship, but he fails to explain how the one is connected to the other.[59] Schiappa points out that Protagoras probably regards the civic virtues not as cooperative virtues but as virtues or excellences that help to ensure the success, prosperity, and stability of the city.[60] Even so, Protagoras does not and apparently cannot explain what he would do if his own or his city's interest were to conflict with the interests of others, as it does in the case of Achilleus and Agamemnon, for example. Second, Protagoras' omission of courage and wisdom from his list of the civic virtues leaves open the question of whether or not and, if so, how these two virtues are related to the others. Of course, we cannot know whether the omission of courage and wisdom is Protagoras' or Plato's, but we can probably assume that Protagoras means to include them since he himself almost immediately introduces them into the discussion (329e).[61] Nonetheless, the question of the relationship of courage and wisdom to the other virtues remains at this point both unasked and unanswered. Third, Protagoras' emphasis upon education as a kind of habituation or social conditioning accomplished in part through the reading and memorization of poetry is problematic because it would seem to reinforce precisely the traditional notion of virtue as courage and skill in battle, inscribed in the Homeric epics, that Protagoras himself apparently wants to oppose. Protagoras probably intends that the study of poetry be undertaken critically—particularly since he makes a point of saying that the poetry is not listened to but read.[62] Nonetheless, his description of the education of children through memorization of poetry, imitation of the actions of its heroes, and reinforcement of the poetry by musical accompaniment would seem to promote its uncritical reception.

Protagoras and Socrates on the Reciprocity of the Virtues

In the *Protagoras,* Socrates addresses the second of these difficulties only. With respect to the first difficulty, Socrates seems to assume without argument that justice is always good for both the individual and the community, that it serves at once both the good of the agent and the good of others.[63] In the *Gorgias,* this difficulty reappears in Socrates' exchanges with both Polus and Callicles. With respect to the third difficulty, as I have indicated, Socrates refuses to take Protagoras seriously and thus avoids rather than addresses the issue of whether the critical analysis of poetry might contribute to a rethinking of traditional notions of virtue. With respect to the second difficulty, the relationship of courage and wisdom to the other virtues, Socrates engages Protagoras' own beliefs to produce accounts of both the reciprocity and the unity of the virtues and to construct an elaborate argument for hedonism, which purports to show that all of virtue is one with the knowledge of good and evil, with the consequence that one cannot be courageous but unjust. The second part of the dialogue (328d–34c) presents Socrates' arguments in support of the reciprocity of the virtues and Protagoras' objection to his arguments on grounds of the relational character of the good. Protagoras' objection resonates throughout the *Protagoras* and beyond, for even if, as some suggest, we read it as a parody of the thought of the more celebrated Protagoras of the *Theaetetus,* we will still be able to hear the voice of Protagoras if we listen, as Bakhtin suggests, to the voice behind the parody, a voice with its own logic, a voice that reveals its own world. In response to Protagoras' Great Speech, Socrates objects that speeches, like books, neither ask nor answer questions and insists upon asking Protagoras a question (328e–29b). He accepts Protagoras' claim that justice, temperance, and holiness are virtues but inquires whether these virtues are parts of a single thing or different names for one and the same thing and, if parts, whether they are parts like the parts of a face or like the parts of gold, with no difference from the whole (329b–d).[64] Protagoras responds that the virtues are parts, like the parts of a face, and that they include courage *(andreia)* and wisdom *(sophia)* as well as the other virtues, also as parts of the whole, so that a person may be, for example, courageous but unjust or just but unwise (329d–30b). Socrates then seeks to show that the virtues are reciprocally related by demonstrating the relationship of each of several pairs of virtues, first, justice and holiness, next, temperance and wisdom, and, then, justice and temperance (330b–33e). Socrates succeeds in eliciting Protagoras' agreement that what is beneficial is good *(agathon)* and apparently intends to argue that a temperate person does what is beneficial and therefore good and that an unjust person does what is harmful and therefore not good (333d–e).[65] Protagoras stops him short of this conclusion, however, observing that the good is elusive and diverse, some things being good for people, some for animals, and some for plants, some things good for one part of a plant and not another, and so on (334a–c).

Irwin claims that Socrates' argument upholds both the reciprocity and the unity theses about the virtues but that Socrates has not sorted out which arguments support which thesis.[66] Socrates seems to think that he has shown that the virtues are one, but in fact he has only shown that certain of the virtues are related reciprocally, one to another.[67] Situated extratextually and contextually, Socrates' argument is nonetheless significant because it shows how he intends to respond to Protagoras' claim that a person could be courageous but unjust or just but unwise. As a response to the cultural conflict about the virtues, Socrates' argument is important not so much because it shows *how* the virtues are related as because it shows *that* they are related, so that one cannot have any one of them without also having the others. Socrates' argument is cut short, however, by Protagoras' explanation of the good as relational, by which he seems to mean that the good is good in relation to something else.[68] C. C. W. Taylor explains that the expression "good for" is similar to expressions such as "taller than" or "half of" in the sense that it implies that a thing has a relation to one thing and not to another.[69] The expression does not imply or support (1) the claim that there is no single set of characteristics or single relation common to all good things, (2) the claim that whatever anyone believes to be good is good for the person who believes it (subjectivism), or (3) the claim that what is good or bad varies with cultural or historical circumstances (relativism).[70] Construed thus, Protagoras' explanation of the relational character of the good seems to bear no direct relationship to his more celebrated views on relativity and may be nothing more than Plato's parody of these views. Even if we read his explanation as parody, however, we can still hear the historical Protagoras, the serious voice, the voice behind the parody, proclaiming the relativity of the things of the world not only *to something* but also *for someone*.[71] Schiappa explains Protagoras' concept of relativity in just this sense: "Plato's accounts of Protagoras' relativism imply that Protagoras believed the 'things' of the world 'are' only *relative to* particular frames of reference. To the form 'A is B' must be added the notion 'for C.' The wind may be cold for one person and not cold for another."[72] Martin Ostwald explains that the same concept, applied to civic affairs, means that whatever things seem just and honorable to a particular city are just and honorable for that city, for as long as it so regards them.[73] Protagoras recalls his explanation of the relational character of the good later in the dialogue when he refuses to say that all pleasant things are good and that all painful things bad absolutely but insists that things may be good or bad or indifferent relative to the rest of his life (351c–d), which is just the sort of estimation that Socrates seeks to provide with his art of measurement. In the *Gorgias,* Socrates himself recalls Protagoras' concept of relativity as the good *for someone* when he observes that different people calculate pleasures differently, so that as a consequence we cannot determine who is right by some independent method of calculation.[74]

Socrates and the Sophists on Cooperative Joint Discussion

Socrates' and Protagoras' account of the relationship of the virtues is interrupted by an apparent digression on Socrates' and the sophists' methods of discussion, in the course of which Protagoras takes his turn at questioning Socrates on the meaning of some lines in Simonides' poem. This third part of the dialogue (334c–48c), though an apparent digression, is important because it establishes the guidelines for conducting a joint discussion and because it recalls the problem of traditional virtue, the problem of the cultural conflict between courage and the other virtues and between courage and justice in particular, the problem that will occupy Socrates and Protagoras throughout the remainder of the dialogue. Bakhtin finds in the Socratic dialogue a creative interplay of ideas between Socrates and the sophists, and the *Protagoras,* most especially, illustrates this creative interplay, both in the development of guidelines for the discussion and in the development of the ideas in the discussion itself. Nonetheless, Socrates, Protagoras, and the other sophists also express strong differences about their preferred methods of discussion.[75] Socrates and the sophists work together to develop guidelines for the discussion, but Protagoras advocates debate and poetic interpretation, and Socrates advocates dialogue or discussion, conceived as rendering and receiving an account for the purpose of testing both the account and the person who holds it. Socrates, unfairly, refuses to take seriously Protagoras' method of interpreting poetry but insists that Protagoras take seriously his own practice of dialogue because he is committed to the mutual testing of accounts in discussion.

Socrates objects to Protagoras' explanation of the relational character of the good because, he claims, he is too forgetful to remember a long speech (334c–d). Protagoras protests that he has frequently engaged in debate but would not have become famous among the Greeks if he had argued as his opponent bid him (335a). Socrates thereupon threatens to leave and break up the discussion *(dialegesthai),* and so Callias and the others intercede, Alcibiades crediting Socrates with skill in rendering and receiving an account *(logos)* and urging Protagoras to discuss with him by question and answer, Critias asking the assembly not to take sides, Prodicus concurring but urging greater attention to the wise, less to the unwise, and Hippias proposing a middle course between long and short speeches and selection of an arbiter or overseer to adjudicate their differences (335a–38a). Socrates declines to name an arbiter but proposes that Protagoras either ask or answer questions, as he prefers, and that the entire assembly jointly oversee the discussion (338b–d).

Protagoras elects to ask Socrates a question. Claiming that skill in poetry is the most important part of a person's education, he asks Socrates to explain some lines in a poem by Simonides, on the very subject that they have been discussing, that is, virtue (338e–39a). According to Protagoras, Simonides claims that "For a man [i.e., person], indeed, to become good *(agathos)* truly is hard" but then objects to Pittacus' saying that "Hard [it is] . . . to be good *(esthlos)*" (339b–c). Protagoras asks Socrates to explain the apparent contradiction, to which Socrates replies that Simonides meant to distinguish between becoming good and being good (339c–40d). Socrates then offers what appear to be ridiculous misreadings of Simonides' poem in the course of which he praises the wisdom of the Spartans and deplores the good person's loss of knowledge (340d–47a). Socrates objects to the poets, for the same reason that he had objected to Protagoras' Great Speech, because they can neither answer his questions nor resolve differences of interpretation (347b–e). He prefers to discuss directly with Protagoras so that they may test *(exelegchein)* each other by turns, making a trial of both the truth and themselves (347e–48a). He insists that this testing be reciprocal and offers to either ask or answer questions so that they might examine the difficulties in their joint pursuit of virtue (348a–49b).

Havelock credits the sophists with developing guidelines for the conduct of discussion, and Schiappa credits Protagoras in particular with developing a technical vocabulary that made possible the critical analysis of poetry.[76] According to Schiappa, Protagoras developed a vocabulary for comparing alternative accounts of the world and for replacing one account with another and so provided the earliest recorded instance of textual criticism.[77] Protagoras' approach to the critical analysis of poetry thus introduces the possibility of not only analyzing but also altering the poetic text. It also introduces the possibility of thereby altering not only the text but also the concepts that are embedded within it. The problem of traditional virtue, as I indicated in chapter 4, was implicit in the stories recounted in Homer's epics and was reinforced through the memorization and oral performance of the poems. The development of literacy and reading practices in the schools, noted in Protagoras' Great Speech, coupled with the development a technical vocabulary for critically analyzing the texts of the poems, thus enabled a rethinking of the traditional concept of virtue embedded within the texts. Socrates' ridiculous misreadings of Simonides' poem may be nothing more than a parody (perhaps Plato's parody) of Protagoras' method of interpreting poetry, but it does not and perhaps cannot conceal the other voices that speak out from behind the parody. Taylor claims that Socrates wrenches the poem from its historical context and interprets it in light of his own interests, presumably to parody Protagoras' method of interpretation.[78] Marina Berzins McCoy and Paul Kameen maintain, however, that Socrates' apparent misreadings contain serious arguments consistent with his arguments elsewhere in the dialogue.[79] McCoy argues that Socrates' distinction between becoming good and being good supports his later claim that virtue is knowledge and his suggestion that human beings can *become* good but cannot *be* good since they cannot achieve continual, unchanging goodness.[80] Kameen argues that the distinction between becoming and being good emphasizes the nature of the exchange between Protagoras and Socrates, an exchange in which both parties are "respectively, and mutually, *becoming* knowledgeable" and in which both are "equally engaged, equally at risk, equally authorized."[81] But Socrates' voice—whether we hear it as parody or as serious argument—is not the only voice that we hear in his reading (and misreading) of Simonides' poem. Behind the voice of Socrates we can hear also the voice of the poet Simonides and perhaps also the voices of Protagoras and Socrates together critically analyzing and perhaps revising the meanings and the values embedded within the poem.

The possibility of revising the traditional notion of virtue through a critical analysis of a poetic text arises in the other lines of Simonides' poem recorded in the course of Socrates' (mis)reading of the poem. If we listen, as Bakhtin suggests, to the voices behind the parody, then we will be able to hear Simonides' further thoughts on traditional virtue and perhaps also Protagoras' and Socrates' further thoughts on Simonides. In these lines, Simonides attributes one's success or failure at becoming or being good to the love either given or withheld by the gods:[82]

For that man [i.e., person] cannot help but be bad
Whom irresistible mischance has overthrown.
Nay more, the virtuous man *(agathos)* is at one time bad, at another
    good *(esthlos)*.
If he hath fared well, every man is good;
Bad, if ill.
Best also for the longest space are they whom the gods love. (344c–45c)

At the same time, he praises those who by their own will and effort become good or at least are not bad: "But I praise and love everyone willingly committing no baseness; for against necessity not even the gods make war" (345d). He seems to equate becoming good (or avoiding evil) with knowledge of what is right for the city: "For my part I am content with whosoever is not evil or too intractable. He who knows Right *(dikē)*, the support of a city, is a healthy man; him I shall never blame, for to blame I am not apt. Infinite is the race of fools. Verily, all things are fair that have in them no admixture of base" (346c). These lines are fragments whose meaning is probably indeterminate. But they seem to provide a commentary upon the traditional virtue of courage celebrated in poems such as "The Greek Dead at Thermopylae" and "The Climb to Virtue," for which Simonides was justly famous. Werner Jaeger believes that the lines provide a commentary on "The Climb to Virtue," which explores the difficulty of scaling to the height of courage *(andreia)*.[83] But Jaeger and others differ about the precise meaning and significance of these lines. Jaeger suggests that Simonides' hymns of victory represent the old tradition but that these lines complicate the traditional view because they assert that only the one whom the gods love can attain virtue.[84] C. M. Bowra maintains that the poem directly challenges the old tradition by suggesting that the old ideal of nobility is impossible because it depends upon the will of the gods and by suggesting a new standard that depends not upon what a person has or is but on what the person does.[85] According to Bowra, this new standard upholds the free will of the individual to do good, construed negatively as whatever is not evil and positively as what is right or just *(dikē)* for the city.[86] Adkins, however, suspects that Simonides may be making his point by juxtaposition, seeking to contrast the one who is not evil or base (and who is therefore as good as one can hope to be) with the one who knows what is right or just for the city (and who is therefore merely healthy or sound).[87] Whatever their precise meaning, these lines recall the traditional ideal of virtue as courage often celebrated by Simonides and thus reintroduce the issue of the relationship of courage to the other virtues and to civic justice in particular. The relationship of courage to the other virtues is precisely the issue that Protagoras and Socrates address in the next part of the dialogue. Behind Socrates' (mis)reading of the poem, therefore, we can hear the voice of Simonides, the poet of the old tradition, and perhaps also the voice of Simonides, the challenger of that tradition, speaking out from behind the parody to remind us of the cultural ideal of courage that persists as the fundamental problem in Protagoras' and Socrates' attempt to provide a satisfactory account of virtue. Moreover, if we suppose that Socrates might take seriously Protagoras' method of critically analyzing poetry, then we might hear other voices speaking out from behind the parody as well—voices such as the those of Protagoras and Socrates together critically analyzing and in the process perhaps also altering the meaning of the Simonides' poem.

Socrates and Protagoras on the Unity of Virtue

Following this apparent digression, Socrates and Protagoras return immediately to the issue raised implicitly in Simonides' poem: the inquiry into the relationship of the virtues and specifically the problem of the relationship between courage and the other virtues. The fourth part of the dialogue (348c–60e) shows how Socrates responds to this problem. Earlier, Protagoras had claimed that virtues such as justice and temperance are good for the city, but he now claims that courage, at least, is different from the other virtues and from wisdom in particular because it derives from nature and nurture—habituation, social conditioning—not from knowledge.[88] Thus he explicitly introduces the possibility that a person might be courageous but unjust and in a way that is especially problematic since he does not explain how the habits thus acquired might be modified or changed. Socrates responds with an elaborate defense of hedonism, which equates the good with the greatest pleasure over the whole of one's life and which requires an art of measurement that will permit one to weigh present and future pleasures.[89] Socrates maintains that wisdom is just this knowledge of the good and that it encompasses all of virtue, which is thus one, a unity.[90] Socrates' account of the unity of virtue draws upon Protagoras' own premises about the virtues to create a cultural hybrid that joins courage to justice, temperance, and the other virtues and thus precludes the possibility that a person might be courageous but unjust. Socrates' account thus compels—or Plato's authorial surplus of meaning thus compels—Protagoras' grudging assent.

Socrates' insistence upon the mutual testing of accounts in discussion helps to explain some of the difficulties in his own account of the unity of virtue. His apparent equation of courage with knowledge construed as professional skill seems to contradict an almost identical argument in the *Laches* but is probably best read as a testing of Protagoras rather than as a statement of Socrates' own belief.[91] Likewise, his attribution of the argument for hedonism to the majority, which leads some readers to believe that the argument could not be Socrates' own, is probably best read as a means of testing his own and Protagoras' belief by examining the merits of the argument itself, irrespective of the persons who support or oppose them.[92] Finally, his proposed art of measurement, which seems to render the testing of arguments unnecessary by establishing a general norm or standard of judgment, is probably best read as a means of calculating goods in relation to each other rather than a means of calculating goods in relation to different persons, which is precisely the art of testing accounts in dialogue that Socrates proposes in the *Gorgias*.

Socrates reminds Protagoras that he had asked him whether justice *(dikaiosunē)*, temperance *(sōphrosunē)*, holiness *(hosiotēs)*, wisdom *(sophia)*, and courage *(andreia)* are one single thing only or parts of one thing, and Protagoras answers that four of the virtues are similar but that courage, at least, is different since many people are unjust and intemperate and unholy and foolish but are nonetheless exceptionally courageous (349a–d). Socrates says that he wants to examine *(episkepsasthai)* what Protagoras says and asks him whether he believes that the courageous are bold *(tharraleos),* whether those who boldly dive into wells or the horsemen or foot soldiers *(peltastēs)* who boldly go to war are those who have knowledge *(epistēmē)* or those who do not, and Protagoras replies that in these as in all other cases the bold are those who have knowledge (349e–50b). Socrates then asks Protagoras whether he believes that some persons who do not have knowledge are also bold and courageous, and Protagoras replies that they are not (350b). Socrates infers that Protagoras apparently believes that the wisest persons are the most bold and therefore also the most courageous, so that, by this account *(logos),* wisdom would be courage (350b–c). Protagoras protests that he has claimed that the courageous are bold but not that the bold are courageous, for he believes that a person may become bold from art or rage or madness but becomes courageous from nature and proper nurture of the soul (350c–51b).

Socrates examines Protagoras—tests his account of courage—apparently to determine whether Protagoras believes, as Laches believes, that knowledge conceived as professional skill constitutes courage, to determine, that is, whether he holds to the traditional ideal of courage. Socrates therefore leads Protagoras through a series of inferences, generally regarding as some of the most fallacious in all of the early dialogues, to precisely this conclusion, which Protagoras rejects.[93] The fallacies or apparent fallacies include the shift from the unidirectional "the courageous are bold" to the bidirectional or biconditional "the courageous are bold (and the bold are courageous)"; the hasty generalization from the divers and horsemen and foot soldiers to all other such cases; and the apparent equivocation from premises about knowledge *(epistēmē)* to the conclusion about wisdom *(sophia).*[94] The apparent equivocation is illusory, however, since, as Taylor observes, both *knowledge* and *wisdom* here, as often, refer to professional skill or technical expertise.[95] Protagoras himself makes the inference from the divers and from others to all other cases, but he rejects the inference from "the courageous are bold" to "the bold are courageous" and therefore rejects the conclusion that knowledge/wisdom (construed as professional skill) is courage as well.[96] By examining Protagoras in this way, Socrates has established that Protagoras does not equate courage with professional skill but that he does attribute courage to nature and nurture or social conditioning. He has not, therefore, merely engaged in a kind of preliminary skirmish, as Gulley suggests, but has identified the problem that he now has to address—the problem of what kind of knowledge does constitute courage.[97]

To address this problem—to show what kind of knowledge constitutes courage (and indeed all of virtue)—Socrates introduces the hedonistic equation of pleasure and pain with good and evil, which the majority of people reject and which Protagoras considers applicable not to the present only but to the whole of his life (351b–e). Socrates and Protagoras propose to examine *(skopein)* the matter, with Socrates leading the inquiry (351e). They agree that wisdom *(sophia)* and knowledge *(epistēmē)* govern human affairs, in opposition to the majority, who believe that many people are so governed by pleasure or pain that, "being overcome by pleasure," they know what is best but refuse to do it (352a–53a). Socrates and Protagoras then set out to show the majority why they are wrong (353a–b). Socrates claims that the majority know that such things as food and drink and sex produce immediate pleasure but future disease and poverty, that physical training and military service produce immediate pain but future health, and he supposes that they believe that things are good or evil because of the greater amount of pleasure or pain that they afford over the long term (353c–54e). Since they apparently agree that pleasure is good and pain is evil, Socrates is able to show them that they are mistaken when they suppose that many people, being overcome by pleasure, nonetheless do what they know is evil (354e–55b). For they acknowledge the absurdity of saying that people, overcome by good, nonetheless do what they know is evil or that people, overcome by pleasure, nonetheless do what they know is painful (355b–e). Socrates supposes that such statements make sense only if one is measuring greater or lesser goods and evils, pleasures and pains (356a–c). He infers therefore that the majority of people require an art of measurement that will enable them to calculate present and future pleasure and pain, each in relation to the other, over the long term (356c–357b). Socrates defers consideration of this art of measurement to another time, but he nonetheless claims to have shown that the experience of "being overcome by pleasure" is due to mere ignorance, the lack of knowledge of relative pleasures and pains, goods and evils (357b–e). He concludes that being overcome by oneself is ignorance, mastering oneself, wisdom, for no one willingly chooses evil rather than good or greater rather than lesser evils (358b–d).

The argument for hedonism purports to show that the majority of people must agree with Socrates and Protagoras that pleasure and pain are equivalent to good and evil considered over the long term, over the course of one's life as a whole. Protagoras himself suggests that such an equation take into account his life as a whole, and Socrates shows that the majority must agree but supposes that they require an art of measurement that will enable them to calculate pleasures and pains, goods and evils, relative to each other over the long term, that is, that they require a certain kind of knowledge. Socrates and Protagoras attribute the argument for hedonism to the majority to show them that they must accept the argument based upon premises that they themselves accept. Irwin maintains that the attribution of the argument to the majority is important because it shows Socrates' willingness to examine the merits of an argument irrespective of the persons who seek to defend or refute it and irrespective of the quality of the defense or the refutation on any given occasion.[98]

Socrates introduces the art of measurement to show the majority how they can calculate relative pleasures and pains, but he defers discussion of this art to some other time. In the *Statesman,* the art of measurement provides a general norm or standard of judgment that would seem to render unnecessary the mutual testing of arguments in discussion. The *Statesman* (283c ff.) distinguishes measurements of quantities relative to each other from measurements of quantities relative to a norm or standard, and the *Philebus* (20b ff.) illustrates the measurement of pleasures relative to a normative conception of the good.[99] The *Gorgias* suggests, however, that the calculation of pleasures and pains is not only relative each to each over the long term but also relative to the person who experiences pleasure and pain, the coward and the courageous person experiencing pleasure or pain differently, for example. The *Protagoras* shows how an art of measurement can solve the problem of calculating pleasures and pains relative to each other over the long term. The *Gorgias* shows that an art of dialogue is necessary to solve the problem of calculating pleasures and pains relative to each person.

Socrates concludes his argument for hedonism by showing Protagoras that courage, too, requires a calculation of present and future pleasures and pains and that courage is, therefore, equivalent to wisdom and so is one with the other virtues. He asserts that no one goes toward what he fears, believing it to be evil, but that everyone, both the cowardly and the courageous, go toward what they can face boldly, so that in this respect the cowardly and the courageous are the same (358d–59d). When Protagoras objects that the courageous go to war but that cowards refuse, Socrates argues that they calculate differently, the courageous person knowing that war is excellent and therefore good and also pleasant, the coward ignorant of what he ought or ought not to fear (359e–60c). He concludes that ignorance of what is and is not to be feared is cowardice, wisdom about what is and is not to be feared, courage, and Protagoras grudgingly nods and then silently gives his assent (360c–e). Socrates' argument purports to establish that courage is equivalent to wisdom, the knowledge of good and evil, and is therefore similar to and indeed is one with the other virtues. R. E. Allen claims that the argument seems to be a reductio ad absurdum of the equation of pleasure with good since it asks us to believe that going to war is excellent and good and therefore also pleasant.[100] Similarly, Charles H. Kahn speculates that hedonism is not stressed in this context "since it is intuitively not very plausible to claim that brave men readily go to war because they find it more pleasant than staying at home."[101] But the point of the hedonistic calculus is that it can correct this faulty intuition. As Irwin observes, "when we consider short-term and long-term pleasures and pains together, we will see that the maximization of pleasure over the longer term, in our life as a whole, requires us to face the pains that the brave person faces."[102] Socrates' argument, of course, extends only to courage. To complete the argument, he would have to show that justice and temperance are subject

to the same kind of calculation of pleasures and pains and are therefore likewise equivalent to wisdom—the knowledge of good and evil—so that all of
virtue is one, a unity.[103] If he were to complete the argument in this way, then
he could claim, for example, that the courage of the person who goes to war
in a just cause is a greater good (and therefore more pleasant)—in the longer
term, over the course of one's life as a whole—than the cowardice of the person who runs away.

COOPERATION OR CONTESTATION?

This limitation notwithstanding, Socrates' argument, coupled with Protagoras' earlier claims, provides a solution to the problem of the cultural conflict
about the virtues in the form of a cultural hybrid that joins traditional courage
to wisdom and so by implication to civic justice and temperance as well. Protagoras has affirmed the civic virtues of justice, temperance, and holiness, and
he has claimed that courage and wisdom, too, are virtues, though he insists
that courage is much unlike the others. He has also affirmed the equivalence
of pleasure and pain with good and evil, over the course of one's life as a
whole, consistent with his earlier explanation of the relational character of the
good. Socrates and Protagoras use these premises to build their joint account
of courage in its relationship to wisdom and thus, implicitly, to the other
virtues as well—uttered, however, in Socrates' voice alone, without acknowledgment of the substantial contribution of Protagoras and the other sophists to
the development of the ideas in the dialogue and without Protagoras' and the
others' explicit assent.

In the conclusion (360e–62a), Socrates claims that he and Protagoras
have switched positions, Protagoras now maintaining that virtue cannot be
taught, Socrates that it can. Gosling and Taylor claim that this reversal is due
to a change in their concept of virtue, from Protagoras' notion of virtue as
habituation or social conditioning to Socrates' notion of virtue as the knowledge of good and evil.[104] Kerferd, however, claims that Protagoras disagrees
with Socrates, that he in fact believes that teaching includes conditioning in
social mores and that such conditioning produces settled states of character
and conduct different from each other and appropriate to the individual
virtues.[105] If Kerferd is correct—and Protagoras' grudging and then silent
assent suggests that he is—then we can see why Socrates insists upon a fundamental change in Protagoras' concept of virtue, for the conditioning in
social mores that Protagoras advocates cannot distinguish the courage of
Achilles from that of Hector, the courage of Xerxes from that of the Spartans
at Thermopylae or the Athenians at Marathon, the courage that sustained the
Athenian empire from the courage of the Meilians or the Syracusans who
opposed it. In the *Protagoras,* Socrates engages dialogue as a method of

cooperative discussion in search of a joint account of the unity of virtue. In the end, however, he opposes Protagoras because he wants him to see that courage as social conditioning is different from courage as knowledge of the other virtues and of virtue itself, to see, that is, that courage that is not joined to justice and the other virtues is not courage at all, but mere boldness. In the *Gorgias,* Socrates opposes Gorgias and others who engage rhetoric as a tool of persuasion in their pursuit of power and pleasure and who espouse courage in pursuit of their own self-interest without regard for justice, temperance, and the other virtues.

6

Dialogue as Carnival

Contesting Cultural and
Rhetorical Practices in the *Gorgias*

The *Protagoras* shows Socrates working with Protagoras and with the other sophists to create a joint account of the unity of virtue, a cultural hybrid that joins the traditional ideal of courage to the civic virtues of justice and temperance and thus rejects the possibility that a person might be courageous but unjust. The *Gorgias* shows Socrates contesting and attempting to refute contemporary cultural and rhetorical practices and at the same time testing his own ideal of the just and virtuous life. Socrates contests Gorgias' view of rhetoric because it seems to permit injustice in the conduct of public affairs. He contests Polus' and Callicles' views of traditional Homeric virtue, *aretē:* Polus' because it represents a conflicted popular morality that even Polus himself does not fully understand, Callicles' because it promotes the self-interested pursuit of power and pleasure without regard for justice. He contests also the cultural ideals and the rhetorical practices of the much renowned Pericles, which he claims are responsible for supporting and sustaining an unjust empire. Finally, Socrates tests his own account *(logos)* of courage as inseparable from justice and temperance and defends his art of dialogue as the only true art of politics because—he claims—this art alone attempts to improve people's lives by making them more just. Traditional readings of the *Gorgias,* as I explained in chapter 2, have found in this earlier dialogue a partial articulation of the rhetoric and dialectic brought to fulfillment in the later *Phaedrus.*[1] According to these traditional readings, the *Gorgias* contrasts the false rhetoric of the sophist Gorgias with the true rhetoric of Plato's Socrates, with

117

its basis in dialectic.[2] More recent interpretations of both the dialogue and the historical figure present a more complex portrait of Gorgias as a philosopher who raises fundamental questions about the relationship of force and persuasion, truth and opinion, and contrasting not only false with true rhetoric but also Homeric courage with civic justice and temperance, Periclean rhetoric with Socratic dialogue, a cultural ideal and a rhetorical practice that sustain an unjust empire with a cultural ideal and a dialogical art that sustain the just life.[3]

Mikhail M. Bakhtin's reading of the Socratic dialogue as a carnivalistic genre supports this more complex reading of the *Gorgias,* emphasizing on the one hand its contrastive features, on the other hand its multiplicity of meaning. In *Problems of Dostoevsky's Poetics* and "Epic and Novel," Bakhtin explains the carnivalistic base of the Socratic dialogue, its debate-like quality—its contrasting of opposites such as light with darkness, life with death, the lofty and the serious with the lowly and the mundane—together with its multiplicity of meaning, its refusal, as Bakhtin says, "to stop and congeal in one-sided seriousness or in a stupid fetish for definition or singleness of meaning."[4] In *Rabelais and His World,* Bakhtin describes the world of the carnival as the site of "intense ideological struggle" through which new cultural and linguistic consciousnesses are born.[5] The *Gorgias* more than other early dialogues illustrates this carnivalesque debate between opposing points of view and this carnivalesque intermingling of the lofty and the serious with the lowly and the mundane, expressed in the "in the style and tone of the marketplace."[6] The *Gorgias* contrasts Gorgias' false with Socrates' true rhetoric, of course, but it also contrasts the traditional Homeric ideal of courage with the newer cultural ideal of civic justice and temperance, the Periclean ideal of empire and Periclean rhetoric with the Socratic ideal of justice and Socratic dialogue. It underscores these contrasts with Socratic degradations, with comparisons of the lofty and the serious to the lowly and the mundane—the comparison of rhetoric to cookery, for example, or the comparison of the purportedly courageous but unjust person to the licentious and shameful catamite. Beyond these simple contrasts, the *Gorgias* also envisions a new cultural and linguistic consciousness born in ideological struggle—the Socratic ideal of the just life and the art of dialogue that sustains it. The dialogue concludes with ominous foreshadowing of Socrates' own trial and death—evidence of Plato the author's essential surplus of meaning—and with Socrates' apparently serious and single-minded monologue, illustrative of his inability either to persuade the other participants in the dialogue to adopt his view of the just and virtuous life or to defend himself at his own trial.[7] But it introduces at the same time new layers of meaning, positing death not as the end but as the beginning of life and dialogue not only as a testing and contesting of others but also and especially as the ultimate testing of oneself.[8] Thus it provides an example of the ultimate self-reckoning—for Socrates and for Athens—that Bakhtin calls "the dialogue on the threshold."[9]

Read in its extratextual historical context and in its contextual relationship to other texts, the *Gorgias* echoes with the sound of many voices, from other dialogues and other more distant texts. Though we might hear in the *Gorgias* the voices of the later *Phaedrus,* we might also hear in Socrates' debate with Gorgias about sophistic rhetoric echoes of similar discussions with Protagoras about sophistic display and poetic interpretation and sophistic/Socratic dialogue, and we might hear in his debate with Polus and Callicles about the exercise of courage and intelligence in the pursuit of power and pleasure echoes of similar discussions with Laches and Nicias and with Protagoras.[10] We might also hear echoes of Socrates' discussions with Protagoras in his debate with Callicles about the problem of hedonism, which the Socrates of the *Protagoras* accepts but which the Socrates of the *Gorgias* rejects, apparently upon the Protagorean principle that the good is relational not only to *some thing* but also to *some one,* the courageous and the cowardly person calculating differently, for example, so that the consistent hedonist cannot distinguish between them.[11] From this perspective, the Socrates of the *Gorgias* seems to offer as an alternative to the hedonistic calculus of the *Protagoras* his own art of dialogue, by which he believes he can establish the knowledge that is virtue.[12] We might also hear in Socrates' concluding speech and in Plato's allusions to his probable trial and death echoes of his more famous defense of his life in the *Apology.* The *Gorgias* echoes as well with voices from other more distant texts. Charles H. Kahn hears in Socrates' debates with Polus and Callicles echoes of Homeric *aretē*—"the ruthless self-assertion of an ambitious individual," who like Achilles strives always to be "first and best and ahead of everyone else."[13] Harvey Yunis hears in Socrates' debates with Gorgias and Callicles echoes of Pericles' speeches on the construction of the middle wall and on the injustice of empire.[14] For Yunis, and perhaps for Plato, these echoes of Pericles' speeches recall not the historical Pericles but Thucydides' Pericles and especially his comparison of the empire to a tyranny, unjust to acquire but dangerous to let go.[15] Still other voices are notably absent from the *Gorgias.* For Plato and his readers, the allusions to Homeric *aretē* may recall the great epic heroes, Achilles and Agamemnon, quarreling over their share of the *prizes* taken in battle. These same allusions, however, will probably not recall the voice of Homer singing the praises of Hector or Odysseus or Penelope or the voice of Simonides singing the praises of the Athenians at Marathon or the Spartans at Thermopylae, voices in praise of the heroes who exercised courage in defense of city, home, and family, men and women who modeled the cultural ideal of civic courage that the Socrates of the *Gorgias* attempts to promote—the same voices that the Plato of the *Republic* so eagerly, and ironically, seeks to silence.

Read extratextually and contextually, the *Gorgias* seems to revisit the problem of the virtues not as a philosophical problem of the relationship of parts/whole or identity/unity but as a problem of cultural conflict between the

Homeric/Athenian ideal of courage and wisdom, conceived as intelligence or practical wisdom, and the newer civic ideal of true wisdom, courage joined to justice and temperance—a conflict that shaped and influenced Athenian politics from Themistocles and Cimon to Pericles to the destruction of the empire.[16] Read thus, the *Gorgias* shows why the cultural conflict about the virtues was so pressing and so important, for the exercise for the traditional ideal—Homeric courage joined to Athenian intelligence in an avowedly unjust cause—would lead, as Plato saw so clearly in hindsight, to the destruction of the empire and the democracy and very nearly to the destruction of Athens itself. The *Gorgias* offers as a response to this problem a new cultural ideal of Homeric courage joined to civic justice and temperance and an art of dialogue by which this ideal can be tested and confirmed, one person at a time. The *Gorgias* shows Socrates contesting with others who practice the politics of empire or the rhetoric that sustains it. He contests Gorgias' notion of rhetoric because it produces belief, not knowledge, about justice and injustice, because, as practiced by Themistocles and Pericles, it produced the belief in the walls and docks and harbors that sustained an unjust empire. He contests Polus' belief in the power of rhetoric to promote injustice because he is convinced that injustice is the greatest of evils and that rhetoric is useless, except as a means of bringing the unjust person to justice. He contests Callicles' belief that the person of virtue *(aretē)* is the person of courage *(andreia)* and intelligence or practical wisdom *(phronēsis)*—the traditional Homeric and contemporary Athenian ideal—because he is convinced that the person of true civic courage is also a person of civic justice and temperance. Finally, he contests Pericles' politics of empire and his rhetorical practice because he believes that neither Pericles' politics nor his rhetoric has shown that it can improve people's lives by making them more just. He acknowledges the possibility of a true rhetoric aimed at improving people's lives but denies that anyone—even Pericles—ever practiced such a rhetoric. He claims that only his own art of dialogue can establish the knowledge necessary for virtuous living and concludes that this art alone, therefore, is the true art of politics, affirmed by his own life.

Gorgias versus Socrates?

Traditional readings of the *Gorgias* have emphasized its significance as an early formulation of the rhetoric and dialectic brought to fulfillment in the later *Phaedrus*.[17] George A. Kennedy identifies the *Gorgias* and the *Phaedrus* as the most important sources for the study of Plato's rhetoric and presents what has become the standard account of the two dialogues. According to Kennedy, the *Gorgias* contrasts the false rhetoric of Gorgias, which produces mere belief, with the true rhetoric of Plato's Socrates, which is based upon, and is productive of, knowledge.[18] Gorgias speaks for rhetoric conceived as persuasion, a rhetoric concerned with justice and injustice, a rhetoric productive of belief, not knowledge.[19] Socrates opposes this rhetoric because it is uninformed by knowledge, including knowledge of justice and injustice, because it is as a consequence a mere image or reflection of justice, in the same way that sophistic is a mere image of legislation, cosmetics an image of gymnastics, and cookery an image of medicine, rhetoric, like cookery, merely serving up to its audience what is temporarily pleasurable.[20] In contrast to Gorgias, Socrates speaks for a rhetoric based upon and productive of knowledge and specifically a knowledge of justice and temperance, the true rhetor seeking always to engender justice and temperance and every other virtue in the people's souls and to remove injustice and intemperance and every other vice.[21] The *Phaedrus* extends and refines the true rhetoric of the *Gorgias* by positing rhetoric as a kind of knowledge based upon, and indeed equivalent to, dialectic—the twin processes of definition and division by which diverse materials are brought together into a single idea or unity and by which these materials are divided into species on the basis of their natural articulations.[22] Like Kennedy, Seth Benardete emphasizes the close relationship of the two dialogues and the contrast between Gorgias' false and Socrates' true rhetoric. According to Benardete, the issue of rhetoric binds the two dialogues together, but whereas the *Gorgias* presents a spurious rhetoric that "captures forever the ghost of justice," the *Phaedrus* presents a genuine rhetoric that is equivalent to Socrates' science of eros and thus is equivalent also to philosophy in its aspiration to transcend itself and become wisdom.[23]

Others find the contrast between Gorgias' false and Socrates' true rhetoric to be less significant than the contrast between Gorgias' false rhetoric and Socrates' dialectic, best represented by the elaborate system of comparisons and contrasts that includes the comparison of rhetoric to cookery—a perfect illustration of the method of dialectic as set forth in the *Phaedrus*. George Kimball Plochmann and Franklin E. Robinson see the contrast between Gorgias' and Socrates' rhetoric as less important than the contrast between Gorgias' rhetoric and Socrates' dialectic, the treatment of rhetoric in the *Gorgias* being merely honorific, the treatment of philosophy as rigorously dialectical as possible under the difficult circumstances of the dialogue.[24] This contrast between rhetoric and dialectic is most clearly evident in the elaborate system of comparisons and contrasts in which rhetoric is shown to be like other forms of flattery such as sophistic, cosmetics, and cookery and unlike true arts such as justice, legislation, gymnastics, and medicine.[25] This system of comparisons and contrasts, according to Plochmann and Robinson, is the most important expression of the dialectical method of the *Gorgias* and in its extended form is the key to the unity of the dialogue.[26] R. E. Allen similarly describes this system of comparisons and contrasts as "an early and very beautiful application of the method of divi-sion, *diairesis,* which is later brought to great prominence in the *Phaedrus, Sophist,* and *Statesman.*"[27]

More recent interpretations have unsettled these traditional readings of the *Gorgias,* presenting, one the one hand, a more complex portrait of Gor-gias and, on the other hand, a more complex set of contrasts—between false and true rhetoric but also between Homeric and Socratic cultural ideals, between Periclean injustice and Socratic justice, between Periclean rhetoric and Socratic dialogue. G. B. Kerferd, Edward Schiappa, and Robert Wardy have challenged the traditional portrait of Gorgias presented in Plato's dia-logue and have drawn a more complex portrait of the historical figure of Gor-gias, rehistoricized as a serious thinker who explored the meaning of persua-sion and its underlying *logos* (Gorgias himself apparently did not use the term *rhetoric—rhētorikē*).[28] Unlike the traditional Gorgias, proponent of a false rhetoric based upon mere belief and concerned with justice and injus-tice alike, this rehistoricized Gorgias explores the complex relationship between force and persuasion, truth and opinion, word and thing. According to Schiappa, Gorgias' *Helen* explores persuasion by means of *logos* as a kind of force, working on the psyche in the same way that astronomers work on the psyche to make opinions appear to be true, contestants in argumentation make them appear pleasing, or rival philosophers show them to be easily changed or in the same way that drugs work on the body, bringing it life or death.[29] Gorgias thus raises fundamental questions about the relationship of force and persuasion, truth and opinion.[30] Kerferd maintains that Gorgias' *On Not Being or On Nature* helps to explain Gorgias' treatment of *logos* in *Helen* because, however inadequate its arguments, however indeterminate its mean-ing, it opens a radical gulf between the word, the thought, and the thing, thus raising the whole problem of meaning and reference.[31] Schiappa argues, how-ever, that through a process of historical contextualization and formalization of its arguments, *On Not Being* can be rendered meaningful as a response to the thought of Parmenides and the later Eleatics.[32] Both Kerferd and Schi-appa agree that Gorgias' *Helen* and *On Not Being* are complex works by a serious thinker. Within Plato's dialogue, which seems to set Gorgias' and Socrates' rhetorics at odds with each other, Alessandra Fussi, too, finds a more complex portrait of Gorgias: "Perhaps Gorgias is right: both the doctor and the philosopher need his services, because bitter drugs can be swallowed more easily with a sweet coating."[33]

Others explore the contrasts between the Homeric ideal of courage and the Socratic ideal of civic justice and temperance, between the Periclean ideal of empire and Socratic justice, between Periclean rhetoric and Socratic dialogue. Kahn notes the contrast between the Homeric cultural ideal of *aretē* and the Socratic ideal of virtue, an ideal that joins the Home-ric virtue of courage and skill in battle to the quiet virtues of justice and temperance.[34] According to Kahn, Socrates refutes each of the other participants in the dialogue by shaming him, by showing him that he does in fact, despite himself, hold to Socrates' own ideal of just and temperate living.[35] Gorgias professes an instrumental view of rhetoric as a morally neutral tool, but Socrates shames him into admitting that he will teach right and wrong, justice and injustice, to anyone who does not know one from the other.[36] Polus disclaims any concern with justice in either rhetoric or politics, but Socrates shames him into admitting that to act unjustly is worse than to suffer unjustly, both for the one who acts or suffers and for society as a whole.[37] Finally, Callicles professes a natural justice that permits the person of courage and practical wisdom to practice an indiscriminate hedonism, but Socrates shames him into admitting that some pleasures are better than others, the courageous person better than the coward, the rational choice of a just and temperate life better than the irrational pursuit of pleasure.[38] Socrates shames them with carnivalistic and degrading comparisons, drawn from the language of the streets.[39] As Kennedy points out, however, while these "Socratic degradations" startle and amuse, they also have a serious purpose.[40] Andrea Wilson Nightingale explains: Socrates' "incessant recourse to 'things vulgar and common'" asks us to reconsider "what is truly vulgar and what noble, what is ridiculous and what serious."[41]

Harvey Yunis emphasizes the contrast between Pericles and Socrates.[42] Yunis claims that the Socrates of the *Gorgias* opposes Athenian rhetorical practice as represented not by the Gorgias of Plato's dialogue but by the Pericles of Thucydides' history and by the Athenian ideal of empire as represented not by contemporary proponents of empire but by its founders—Miltiades, Cimon, Themistocles, and, especially, Pericles.[43] According to Yunis, Socrates opposes Periclean rhetoric because it supports the Periclean ideal of empire: "Plato's cardinal objection to Periclean rhetoric is fundamentally an objection to the public, authoritative encouragement of brute power and wealth—empire—in preference to the real political virtues of knowledge and justice."[44] The Pericles depicted in Thucydides' history engages an "instructional rhetoric" to ensure a consistent, long-term understanding of the Athenian policy of empire.[45] The Socrates of Plato's dialogue opposes this rhetoric because it fails to exert any long-term influence on policy and especially because it fails to improve people's lives by making them more virtuous.[46] According to Yunis, however, Socrates offers no alternative to Periclean rhetoric as a form of "mass political education," and he offers no reason to believe that he himself was any more successful than Pericles at improving people's lives: "Plato provides in the *Gorgias* a new argument which shows that although Socratic discourse cannot be deemed to have improved the Athenians, far from contributing to their corruption, Socrates stands aloof, failing to communicate with them at all."[47] Wardy and Nightingale, however, maintain that Socratic dialogue is itself an alternative form of political discourse aimed at improving people's lives. Wardy claims that Socrates opposes the "loyal imperialism" of Pericles and other Athenian politicians and offers himself as the only true politician because he alone practices an art of dialogue aimed at a "shared truth" or shared *logos* for the good of others.[48] Nightingale similarly recalls Socrates' claim that he alone practices "the true political art" and suggests that Socrates' departure from his dialogical/dialectical method at the end of the dialogue is not a repudiation but a vindication of his method through the *deus ex machina* of divine judgment.[49]

CARNIVALISTIC DEBATE: CONTESTING CULTURAL AND RHETORICAL PRACTICES

Traditional readings of the *Gorgias* thus emphasize the contrast between the false rhetoric of Plato's Gorgias and the true rhetoric and dialectic of Plato's Socrates previewed in the *Gorgias* and brought to fulfillment in the *Phaedrus*. More recent readings of the *Gorgias* suggest, however, a more complex set of contrasts that set Socrates not only against Gorgias and others who participate directly in the dialogue but also against Pericles, his pursuit of empire, and his rhetoric. Bakhtin's reading of the Socratic dialogue as a carnivalesque genre supports these more recent readings of the *Gorgias* as a complex set of contrasts dramatized as carnivalistic debates between elemental forces and made close and familiar by Socrates' degrading comparisons of the lofty and pretentious ideals of Gorgias, Polus, Callicles, and even Pericles to the lowly and mundane language and imagery of the streets—the language of the marketplace.

Read in its extratextual context and in its contexual relationship to the *Laches* and the *Protagoras,* the *Gorgias* seems to revisit the problem of the cultural conflict between courage and the other virtues, set against the immediate background of the Athenian politics of empire. Read in its contextual relationship to the *Protagoras* in particular, the *Gorgias* also seems to revisit the problem of hedonism, which the Socrates of the *Protagoras* upholds because it provides a means of calculating goods relative to each other but which the Socrates of the *Gorgias* rejects because it does not provide a means of calculating goods relative to someone and therefore does not provide the kind of knowledge that enables the hedonist (or indeed any one of us) to distinguish one good from another, each of us calculating goods quite differently. Socrates therefore offers in place of the hedonistic calculus of the *Protagoras* and as a response to the problem of the cultural conflict about the virtues his own art of dialogue, by which means alone he believes he can acquire the knowledge necessary for virtuous living. In the *Gorgias,* Socrates conceives this art as a means of contesting and refuting the cultural ideal that joins traditional Homeric courage to contemporary Athenian intelligence in the pursuit of empire and the Periclean rhetoric that sustains it and equally as a means of testing his own account *(logos)* of courage as inseparable from civic justice and temperance.

The *Gorgias* is structured as a series of debates between Socrates and the other participants, Gorgias, Polus, and Callicles. Kennedy describes it as a series of confrontations between Socrates and the three rhetoricians, each more sophistic and less sympathetic to Socrates than the last.[50] But the *Gorgias* may also be read as a series of debates between false and true rhetoric, between Homeric courage and Socratic (and Protagorean) justice and temperance, between Periclean acquisitiveness and injustice and Socratic justice, between Periclean rhetoric and Socratic dialogue—debates (as Bakhtin describes them) between elemental forces of life and death, darkness and light, conducted in the language of the streets.[51] As in the *Protagoras,* we can have no doubt that Plato takes Socrates' side in the debate, and we can detect his authorial hand—his essential surplus of meaning—in his manipulation of the arguments in Socrates' favor.[52] Richard Leo Enos maintains that the shift from an oral to a written medium so transforms the early Socratic dialogues that they become dialogical in form and dialectical in appearance only.[53] According to Enos, Plato's *Gorgias* is "one detailed argument of proposition under the guise of a dialogue," and his mode of questioning is "a heuristic employed not to discover Truth but rather to create his interpretation of reality in the minds of readers."[54] Nightingale similarly argues that *Gorgias* resorts to mythic harangue and the *deus ex machina* of divine judgment to rescue Socrates from his inability to persuade his opponents to embrace the philosophical life.[55] But the *Gorgias* contrasts not only Gorgias' false and Socrates' true (albeit unsuccessful) rhetoric and dialectic but also Homeric and Socratic virtue, Periclean rhetoric and Socratic dialogue. Moreover, Nightingale observes, the closing myth is not only a divine rescue but also a divine reversal of human judgment that transforms death into life on the Islands of the Blessed.[56] From Bakhtin's perspective, therefore, we might hear in Socrates' exchanges with his opponents not Platonic monologue but Socratic dialogue conducted in the manner of carnivalistic debate, and we might hear in his final mythic harangue not Platonic myth but Socratic "dialogue on the threshold," not an anticipation of the mythic quality of later dialogues such as the *Phaedo* and the *Republic* but an echo of the confessional quality of the earlier *Apology*.[57]

Contesting Rhetorical Practices:
Socrates versus Gorgias and Polus

At the beginning of the *Gorgias,* Socrates and Gorgias initiate an inquiry into the nature of rhetoric. Socrates contests Gorgias' rhetoric because it is based upon belief, not knowledge, about justice and injustice. At the end of the dialogue, Socrates offers as an alternative to Gorgias' rhetoric not a true rhetoric based upon justice but an art of dialogue by which he believes he can produce the knowledge necessary for virtuous living. Socrates' argument is practical, not theoretical. He rejects the true rhetoric based upon justice because, however desirable, it does not exist and has never existed in practice, not even in the rhetoric of the much renowned Pericles. He advocates his own art of dialogue because his lifelong practice of the art has demonstrated to him that people who hold false, immoral beliefs can always be shown to hold at the same time true, moral convictions that conflict with their false beliefs. Moreover, his lifelong practice of his art of dialogue has also demonstrated him that his own moral beliefs, in particular his belief that courage is inseparable from justice and temperance, will always withstand the test of dialogical questioning. As I indicated in chapter 2, Socrates is frequently viewed from the perspective of Aristotle's *Metaphysics* as the originator of the inductive method in search of universal definitions, the basis of Aristotle's syllogistic and enthymematic reasoning. As Thomas C. Brickhouse and Nicolas D. Smith point out, however, Socrates never claims that he finds these universal definitions, only that he seeks them, repeatedly testing others in discussion and always finding that those who oppose his views—for example, his view of the just life—show inconsistencies in their own beliefs and thus show themselves to be ridiculous.[58] Socrates claims only that he has tested both others and himself frequently enough to acquire the kind of knowledge necessary for a virtuous and fulfilling life, not the kind of knowledge that constitutes true wisdom.[59] Socrates may be said to practice induction, therefore, only in the sense that he has gathered sufficient evidence through repeated testing of his beliefs to be confident that he has established the general moral truth that the just life is the only life that is worth living.[60]

The *Gorgias* may be divided into three main parts, corresponding to the three main topics of debate (rather than the three main speakers), plus the closing myth.[61] In the first part (447a–66a), Socrates debates with Gorgias and Polus the nature of rhetoric and contests their apparent belief in a rhetoric indifferent to injustice—best exemplified by Pericles—as an appeal to mere pleasure akin to sophistic, cosmetics, and, especially, cookery. In the second part (466a–500a), Socrates debates with Polus and Callicles the cultural ideal of courage joined to intelligence or practical wisdom and contests their commitment to this ideal as a self-interested pursuit of power and pleasure at odds with civic justice and temperance. In the third part (500a–527e), Socrates debates with Callicles and contests his belief that Athenian politicians from Miltiades to Pericles were good orators and good men because he does not believe that they either attempted to improve or succeeded in improving people's lives. At the same time, he tests his own ideal of virtue as courage joined to justice and temperance and rejects even a rhetoric committed to the pursuit of virtue in favor of his own art of dialogue on grounds that no one—not even Pericles—ever practiced such a rhetoric and that he alone practices the true art of politics. In his closing myth, he offers his own life as evidence that the just life is the only life worth living.

The first part of the dialogue (447a–66a) begins abruptly with Socrates' suggestion that he and the others—Callicles, Chaerephon, and Polus—inquire into the nature of Gorgias' art (447a–c). Gorgias names his art *rhetoric (rhētorikē)* and explains that rhetoric is the art of persuasion with speeches in the law courts, the Council, or the Assembly (448e–49a, 452e). Socrates contrasts Gorgias' rhetoric with his own practice of discussion *(dialegesthai)* and presses Gorgias to identify the substance or subject matter of rhetoric, and Gorgias explains that rhetoric is concerned with justice and injustice and produces belief rather than knowledge (448d–e, 454b, 454e–55a). Socrates protests that in public assemblies craftspeople, not rhetoricians, give advice on issues such as the construction of walls and harbors and docks, but Gorgias points out that in fact rhetoricians such as Themistocles and Pericles, not craftspeople, gave advice on the walls and harbors and docks and that as a result these structures were actually built, and Socrates agrees (455a–e).[62] Gorgias concludes that rhetoricians, not craftspeople, have the power to win over a multitude and claims that if they use this power unjustly they, not their teachers, should be hated and expelled (456a–57c). Socrates then inquires whether the rhetorician must know what is good or bad, noble or base, just or unjust, and Gorgias replies that the rhetorician must know such things, that he will teach them to his students if they do not know them, and that a person who knows what is right and just will do what is right and just (459c–60a). Socrates points out that Gorgias has contradicted himself, that he cannot, on the one hand, disclaim responsibility for his students' injustice and, on the other hand, claim that since he teaches justice his students will know and do what is just (460c–61b).

Socrates contests Gorgias' view of rhetoric because it seems to permit injustice in the conduct of public affairs, as illustrated in the persons of Themistocles and Pericles. Socrates catches Gorgias in contradiction by drawing forth and juxtaposing his beliefs that (1) the rhetorician might use rhetoric unjustly, (2) Gorgias will teach his students justice and injustice if they do not already know these things, and (3) a person who knows what is just will be a just person and so will do what is just—the latter two claims conflicting with the first.[63] Kennedy suggests that Gorgias makes strategic mistakes when he claims that rhetoric deals with justice and injustice and produces belief, not knowledge, for, as Aristotle demonstrates, rhetoric deals with a wide range of subjects and with either knowledge or belief, depending upon the evidence at hand.[64] Gorgias' mistakes, Kennedy suggests, may be due to the historical Gorgias' low opinion of knowledge, as exhibited in *On Not Being or On Nature*.[65] As Kerferd and Schiappa point out, however, the historical Gorgias was deeply concerned with the problem of knowledge and maintained rather the profound difficulty of knowing than the unimportance of knowing.[66] Moreover, the Gorgias of the dialogue was probably unable to contemplate the possibilities of rhetoric as a disciplinary activity, as developed by Aristotle, for example, since the name *rhetoric (rhētorikē)* apparently originated in the *Gorgias,* and the disciplinary activity did not develop until much later.[67] Gorgias' problem thus seems to lie much deeper. Gorgias could maintain an instrumental view of rhetoric, such as Aristotle's, without inherent contradiction, but, as Kahn observes, he cannot maintain that such a view is morally and socially compatible with his claim to teach the art of political leadership in the law courts and other public assemblies.[68] The problem is illustrated in the persons of Themisticles and Pericles. As Kennedy observes, Socrates unrealistically claims that only an expert has the requisite knowledge to give advice on issues such as the construction of walls and harbors and docks.[69] Gorgias corrects him, therefore, pointing out that Themistocles and Pericles also gave such advice, and Socrates agrees. Terence Irwin explains the problem: "An unjust carpenter is capable of making a perfectly good bed; we might buy his bed if we make sure that he does not cheat or overcharge us. . . . If an orator is unjust, however, can we still rely on his ability to give us good advice?"[70] Bakhtin's observation that in the Socratic dialogue the idea is still organically combined with the person who holds it helps us to understand why the problem proved to be so intractable.[71]

Polus next asks Socrates to present his own view of rhetoric. Polus argues that Gorgias was ashamed to say what he really thinks and so claimed to know and to teach what is good and noble and just (461b–c). Polus nonetheless acknowledges Gorgias' defeat and asks Socrates to explain what kind of art he thinks rhetoric is. Socrates responds that rhetoric is not an art but a knack for producing pleasure, akin to cookery (462b–e). He explains that the true arts—justice, legislation, gymnastic, and medicine—seek the greatest good of the soul and body but that the false arts, or arts of flattery—rhetoric, sophistry, cosmetics, and cookery—disguise themselves as true arts and seek not the greatest good but the pleasure of the moment (463a–64e). Rhetoric thus resembles cookery since both are false arts of flattery, rhetoric corresponding to the true art of justice in the same way that sophistry corresponds to legislation, cosmetics to gymnastic, and cookery to medicine (465a–e).

Socrates thus decrowns Gorgias and Polus, carnivalizing their view of rhetoric, bringing it down to earth, degrading it by comparing it to the lowly and mundane art—the false art—of cookery. Kennedy suggests that Socrates' comparison might have been provoked by the brash personality of Polus and might not have been expounded to Gorgias directly.[72] But the comparison is surely addressed, directly or indirectly, to both of them and is addressed not only to their ideas but also to their persons. Bakhtin observes the power of Socrates' lowly images to bring serious and lofty ideas down to earth, to bring the world closer to us, so that we can investigate it freely and fearlessly.[73] He also observes the power of these images to bring people down to earth, to familiarize relationships and to remove the distance between them, often by ritually crowning and decrowning them.[74] In the *Gorgias,* Socrates enacts such a ritual crowning and decrowning, degrading and shaming Gorgias and Polus, undermining their lofty pretensions with lowly images and carnivalistic laughter. Moreover, the comparison does not terminate at this point in the dialogue but continues—almost as if uninterrupted—after a long discussion of the virtues and then is directly applied not to Gorgias' (or Polus') view of rhetoric but to the Athenian practice of rhetoric as exemplified by Themistocles, by Cimon, and, especially, by Pericles (500e–505d). Socrates contests Gorgias' rhetoric because it is inconsistent, because it claims to teach justice but disclaims any responsibility for its students' injustice. Socrates will contest Pericles' rhetoric because, like the false art of cookery, it seeks not the greatest good of the soul and body but the pleasure of the moment. First, however, Socrates contests the cultural ideal of virtue that informs and shapes Periclean rhetoric.

Contesting Cultural Beliefs:
Socrates versus Polus and Callicles

The problem of rhetoric as set forth in the *Gorgias* is not theoretical but practical. Gorgias could eliminate the conceptual inconsistency in his view of rhetoric if he simply proclaimed an instrumental view of rhetoric and disclaimed any commitment to teach what is and is not just. But he cannot in practice disclaim a commitment to teach what is just and at the same time claim to teach the art of political leadership.[75] Socrates' further discussions with Polus and Callicles in the second part of the dialogue (466a–500a) show why he contests Gorgias' teaching and Pericles' practice of rhetoric, for Polus and Callicles apparently represent the traditional cultural ideal of *aretē* as courage and intelligence or practical wisdom, an ideal that informs and shapes Athenian rhetorical practice, indirectly and confusedly in Gorgias' teaching, directly and explicitly in Pericles' practice. Polus claims that orators and tyrants have the greatest power in cities because they can do whatever they wish in pursuit of their own interest. Socrates contests Polus' view by showing him that orators and tyrants may do what they want but do not in fact do what they wish because they do not do what is really good for themselves, because they do not understand that to commit is worse than to suffer injustice. Callicles claims that a standard of justice based upon nature rather than mere convention legitimates the self-interested pursuit of power and pleasure, the exercise of courage and intelligence without regard for (conventional) justice and temperance. Socrates contests Callicles' view by showing him that he himself believes that some pleasures are better than others, that the person of courage and intelligence is better than the shameful catamite or the foolish coward, that in fact the good, not the merely pleasurable, is the end of all our actions. Kahn maintains that Polus and Callicles represent the traditional Homeric ideal of *aretē,* courage and intelligence in the pursuit of success, power, and wealth—the ruthless self-assertion of the ambitious individual, who like Achilles strives always to be first and best—in contrast to the civic ideal of justice and temperance in the exercise of civic duty.[76] Callicles' linking of courage and intelligence suggests that he may represent more specifically the contemporary Athenian transformation of the traditional ideal—traditional Homeric courage joined to contemporary Athenian intelligence—a suggestion reinforced by the echoes of Periclean rhetoric in Callicles' defense of natural justice and by the reappearance of Pericles himself in the third part of the dialogue.[77] Socrates' refutation of the Athenian cultural ideal of virtue requires a rejection of the indiscriminate hedonism of the *Protagoras* because it leads Socrates to acknowledge, as Callicles too acknowledges, that pleasures are relative not only to each other but also to someone, that they are not only quantitatively but also qualitatively different, the courageous and the cowardly person, for example, calculating differently, the cowardly person experiencing perhaps the greater pleasure in the present but the courageous person the greater pleasure, and thus the greater good, over the longer term. Socrates' refutation of this ideal also helps to explain his rejection of Periclean rhetoric, for Socrates apparently believes that Pericles' policy of empire and perhaps even his person were neither courageous nor just, his rhetoric a pursuit of immediate pleasure rather than civic virtue, his legacy the destruction of the empire rather than the stability and security of the city.

Polus denies Socrates' claims about rhetoric, for he believes that orators and tyrants have great power in their cities to do whatever they please (466b–c). Socrates disputes this claim because he believes that orators and tyrants do what they think is best but do not do what they really wish to do because they do not understand that to commit is worse than to suffer injustice and that one who commits injustice is not only unjust but also unhappy (466d–67b, 469b–c, 470c–e). Polus attempts to defend his claim with an argument by example, citing Archelaus of Macedonia, the son of a slave, ruler by treachery and murder, the most unjust but also, presumably, the happiest person in all of Macedonia (471a–d). Socrates objects that Polus makes his case by rhetoric *(rhētorikē)* rather than by discussion *(dialegesthai),* calling upon witnesses rather than attempting to refute *(elegchein)* him; he challenges Polus either to refute him or to permit him to refute Polus, thereby confirming their account *(logos)* by acting either one as a witness to the other (471d–72d, 473d–74b).[78] Polus then reasserts his claims that to suffer is worse than to commit injustice and that the unjust person is also a happy person, and Socrates attempts to refute him (472d–73d). Polus denies that to commit is worse than to suffer injustice and asserts that neither he nor anyone else would choose to suffer rather than to commit injustice (474b). Socrates then asks Polus whether to commit injustice is more shameful or ugly *(aischron)* and, of so, more painful or more evil than to suffer injustice, and Polus admits that to commit injustice is both more shameful and more evil (474c–75c). He admits, furthermore, that he would not choose what is more evil and more shameful rather than less (475d–e). Socrates concludes that neither Polus nor anyone else in the world would choose to commit rather than to suffer injustice (475e). He nonetheless asserts that to commit injustice is not the greatest but merely the second greatest of evils, the greatest evil being to commit injustice but not to pay the penalty, the best use of rhetoric being therefore to expose injustice and thereby to bring the unjust person to justice (479c–d, 480b–d).

Kahn argues that both Polus and Callicles uphold the traditional Homeric ideal of *aretē* but that Polus maintains both Homeric courage and self-assertiveness and civic justice and temperance and thus represents a conflicted popular morality that he does not fully understand.[79] Socrates decrowns Polus, undermining his lofty moral ideas with a wry irony (Bakhtin calls it "reduced carnival laughter"), refuting him by revealing to him the inconsistency in his moral beliefs.[80] Socrates expresses the surprising and ironic convictions that orators and tyrants do what they think is best but nonetheless do not do what they really wish, that they do not understand that to commit is worse than to suffer injustice, that they are therefore not only unjust but also unhappy, and he refutes Polus by showing him that he, too, despite himself, shares these convictions. Socrates does not refute Polus in rhetorical fashion, however, but in discussion conducted in the manner of a carnivalesque debate, drawing forth and juxtaposing his inconsistent and conflicted beliefs not for the purpose of merely testing him—as he had tested Laches and Nicias, for example—but for the purpose of contesting and refuting beliefs that he is convinced are dangerous, destructive, and simply wrong. Polus has presumed that do suffer is worse than to commit injustice and that an unjust person is a happy person, but Socrates leads him to acknowledge that to commit injustice is more shameful, and worse, than to suffer injustice, that he would not choose what is worse and more shameful over what is better and less shameful, that he therefore would not choose to commit rather than to suffer injustice, and that as a consequence it is better for him to suffer than to commit injustice.[81] Has Socrates in fact successfully refuted Polus?[82] Gregory Vlastos argues that when Socrates asks Polus whether it is more shameful and, if so, more painful or more evil, to commit or to suffer injustice, he fails to ask, "More painful *for whom?*" with the consequence that Polus might have escaped Socrates' trap if he had answered his question from the perspective of the observer, the answer to the question being, from this perspective, indeterminate, that is, answerable either way.[83] Kahn, Irwin, and others maintain, however, that Socrates clearly means more shameful, more painful, or more evil *for the*

agent, not *for the observer,* and that he has immediately closed Polus' escape
route when he leads him to assert that to commit is worse than to suffer injustice, *worse* clearly meaning *worse for the agent* since the justice and happiness of the agent is precisely the issue in dispute.[84] Scott Berman pointedly
observes that a comparative statement always implies a comparison relative
to someone and that Polus surely means "*my* suffering injustice is worse than
my doing injustice *relative to* securing my own happiness."[85] Whatever the
merits and limitations of Socrates' argument, Polus and Callicles, at least,
believe that it has successfully refuted Polus (475d–3, 482c–e). Socrates'
argument, moreover, is significant for the progress of the dialogue as a whole
since it shows that justice and injustice, happiness and unhappiness, are relative to one's perception. Thus it recalls Protagoras' suggestion that the good
is relative not only to *some thing* but also to *some one,* and it anticipates
Socrates' argument against Callicles' hedonism, his claim that the courageous
and the cowardly person calculate pleasures differently, with the consequence
that the consistent hedonist cannot distinguish between them.

Callicles, in turn, protests Socrates' treatment of Polus, pointing out
that just as Socrates has shamed Gorgias into claiming to teach justice, so
also he has shamed Polus into conceding that to commit is more shameful
than to suffer injustice (482c–e). Callicles refuses to make any such con-
cession. He claims that Socrates dupes Polus by clever trickery, by failing
to distinguish between nature and convention, so that when Polus acknowledges that to commit is more shameful than to suffer injustice according to
convention, Socrates presumes that he means more shameful according to a
natural principle (482e–83a). Callicles insists, to the contrary, that conventions and laws are merely attempts by the majority who are weak to gain
advantage over the few who are strong, that nature herself reveals a principle
of right *(dikē)* according to which the better and stronger person should have
rule and advantage over the weaker (483b–84c). Socrates claims that Callicles
will be the best sort of person to test *(basanizein)* his own beliefs because he
is wise, kind, and candid enough to say what he really thinks, so that whatever they agree upon will be the perfect truth (486e–87e). He asks Callicles
what sort of person the better and stronger person might be, and Callicles
responds that the better person is a person of courage *(andreia)* and also a person of wisdom or intelligence *(phronēsis),* a person who has strong desires
and who as a person of courage and intelligence is able to satisfy those desires
(491c–92a).[86] Socrates maintains, to the contrary, that the person who would
rule over others must first rule over the self—must achieve self-mastery or
temperance—and that the person who fails to rule the self is no better than the
licentious and shameful catamite (491d–e, 494e).[87] Socrates elicits Callicles'
belief that the satisfaction of desire—pleasure—is equivalent to the good and
then argues, first, that although we can feel pleasure and pain at the same time,
we cannot fare well and ill at the same time, with the consequence that plea-

sure is not equivalent to the good, and, second, that although the courageous and wise person is a good person, the courageous and wise person does not necessarily experience greater pleasure than a cowardly and foolish person, again with the consequence that pleasure and the good are not necessarily equivalent, the good, not the pleasant, being the end of all of our actions (494e–95a, 495c–500a).[88]

Unlike Polus, who represents a conflicted popular morality that he does not fully understand, Callicles professes a consistent moral outlook based upon Homeric courage and Athenian intelligence in the pursuit of power, success, and pleasure without regard for conventional notions of justice and temperance.[89] Socrates decrowns Callicles by carnivalizing his self-proclaimed morality, shames him by showing him that his moral position is not as consistent as he believes it to be, brings him down to earth by comparing his ideal life of indiscriminate hedonism to the shameful life of the licentious catamite or the foolish coward. Callicles claims to uphold an indiscriminate and unrestricted hedonism but fails to foresee the consequences of his belief.[90] He supposes that the end of all our actions is pleasure—the maximum satisfaction of desire—and that the person of courage and practical wisdom deserves as a matter of natural right to have more pleasure than others. He fails to see that his professed moral outlook is inconsistent with an indiscriminate hedonism, that not all pleasures are equal, that the pleasure of the courageous and intelligent person is not the same as the pleasure of the catamite or the coward. Kahn notes that Callicles might have had a more defensible position if he had maintained, for example, the selective hedonism of the successful politician, who restrains some desires for the sake of others, and speculates that Plato may have opted for an indiscriminate hedonism because it would have appealed to the self-indulgent young men of his time or because it seems to offer a solution to the problem of knowing how to live the good life by appealing to obvious facts about pleasure and pain.[91] The Socrates of the *Protagoras,* of course, has maintained just such a position, which the Socrates of the *Gorgias* now explicitly rejects, and Plato may also have opted for an indiscriminate hedonism in the interest of returning to a problem that he had left unresolved in the earlier dialogue.[92] In the *Protagoras,* Socrates had proposed but had not explained the hedonistic calculus that would permit us to know how to live the good life by enabling us to calculate relative pleasures and pains, goods and evils, over the course of our lives as a whole. In the *Gorgias,* Socrates recalls the problem of the relativity of the good and in particular the problem of the good as relative not only to some thing but also to someone. Kahn notes that this problem appears in any attempt to define hedonism in terms of the subjective quality of the agent's experience—for (as Aristotle remarks) the virtuous person takes pleasure in acting virtuously, the vicious person in acting viciously.[93] Irwin observes, moreover, that the problem arises in any purely quantitatively comparison of pleasures, such as the proposed hedonistic calculus: "If cowardly people's values determine their pleasures, and brave people's values determine their pleasures, we cannot decide who is right by some independent calculation of pleasure."[94] The Socrates of the *Gorgias* resolves the problem by turning away from hedonism and from the hedonistic calculus of the *Protagoras* and proposing instead his own art of dialogue, by which means alone, he believes, we can acquire the knowledge necessary for virtuous living.[95]

Contesting the Politics and Rhetoric of Empire: Socrates versus Callicles and Pericles

Callicles has maintained the exercise of courage and intelligence—the Homeric and Athenian ideal—in the pursuit of power and pleasure and without regard for justice. Socrates has shown him that he cannot maintain this position consistently, that he cannot uphold an indiscriminate hedonism, since he is unwilling to grant that the pleasures of the courageous and the cowardly person are indistinguishable, the one no better than the other. Immediately following this refutation of Callicles, Socrates returns abruptly to the discussion of rhetoric and repeats his claim that rhetoric, like cookery, is concerned with only the pleasure of the moment. Socrates turns in the third part of the dialogue (500a–527e) to a positive account of the harmony and order of the soul, the relationship of the virtues, and the role of the true orator.[96] But he also returns to his earlier discussion of the false rhetoric that seeks only pleasure and explicitly associates this rhetoric with the great Athenian political leaders of the past and especially with Pericles, thereby indicating that the carnival— and the debate—is not yet finished. The carnivalesque atmosphere persists in Socrates' elaborate and lowly comparisons of Periclean rhetoric to the slavish and menial treatments of the body by cooks and shopkeepers and winemakers, and the debate unfolds as a contrast and a contest between Periclean intemperance and injustice and Socratic justice, between Periclean rhetoric and Socratic dialogue.[97] Socrates maintains that the harmonious and orderly soul is the soul that is at once just and temperate and holy and also courageous and that the true orator is the orator who seeks to engender these qualities in the souls of others. He thus articulates a new cultural ideal that joins Homeric courage to civic justice and temperance and a new and true rhetoric that sustains, or ought to sustain, this ideal.[98] Nonetheless, he contests Callicles' claim that such an ideal of virtue and such an ideal of rhetoric exists or has ever existed and blames the greatest of Athenians—Themistocles, Cimon, and especially Pericles—for their failure to pursue these ideals, for their practice of a servile rhetoric akin to cookery, for their intemperate and unjust pursuit of empire, and for its inevitable destruction. He does not blame Miltiades, the hero at Marathon, however, perhaps because he recognizes that the persons responsible for Athens' undoing were not the Athenians or even the Spartans who defended their cities, homes, and families but the architects of empire who succeeded them. Socrates concludes, therefore, that he alone practices the true art of politics, the art of dialogue, affirmed in his concluding myth and in his own life.[99]

Reminding Callicles that he has acknowledged that some pleasures are better than others, Socrates returns to his comparison of rhetoric to cookery, observing that both are concerned with the soul's pleasure, without regard for which pleasures are better or worse, concerned, that is, with mere gratification and with the gratification of the many as well as the one (500a–501d). Socrates inquires whether the kind of rhetoric addressed to the many aims to make them as good as possible or merely to gratify them and, if the former, whether anyone has ever practiced such a rhetoric (502d–3b). Callicles claims that Themistocles, Cimon, Miltiades, and Pericles were such men as Socrates describes (503c). Socrates maintains, to the contrary, that a soul that is regular and orderly is a soul that is just and temperate and holy and also courageous and that the true orator will with every word and action seek to engender these virtues in the souls of other citizens (503d–4e, 507a–c).[100] He claims no certainty for the truth of his own account *(logos)* of virtue but claims also that neither Callicles nor anyone else has ever successfully challenged his reasons of steel and adamant but instead in trying has shown himself to be ridiculous (508c–9a). As for the great Athenians of the past, Socrates claims that neither Pericles nor Cimon nor Themistocles nor Miltiades ever practiced a true art of rhetoric since all of them were treated harshly by those in their care, and he blames all but Miltiades for filling Athens with harbors and arsenals and walls and tribute, with no regard for justice and temperance, and for the foreseeable loss of all that Athens has had and all that it has more recently acquired (516b–e, 518e–19b).[101] He therefore claims that he alone attempts to practice a true art of politics *(politikē technē),* that he alone practices an art aimed not at gratification, not at what is most pleasant, but at what is best for those in his care (521d–e). He admits that if brought to trial he will be like a doctor brought before children on a charge by a cook, but he nonetheless refuses to practice a flattering rhetoric and expresses willingness to accept his death as a consequence (521e, 522d–e). He concludes with a mythic tale of a divine judgment that separates the just from the unjust and urges Callicles to prepare for his own trial and judgment and to practice rhetoric only for the purpose of promoting what is just (523a–24a, 527a–c).

Socrates decrowns the great Athenians of the past, as he has decrowned Gorgias, by comparing their rhetoric to cookery and by contrasting their false rhetoric to a true rhetoric that would promote what is just—if ever there were such a rhetoric—and to the true art of politics—the art of dialogue—that does indeed, so Socrates believes, promote what is just.[102] Thus he not only contests the cultural ideals and rhetorical practices of his time; he seeks also to transform these ideals and these practices into a new cultural and linguistic consciousness, a new moral vision with transformative and redemptive power. Kahn argues that Socrates has solved the problem of virtue that had persisted in Greek thought from the time of Homer by joining the competitive to the cooperative virtues—self-regarding courage to other-regarding justice and temperance:

> It was one of Socrates' greatest achievements to reshape these two conceptions into a new and consistent moral ideal, the unity of the virtues founded on wisdom and on the cooperative excellences, pushing justice to new and revolutionary demands ("never harm anyone, even an enemy"), but remaining faithful to the old ideal of manliness by fearlessly risking and finally giving up his life in the cause of justice and loyalty to moral principle.[103]

Kennedy maintains that the true philosophical rhetoric of the *Gorgias* is a rhetoric that promotes these virtues and that such a rhetoric represents an advance over either Polus' view of rhetoric as flattery or Socrates' earlier view of rhetoric as a means of bringing the unjust person to justice.[104] Yunis, however, claims that the more immediate and pressing issue in the *Gorgias* is the contest between rhetorical practices well established in contemporary Athenian politics and an alternative rhetorical ideal that finds its fulfillment not in the *Gorgias* but in the *Republic,* in the person of the "philosopher-*rhētōr*" who is also the philosopher-king.[105] According to Yunis, Gorgias, Polus, and Callicles represent and defend established forms of deliberation and discourse best represented by the Pericles of Thucydides' *History*.[106] Plato's Callicles and Thucydides' Pericles converge strikingly, Yunis claims, in Pericles' justification of Athens' defense of its empire as unjust to take but dangerous to let go.[107] Plato's Socrates opposes the Periclean policy that has transformed Athens into a large-scale tyrant, "powerful, corrupt, and insatiable."[108] He opposes Periclean rhetoric because it has made Athens more wealthy and more powerful but not better and more just.[109] But the Socrates of the *Gorgias* does not, Yunis believes, offer any alternative to Periclean rhetoric as a solution to the problem of "mass political education."[110] The Socrates of the *Gorgias* rejects discussion with the many but leaves open the possibility of the "discourse of command" elaborated in the *Republic*—the discourse of the political expert who as philosopher-*rhētōr* must persuade the masses that the philosopher will be the best ruler but who as philosopher-king has only to issue authoritative advice, which all must obey.[111]

The Socrates of the *Gorgias* does indeed reject the notion of mass political education, conducting his discussions with others one person at a time not to persuade them that what he knows is true but to demonstrate to them the conflicts and contradictions in their own beliefs and also to test his own beliefs by inviting and indeed challenging others to refute him. Socrates insists upon discussing *(dialegesthai)*—rendering and receiving accounts— with the one rather than with the many not because he believes that he can persuade either one person or many to accept his own account *(logos)* of virtue but because he believes that he can show—and indeed has shown—that no one has ever been able to offer an alternative account without showing himself to be ridiculous (474a, 509a). He claims that he does not know the truth of his own account but invites and encourages others to refute *(elegchein)* him (505e–6a). He claims no knowledge beyond the knowledge that results from such a repeated testing of his beliefs.[112] Yunis maintains that the Socrates of the *Gorgias,* unlike the Socrates of the *Apology,* acknowledges the failure of philosophy as a form of political discourse.[113] The Socrates of the *Apology* recognizes the tension between philosophy and politics but engages an eloquent if unconventional rhetoric in his own defense.[114] The Socrates of the *Gorgias,* like the philosopher-physician, who falls silent at the charge of the prosecutor-cook before the jeers of the children-jurors, acknowledges the unbridgeable chasm between philosophy and politics, renounces discourse with the many, and withdraws from politics altogether.[115] Nightingale, how- ever, recalls Socrates' claim that he alone practices the true art of politics and argues that he is distinguishing not philosophy from politics but two different kinds of political discourse: a rhetoric that serves the aspiring politician equally well in either a democracy or a tyranny and a kind of philosophical discourse that serves justice in ethics and politics and thus includes practical and political activities.[116] Wardy similarly argues that Socrates' claim that he alone practices the true art of politics, though "perplexing and outrageous," is nonetheless warranted, his conclusion inescapable, for "Socrates is unique in his unwavering commitment to a *logos* which is capable of doing his fellow- citizens good."[117]

Whether or not Plato actually *read* Pericles' speeches, as re-created by Thucydides, he must surely have *heard* echoes of his voice in the lives of contemporary Athenians, in men like Polus and Callicles. He may also have heard echoes of the voice of Homer singing in praise of traditional *aretē,* of courage and skill in battle, of men such as Achilles and Agamemnon. Appar- ently he did not hear, as Athens did not hear, the voice of Homer singing in praise of heroes such as Hector and Odysseus and Penelope or the voice of Simonides singing in praise of the Athenians and the Spartans who with- stood the Persian invasions, of the men and women who gave their lives in a just defense of their cities, their homes, and their families. But in the dark days of the end of the empire and the democracy, in the darkness of Socrates' trial and death, Plato must surely have heard—and he wants his readers to hear—the voice of Socrates himself, which must have seemed to him to be a very lonely and heroic voice speaking out against the tyranny and injustice of his time.

Dialogue on the Threshold:
The Contest of the Just Life

The ending of the *Gorgias* seems at worst a "retreat into rhetoric," a "mythic harangue" by a "mob-orator," at best an anticipation of the elegantly poetic myths of later dialogues such as the *Phaedo*, the *Republic*, and the *Phaedrus*.[118] Following Bakhtin's suggestion, however, we might read the ending of the *Gorgias* in its contextual relationship to the *Apology* as a "dialogue on the threshold"—a summing-up of Socrates' life and also a representation of Callicles as a person on the threshold of a final decision about his life.[119] From this perspective, we will see the *Apology* as Socrates' confession of his life, his defense of his lifelong mission of inquiry into the truth for the purpose of living virtuously, addressed to his divine rather than to his human judges, and we will see the ending of the *Gorgias* as both Socrates' confession of his life and a challenge to Callicles and to contemporary Athenians and to every one of Socrates' listeners and every one of Plato's readers to prepare themselves for their own dialogue on the threshold, their own confession of their lives before their divine judges—a challenge that Socrates describes as a contest *(agōn)*—indeed the greatest of all the contests on earth.

In *Problems of Dostoevsky's Poetics,* Bakhtin explains the dialogue on the threshold as a summing-up and confession of a person standing on the threshold, provoked by the extraordinary situation of impending death.[120] He notes the limits of the Socratic dialogue on the threshold, due to its historical and memoirist nature, but nonetheless credits the *Apology* in particular with giving birth to the genre and even pointing the way to its future development in its vision of Socrates conducting discussions with others from distant times in the next life as he has in his life on earth.[121] Some readers of the *Apology* take Socrates' defense of himself to be a serious attempt at persuasion and thus an illustration of the true philosophical rhetoric developed in the later *Gorgias* and *Phaedrus.*[122] Brickhouse and Smith claim that Socrates' own moral and religious commitments require that he present a sincere and effective defense to his jury and claim, moreover, that such a defense is consistent with the goal of a philosophical rhetoric, with its scrupulous regard for truth in the service of justice.[123] Others note that Socrates' defense conforms to the standard structure of Greek forensic oratory and that all three of his speeches emphasize his commitment to truth and virtue, to an art of rhetoric based upon knowledge and directed toward justice and the good of the soul.[124] Allen says simply: "The *Apology* is philosophical rhetoric, aimed at truth and indifferent to gratification and pleasure."[125]

Bakhtin's reading of the *Apology* as a dialogue on the threshold suggests, however, that we take Socrates' defense to be not so much an attempt to persuade as to confess, to sum up his life and to say, as Fyodor Dostoevsky says of Don Quixote: "Here is my conclusion about life, can you judge me for it?"[126] The Socrates of the *Apology* repeatedly affirms his commitment to seek truth and to live virtuously (29d–31b, 32e–33a, 36c, 41e) and to test both his own and others' knowledge of that truth in discussion *(dialegesthai),* both in this world and the next (21b–23d, 41b–c).[127] He disclaims any knowledge of his own (21b–d) but nonetheless concludes that the unexamined life is not worth living (38a). Given these commitments, he can propose, ironically but also quite seriously, that he be honored with free meals at the prytaneum or town hall *(prutaneion)* (36e–37a).[128] He can offer this proposal seriously because he views his life from the perspective of his final judgment, before the true judges—Minos, Rhadamanthus, Aeacus, and Triptolemus—and because he anticipates his journey through death to a better place, where he can continue his practice of testing and questioning without threat of death, immortal and in every respect happy (40c–41c).

Elsewhere in *Problems of Dostoevsky's Poetics,* Bakhtin notes that Dostoevsky always situates people on the threshold of a final decision, at a moment of crisis, a turning point for the soul.[129] At the end of the *Gorgias,* Socrates creates such a moment of crisis, a threshold of final decision, for Callicles, for contemporary Athenians, and for each of us. Nightingale describes the ending of the *Gorgias* as "mythic harangue."[130] Allen describes it as rhetorical argument, an attempt to persuade Callicles to pursue a life of virtue.[131] Bakhtin would likely explain it as dialogue on the threshold, a situating of the characters in the dialogue on the threshold of one of life's great decisions. The ending of the *Gorgias* recalls the *Apology,* with its allusions to Socrates' trial and death (486a–b, 511b–c, 521e–522a) and with its repetition and elaboration of the myth of the final judgment (523a–26d). It is, like the *Apology,* a dialogue on the threshold, but it is a different kind of dialogue, a situating not only of Socrates but also of Callicles—and so too Socrates' listeners (and Plato's readers)—on the threshold of life's greatest challenge and life's greatest contest—the challenge to live a life of justice and virtue. Socrates tells a story of final judgment: Zeus has ordered the divine judges—Minos, Rhadamanthus, and Aeacus—to review defendants at trial unclothed, without witnesses, and after their death, to ensure their just judgment (523a–24a). Rhadamanthus and the others see their souls unclothed and judge them, sending the wicked to Tartarus, to suffer their punishment, and sending the holy, who have lived in truth, to the Isle of the Blessed (524e–26c). Convinced by this story, Socrates commits himself to the pursuit of truth and virtue (526d–e). He invites both Callicles and others to join him in this pursuit, this contest *(agōn)* worthy of all other contests on earth (526e). He reaffirms his account, his *logos,* which neither Polus nor Callicles has been able to disprove, that doing wrong is worse than suffering it (527a–b), and he urges Callicles to join him in the pursuit of the just life and the practice of a just rhetoric, postponing politics until they have learned to live and die in justice and in the other virtues (527c–e).

Yunis argues that Socratic dialogue was no more successful than Periclean rhetoric, as judged by its results, since Socrates, too, like the other great

Athenian statesmen, was treated harshly by those in his care, those whose lives he sought to improve.[132] Nightingale notes, however, that Socrates in his concluding myth looks not to this life but to the next for evidence of the worth of his life and art.[133] She acknowledges Socrates' failure to persuade others, and to persuade Athens, to accept the life of virtue and claims that Plato seeks to vindicate him through recourse to a *deus ex machina,* the myth of divine judgment that concludes the dialogue.[134] But she also observes that the myth opens up a broader perspective, "a god's-eye view of the issues dealt with in the dialogue," a view that replaces human with divine judgment, that sees only the virtue that lives in one's soul, and that sees death not as the end but as the beginning of life.[135] Situated thus at the threshold of the next life, Socrates invites Callicles and invites also his listeners (and Plato's readers) to join him. But Callicles stands mute before him, like many other contemporary Athenians, who listened to Pericles and perhaps to Thucydides but who did not listen either to Socrates or to the other voices—from Homer to Simonides to Protagoras—who might have helped them to understand courage in its relationship to civic virtue, true courage as courage in a just cause, who might therefore have helped them to grasp the meaning of the just life.

EPILOGUE

Dialogical Rhetoric in
Print and Digital Media

Dialogue—and dialogical rhetoric—seems to emerge at times of cultural conflict and seems to be possible in any medium—oral, print, and digital. According to Don H. Bialostosky, Mikhail M. Bakhtin developed his concepts of dialogism, heteroglossia, and carnival as a response to the cultural crisis of the individual author confronted by the authoritative knowledge accumulated within traditional disciplinary texts.[1] According to Charles H. Kahn, Harvey Yunis, and others, the Socrates of the early dialogues practiced his art of dialogue in response to the crisis of a culture caught in a conflict between the Homeric ideal of excellence as courage and skill in battle *(aretē)* upheld within the Greek oral tradition and the civic ideal of justice and temperance upheld, at least in principle, in contemporary political thought—by Protagoras, for example, and by Socrates himself.[2] This cultural conflict became a crisis of survival for the Athenian democracy and for Athens itself as the Pericles of Thucydides' *History* engaged his rhetoric as a tool of persuasion in pursuit of an unjust empire and so, the Socrates of the *Gorgias* suggests, set Athens on a path toward moral decline and physical self-destruction.[3] Our own culture presents a similar crisis of confidence in traditional authority brought about by the transition from an industrial to an information culture and from the culture of the printed book to the culture of the new digital media—the electronic book, the digital library, the networked classroom, and the World Wide Web.[4] It apparently also presents new possibilities for dialogue—interactivity and intersubjectivity, participation and collaboration, conflict and contestation—in the context of the new digital media.[5]

Dialogue thus seems to be possible in any medium. The Socrates of the early dialogues engages oral dialogue to contest both oral poetry and oral rhetoric. The Socrates of the *Republic* contests oral poetry in what seems to be a fixed and finalized written text. But the Socrates of the *Phaedrus* contests written texts, in a written text, for the same reasons that the Socrates of the early dialogues contests oral poetry and oral rhetoric. The Plato who preserves Socrates' oral arguments in written texts preserves at the same time the voices of Protagoras and Gorgias, Homer and Simonides, Pericles and Thucydides, and, in the *Phaedrus,* Lysias and Stesichorus, among many others. Bakhtin finds dialogue in every utterance, both oral and written, and he develops his most important concepts on the basis of written literary texts. Some contemporary critics note the challenge to the cultural authority of the printed book brought by the new digital media but also note resemblances between the new digital and the old oral media. We should therefore—as Kathleen E. Welch reminds us—be suspicious of any strict binary opposition between orality and literacy or between orality/literacy and the new digital media.[6] We should thus think of dialogue not as a characteristic of any given medium but as a mode of *consciousness* (to use Welch's term), as a willingness to read and write and think with others, to ask them to help us to see what is behind our heads, to see the conflicts and contradictions in our own beliefs.[7] Bakhtin's Socrates—the Socrates of the early dialogues—tells us that we think with others not by seeking to persuade others to accept beliefs that we already know to be true (for they may turn out to be partial or conflicted) but by entering into an exchange of utterances for the purpose of testing and contesting and creating ideas in cooperation and sometimes in conflict with others. Bakhtin's Socrates illustrates these possibilities in oral discourse. In this epilogue, I illustrate these possibilities in print and digital media.

CULTURAL CONFLICT AND OLD/NEW MEDIA

The objections to older media, both in Plato's time and in our own, serve as a useful reminder that the controversy between old and new media is not so much a controversy about the relative merits of oral or print or digital media as it is a controversy about the cultural authority presumed to be embedded within older media. The Socrates of the early dialogues offers his art of dialogue as an alternative to Protagoras' methods of display and poetic interpretation and Gorgias' and Pericles' rhetorical pedagogy and practice for the purpose of testing and contesting the traditional concept of *aretē* embedded within the Greek oral tradition. The Socrates of the later *Phaedrus* proposes his dialectical method of question and answer and protests the practice of writing for the same reason that the Socrates of the earlier dialogues protests oral poetry and oral rhetoric: writing is no better than either poetry or speech-making at asking and answering questions. Like the *Republic,* which provides an alternative to traditional *aretē* in a strict class system in which each of the virtues has its specific role or function, the *Phaedrus* provides an alternative in an ideal world in which each of the virtues exists in its absolute and eternal Form.[8] So we might well suppose that the Socratic practice of questioning and answering has no place in the later dialogues and survives in the *Phaedrus* as a mere remnant of the earlier period were it not that the very composition of the *Phaedrus* invites an exchange of questions and answers in the manner of the earlier dialogues. As I noted in chapters 1 and 3, Bakhtin probably overstates his distinction between the earlier and the later dialogues, and some readers of the *Phaedrus* have found in the apparent disunity of the dialogue and in its multiplicity of voices a new (for Plato's readers) kind of writing that invites us to continue to ask and to answer questions.[9]

As I explained in chapter 2, the *Phaedrus* has two main parts: first, a sequence of three speeches and, second, an exposition on dialectic, rhetoric, and writing, including a defense of dialectic as a method of question and answer.[10] The apparent disunity between the two parts of the dialogue is evident in the thematic and structural differences between the mythic/poetic speeches on love in the first part and the philosophical discussion on dialectic, rhetoric, and writing in the second part.[11] Some readers find an underlying unity between the two parts. Charles L. Griswold Jr. argues that the various dramatic, structural, and thematic threads in the dialogue harmonize in a "difficult, but beautiful, dialectic of self-knowledge."[12] Seth Benardete sees rather a tension between self-knowledge and knowledge in the two parts of the *Phaedrus,* brought together in a "nonevident unity" by Socrates' erotic art, which "seems to be a special case of the union of soul and mind."[13] George A. Kennedy finds a structural unity between the two parts in the balance between the illustration of rhetorical forms in the first part and the conceptualization of rhetorical composition in the second.[14] Others view the apparent disunity between the two parts of the dialogue as a deliberate attempt to invite and encourage an ongoing exchange of questions and answers. James L. Kastely argues that the two parts of the dialogue reflect a division between the personal and the political, between the rhetoric of love and the rhetoric of the polis, between intimate conversation and public discourse.[15] Kastely urges us, therefore, to question attempts to find unity and harmony in the *Phaedrus* and so "to recover the world as a place of conflict and choice," a place in which "we negotiate the legitimate but conflicting demands that we feel as erotic and political beings."[16] Both R. Allen Harris and Paul Kameen observe the destabilizing effect of the multiplicity of voices in the *Phaedrus.*[17] Harris notes, for example, that Phaedrus delivers a speech composed by Lysias and that Socrates delivers two speeches, one of which he attributes to a certain crafty boy (237b) and later to Phaedrus (243a), another of which he attributes to Stesichorus (244a).[18] Socrates also speaks in the voice of Theuth, speaking to

Thamus (274e–75b), or perhaps Plato speaks to his readers "pretending to be Socrates, pretending to be Theuth talking to Thamus, as he talks to Phaedrus," with the result that we are left wondering "who, exactly, is in charge?"[19] Similarly, Kameen wonders why, in his second speech, when he addresses "the most crucial question of this dialogue, perhaps even of the whole Socratic ethic," Socrates resorts to metaphor, despite his expressed contempt for poetic discourse.[20] Socrates' second speech thus "raises a very fundamental question about either the degree to which Socrates wants to stand squarely behind the assertions of his second speech or the degree to which he wants to stand squarely behind his express contempt for poetic semblances."[21]

Socrates' invitation to continue the exchange of questions and answers is explicit in his discussion of writing at the end of the dialogue. In the *Protagoras,* Socrates objects to speeches because, like books, they neither ask nor answer questions (328e–29b), and he objects to the poets for the same reason (347b–e). In the *Phaedrus,* he objects to writing because it resembles a painting, which depicts creatures who appear to be living beings but who, if you ask them a question, maintain a solemn silence (275d). Socrates thus seems to object not so much to a specific medium of expression but to any medium—a speech, a book, a painting—that does not permit the asking and answering of questions. Thus he reaffirms his dialectical method as a process of questioning and answering, which he believes will ensure that intelligent words will live in other minds capable of continuing the process forever (276e–77a). Given these implicit and explicit invitations to continue the exchange of questions and answers, we might feel that we have a right to ask Socrates some questions about the arguments that he presents in the *Phaedrus* and so to test and perhaps contest his own accumulated cultural authority. With Harris and Kameen, we might want to point to the multiple perspectives and contradictions in his arguments and ask him who and what he speaks for and what he really believes. We might want to recall the vision of absolute and eternal justice, temperance, and knowledge in the metaphor of the winged horses (247d–e) and ask him if he believes that courage is among the absolute and eternal Forms in the region above the heavens. If so, then we might want to ask him if he believes that a person can exercise courage in battle only or in any attempt to exert power over others, or if he believes that such an exercise of power can be called *courageous* if it is not also just, or if he believes that courage belongs to men only if it can also belong to women. We might also want to ask him if he objects to writing of any and every kind or only to a kind of writing that cannot ask or answer questions, a kind of writing that therefore cannot be held accountable for what it claims to be right or courageous or just. We might question him, that is, about his own cultural values and beliefs and his own rhetorical practices and thereby test and if necessary contest the cultural authority embedded within the text of the dialogue that has been handed down by Plato to all of us—in a new kind of writing that now seems old to many of us.

Some contemporary critics of the old print and the new digital media similarly call into question the cultural authority of the old media and thus provide another reminder that the controversy is not so much about old and new media as it is about the cultural values and beliefs presumed to be embedded within them. These critics characterize the old textual rhetoric as fixed and authoritative, linear and hierarchical, and they envision new forms of rhetoric and dialogue as dynamic and interactive networks of associations filled with a multiplicity of languages and voices.[22] In place of the traditional knowledge that they find inscribed and enshrined in printed texts, they promise the individual freedom to think and to read and to write creatively in digital space.[23] Richard A. Lanham observes that traditional cultural knowledge has long been associated with the printed book and is still frequently presented to us as "a print-stable collection of Great Ideas enshrined in Great Books."[24] Jay David Bolter explains that this body of traditional cultural knowledge was preserved historically in great books amassed in libraries and condensed in encyclopedias, which organized and controlled information in order to make it more readily accessible to readers.[25] In the encyclopedias, the organization of information was first associational, then hierarchical, then alphabetical (linear); in the libraries, it was both topical and alphabetical.[26] Myron C. Tuman maintains, moreover, that more recent cultural knowledge is not only preserved but also extended by print literacy since both science/technology and ideology (critique) are grounded in careful literate discourse and since the power of literate discourse is grounded, in turn, in the demonstrable power of industrial technology: "Our commitment to the notion that print literacy is capable of reshaping our world is itself the product of our deep cultural experience of the tangible power of industrial technology in controlling and reshaping the world for our betterment."[27]

These critics of old and new media thus challenge not only the old technology of the printed book but also the cultural knowledge presumed to be inscribed and enshrined within it. In place of the traditional knowledge inscribed in printed texts, they promise a new rhetoric and a new dialogue that encourage individual freedom to think and read and write creatively within a dynamic and interactive network of associations filled with a multiplicity of languages and voices.[28] Lanham foresees a rebirth of the art of rhetoric as the traditional art of persuasion—the art of persuasion, however, as it was practiced in the early oral period of the Homeric epic, in the speeches of heroes animated by competition, by "a truly Homeric urge to always be the best."[29] He envisions a new digital rhetoric that is dynamic rather than static; constantly changing rather than fixed; and general, chaotic, and centripetal rather than specialized, delimited, and predictable.[30] Bolter similarly envisions new forms of digital writing that return to the older tradition of oral discourse—not the persuasive discourse of the Homeric heroes but the dialogical discourse of Socrates and his partners in discussion—a discourse that is conversational rather than monological, associative and hypertextual rather than linear and hierarchical, a discourse that is part oral, part written, that offers readers at least some control of the argument and some responsibility for its outcome.[31] Bolter claims that the new digital (and dialogical) writing offers greater individual freedom not only to read but also to associate with others in shifting networks of association rather than in hierarchical structures of control and interpretation—networks of association that are horizontal and associative rather than vertical and hierarchical.[32] Welch turns rather to Isocrates as a model for the new "electric rhetoric," which she characterizes as additive, associative, and situational rather than hierarchical, logical, and abstract, as both agonistic and also collaborative, empathetic, and participatory.[33] Tuman sees similar contrasts between the old and new media but finds a precedent for the new media in Bakhtin rather than in the early Greeks—Homer, Socrates, and Isocrates.[34] Like Bolter, Tuman sees potential for individual freedom in the new digital media—freedom from the authoritative discourse that we are asked to accept because of the status of those who speak it, freedom to accept our own internally persuasive discourse, a freedom exercised, however, not in isolation from others but in the context of the chorus of languages, the multiplicity of voices (Bolter would call it a *network of associations*), that—together—we all speak and write.[35] This freedom, however, is not necessarily or inevitably characteristic of digital space, and we need only recall the persistent practice of *flaming* in digital spaces or the potential for mass marketing via the Internet and the World Wide Web to recognize that freedom for one is not necessarily freedom for everyone—freedom to interact and conflict and collaborate, to test and contest and create ideas in cooperation or in conflict with others.[36]

TESTING CULTURAL DIFFERENCES IN PRINTED TEXTS

Printed texts seem to be more fixed and authoritative than oral or digital media, more resistant to the exchange of utterances that Bakhtin finds in the Socratic dialogue. Bolter, however, observes the possibility of dialogue in printed texts, citing instances such as the characteristic "fragmentation and interruption" of Roland Barthes' texts, the complex interconnected network or "hypertext" of Ludwig Wittgenstein's *Philosophical Investigations,* and the nonlinear, asymmetrical typography of Jacques Derrida's *Glas.*[37] According to Bolter, both Barthes and Wittgenstein experiment with the conventions of the printed book, and Derrida so departs from these conventions that he creates not a book but an "antibook."[38] Moreover, even conventional printed books permit an exchange of utterances, both within and also between and among individual texts. Dialogical anthropology, for example, has long recognized the possibility of dialogue as an exchange of speaking subjects in printed texts.[39] One of a variety of responses to traditional "realist" or "scientific" anthropology, which maintains the authority of the anthropologist/author as neutral observer/reporter of cultural behavior, dialogical anthropology has been described as "a subspecies of broader processes of social interaction that are constitutive of social knowledge," a means by which anthropologists and informants and readers negotiate "radical cultural difference."[40] Conceived initially as an unequal exchange between anthropologist and informant, it has come to be seen as a complex process of exchange between anthropologist and informants and readers, a process of drawing forth and juxtaposing cultural differences for the purpose of testing them, each against the others, a process that Bakhtin in his discussion of the Socratic dialogue calls *anacrisis* and *syncrisis*.[41] Emily Martin's *Flexible Bodies* provides a particularly rich example of this kind of dialogue in printed texts—rich as a challenge to traditional cultural authority, on the one hand, and as an illustration of the persistence of traditional cultural values, on the other. In a complex series of juxtapositions, Martin shows how the new concept of *flexibility* is replacing traditional views of immunology and how this new concept nonetheless retains traditional values, including the ancient ideal of *aretē*—courage and skill in battle—situated, however, within the context of the contemporary struggle against AIDS.[42]

Kevin Dwyer's well known and widely cited *Moroccan Dialogues* illustrates the problem of the unequal exchange in the dialogue between anthropologist and informant and the inevitable presence of the anthropologist/author's hand—the author's "essential 'surplus' of *meaning*"—in the textual reconstruction of the dialogue.[43] George E. Marcus and Michael M. J. Fischer claim that even Dwyer's "lightly edited transcripts of field interviews" reveal the limitations of the anthropologist's "neat textualization of the immediate experiential data of fieldwork" and thus reveal as well the vulnerability of all of the participants—anthropologist, informants, readers—in the ethnographic project.[44] Dwyer himself acknowledges "the structured inequality of the partners" in the dialogue and the "radical recasting of experience" that inevitably occurs in the transformation of the experience of the dialogue into a printed text.[45] From a broader historical perspective, James Clifford and Vincent Crapanzano recall Plato's textualization of the Socratic dialogues and the inevitable reconstruction of experience that such a process entails.[46] Crapanzano asks us all to recognize, as Socrates himself would have recognized, that "Plato's compromise—the written dialogue—is indeed written and subject to all of the uses and misuses of the written, the quoted, word."[47]

Despite this persistent authorial presence (inevitable, perhaps, except in the context of a truly artistic creation such as the polyphonic novel), dialogical anthropologists have recognized the significant contribution of all of the participants—anthropologists, informants, readers—in the dialogical exchange. Citing the multiplicity of voices that Bakhtin finds in every utterance, they have endeavored to relinquish their own surplus of meaning and have invited this multiplicity of other voices into their texts for the purpose of juxtaposing and so testing all of them. Clifford, for example, citing Bakhtin's "concrete heteroglot conception of the world," claims that ethnographic writing "cannot be construed as monological, as the authoritative statement about, or interpretation of, an abstracted, textualized reality," for it is "shot through with other subjectivities and specific contextual overtones."[48] At an extreme, he suggests, this writing resembles Bakhtin's polyphonic novel.[49] Similarly, Bruce Mannheim and Dennis Tedlock, explaining Bakhtinian "intertextuality" as a complex web of juxtapositions of various linguistic registers, genres, and styles, claim that ethnographic writing cannot be based "solely on the two-sided interaction between ethnographers and interlocutors, each as an embodiment of a social position."[50] Ethnographers, they claim, both observe and create culture and so (like Bakhtin's polyphonic author) must enter into the same historical moment and the same critical plane as both their informants and their readers.[51] In doing so, they juxtapose and test their own and their informants' and their readers' beliefs, each against the others, relinquishing any vantage point of authority that would allow them to judge which of these beliefs are right or wrong. In an unusually self-reflective example of this kind of ethnographic writing, David J. Hess in *Science in the New Age* juxtaposes three cultures or belief systems about the paranormal—New Age, Parapsychology, and Skepticism—plus his own belief system—the human sciences—for the purpose of testing the sometimes unstated and often untested assumptions and values implicit in each of them.[52] Hess does not attempt to determine whose beliefs are right or wrong but rather to raise questions that invite each culture to reflect critically upon others' and especially its own beliefs—thus instantiating his own vision of the human sciences as a dialogical enterprise.[53]

Martin's *Flexible Bodies* similarly juxtaposes complex sets of beliefs about immunology.[54] Though she does not cite them directly, her image of contemporary warriors in the contemporary battle against AIDS recalls the ancient ideal of *aretē* and tacitly recalls also the folly and injustice that Socrates, too, perceived in this ideal. Martin's complex study cannot be reduced to a simple summary, but some of the main lines of development in her exposition illustrate how the juxtaposition of diverse cultural beliefs serves to test each of them against the others and at the same time invites both author and readers to test their own beliefs as well. Martin juxtaposes historical and contemporary views of immunology, a range of contemporary perspectives on immunology, and a variety of "configurations" and "practicums" in which the new concept of *flexibility* is developing simultaneously in complex systems of all kinds, including the immune system.[55] One of the main threads in her exposition is the shift in understanding from the concept of the immune system as a body at war with forces outside itself to the concept of the immune system as a complex system, at its best a resilient and flexible system, at war within the body itself.[56]

As Martin illustrates, however, even the new concept of a complex and flexible immune system retains elements of the older concept of warfare and echoes of the ancient ideal of *aretē*—courage and skill in battle—associated with warfare since the days of the early Greeks.

From the early through the middle of the twentieth century, Martin shows, the body was viewed as the site of battle against germs and viruses that attacked the body from outside, and bodily hygiene was viewed as the most important defense against disease.[57] At this time, the concepts of *body* and *system* were essentially synonymous ways of thinking about any bodily function.[58] Beginning in the 1950s, the body gradually came to be viewed—in obviously masculine metaphors—as the site of an internal battle between the immune system and the hostile microorganisms that seek to destroy it, between the Rambo-like, Mister T-like T cells called *killer cells* and the disease-causing microorganisms that invade the body from outside. Eventually, as Martin reveals in her interviews with nonscientists, practitioners, and scientists, the immune system comes to be viewed not simply as a military defense system but as a complex system capable of changing, adapting, and even learning about itself and the microorganisms—some good, some bad—that with it cohabit the human body.[59] This concept of a complex system capable of learning about itself is not peculiar to the immune system but is reflected in a wide array of ideas and practices, or "configurations," and is developed through a variety of processes, or "practicums," which permit (but do not guarantee) change through training and education, consistent with the most fundamental tenets of a liberal democracy.[60] Thus complex and flexible systems appear not only in immunology but also in configurations such as human resource management, computer software, economics, New Age philosophy, government organizations, psychology, and feminist theory, and they are developed through training and education, or practicums, such as laboratory research, media saturation, or management-training exercises, in the same way that the immune system itself is developed—trained and educated—through vaccinations and assessed and monitored through tests and measuring devices.[61]

These changes notwithstanding, the concept of the complex, flexible immune system nonetheless retains echoes of the older concept of warfare in ways that seem to illustrate the folly and injustice of the older concept. As Martin illustrates in her final chapter, the concept encourages a kind of post-Darwinian belief that some people have a stronger immune system than others and that these stronger and more courageous people will triumph in the battle against disease, even against deadly new diseases such as AIDS. This belief in a macho strength and courage, akin to the ancient Greek ideal of *aretē,* is equally accessible to both men and women:

> One medical resident I heard about, dismissing the possibility of contracting HIV infection from blood in the emergency room where

he worked, claimed that his immune system could "kick ass." . . .
And, in an invidious twist, the local newspaper reported that "5
Texas girls say they had sex with an HIV-infected male to get into
gang": "If the test came up negative, then it was like they were brave
to have unprotected sex and they were tough enough and their body
was tough enough to fight the disease."[62]

This belief stands in striking contrast to the concern that a community leader
expressed about the threat of AIDS to his community:

We think it [AIDS] could kill us. It could just kill a lot of people in
our community, that's what I think about. Because, with AIDS, the
way they say that you get AIDS, we got a lot of relationships here,
because they say that you get AIDS through needles, and a lot of our
people shoot up. They say you get AIDS through gay sex, and a lot
of our people function as prostitutes, and are [a] really sexually
active population, so, and then you get it through having relations
with one another, and you pass it by being close to one another, and
our people are very close to one another.[63]

In this context, the folly and injustice of the macho ideal of strength and
courage seems clear enough. But Martin does not draw this conclusion. In
fact, she carefully avoids drawing any conclusion.[64] She simply juxtaposes
these passages and invites her readers to draw their own conclusions for themselves, thus initiating, rather than ending, the dialogical exchange between her
informants, her readers, and herself.

CONTESTING CULTURAL AUTHORITY
IN DIGITAL DISCUSSION GROUPS

In contrast to print media, digital media seem to offer greater opportunities for
dialogue—opportunities for individuals to test and contest their own and others' ideas and themselves and to create new ideas in collaboration with others.
Some observers of digital discussion groups such as listservs, networked
classrooms, and MUDs and MOOs emphasize the opportunity afforded by
these media to explore self-identity and to contest traditional structures of
authority.[65] These observers, however, present conflicting evidence on the
potential of digital discussion groups to contest authority within these
groups.[66] They have only begun to explore the potential of digital discussion
groups to contest authority outside these groups, in the larger physical and
social world.[67] As I explained in chapter 3, Bakhtin views the carnival as an
opportunity not only to contest but also to transform official languages and

cultures. Some digital discussion groups, most strikingly the MUDs and MOOs, recall this carnivalesque atmosphere, with its marketplace language and its opposition of official languages and cultures. These digital discussion groups seem to have potential to effect transformations in the larger physical world by offering lessons in social justice, through direct experience with the cultural codes and values that structure and inform our relationships with others.[68] My own experience in a digital classroom with colleagues Laura J. Gurak and Stephen Doheny-Farina and a select group of graduate students illustrates this potential.[69]

Digital discussion groups appear to offer opportunities to explore one's own self-identity in processes that are both individual and social. Sherry Turkle notes the postmodern phenomenon of multiple and fluid self-identity and observes the opportunity to explore and to create multiple identities or personae in digital discussions, especially in MUDs and MOOs.[70] Bolter similarly observes the opportunity afforded by MOOs and chat rooms "to examine the politics of identity through the lenses of race, gender, and class."[71] Others claim that the formation of individual self-identity is inherently social. Lester Faigley, for example, describes the "achieved utopia" of the networked classroom in which students discover their "authentic selves" by trying on and exchanging identities, even from one message to the next.[72] He maintains, however, that this process of identity formation is not individual but social, a process of equal participation between student and student akin to the Bakhtinian struggle between "the monologic centripetal forces of unity, authority, and truth and the dialogic centrifugal forces of multiplicity, equality, and uncertainty."[73] Tuman similarly describes the process of achieving individuality in the context of the networked classroom as a Bakhtinian challenge to authoritative discourses captured in printed texts and as an opportunity to develop one's own internally persuasive discourses.[74] He, too, maintains that this process is inherently social—a collaboration in which "the written exchange or dialogue occasioned by a text" is at least as important as the text itself.[75] Whereas Faigley views this process as "inherently agonistic," however, Tuman views it as cooperative and communal—an antidote to individual self-absorption and moral blindness.[76] Tharon W. Howard claims that it is both individual and social, both agonistic and cooperative, that it embraces both "rhetorics of accommodation" and "rhetorics of resistance," both "individualistic" and "constitutive" views of community.[77] Rejecting the inside/outside binary that sustains these distinctions, he embraces Valentin Voloshinov's view of individuals as socially organized and therefore capable of language, meaning, and even consciousness itself.[78]

Digital discussion groups apparently also offer opportunities to contest authority both within and outside these groups. Bakhtin envisions the carnival as an opportunity both to contest and to transform official languages and cultures, as illustrated, for example, by the revival of classical Latin and the development of vernacular languages in Rabelais' time, which not only con-tested but also transformed the official language and culture of church and state. Nonetheless, some of Bakhtin's critics have observed that his vision of the carnival as a linguistic and cultural event has little power to contest and to change institutional structures of authority and control. Peter Stally-brass and Allon White insist that carnivalesque practice is politically mean-ingless if it does not address "the question of the *domain of discourse*" and the degree to which this practice "has actually shifted or realigned domains."[79] Feminist critic Clair Wills explains that the challenge of femi-nist poetry is a literary challenge, an attempt to change literary forms, and through this challenge an attempt to change also the forms of cultural authority, such as the literary canon, the repository of the values of the dom-inant culture.[80] She, too, insists that this challenge must also be directed toward "the sites of discourse," the dominant literary institutions, such as publishing houses, lest it become objectified and marginalized within them.[81] Some observers of digital discussion groups point to similar prob-lems. Faigley, for example, acknowledges that the utopian dream of an equi-table sharing of classroom authority is achieved in the networked class-room—but only for the duration of the class discussion.[82] Howard shows, moreover, that forces outside the discussion group can actually constrain the choices of individuals within the group. Describing his experience with an academic listserv, he observes that commitments and allegiances to profes-sional and social groups outside the listserv constrain individual choice, with the consequence that some individuals complain or withdraw or decline to participate in digital discussions when confronted with other per-sonal or professional commitments or when intimidated by participants per-ceived to have greater cultural authority by virtue of their professional sta-tus or position outside the group.[83] Though his rhetoric of accommodation/resistance offers the promise of resistance and change, his experience suggests that digital discussion groups may not only fail to trans-form the larger professional and social worlds outside these groups but may actually be constrained by them.[84]

These difficulties notwithstanding, other observers of digital discussion groups speculate about their potential to contest and transform traditional structures of authority—official languages and cultures—and thereby to pro-vide a model for social change not only within but also outside these groups. Beth Kolko argues that the challenge to traditional structures of authority in digital discussion groups such as MUDs and MOOs is nothing less than a quest for social justice.[85] In a characterization that resembles Bakhtin's view of the carnival, Kolko describes the real-time chat space of the MOO as a realm of dialogue: a site of oppositional discourse, parody, and resistance; a site of collision between languages, worldviews, and cultural expectations; and a place for play, pun, and slippage.[86] Kolko notes, moreover, that this site of dialogical opposition, collision, and play is also a site for lessons in social justice, in the exercise of power relationships informed by cultural codes of race, class, geography, and gender—lessons from the virtual world that are equally valuable in the physical and social world beyond it.[87] Laura Gurak, Steve Doheny-Farina, and I offer a similar description of the carnivalesque quality of our own experience in a MOO discussion group and show how the development of our discussions over a period of time successfully contested traditional structures of classroom authority.[88] I believe that these discussions also illustrate the potential of the MOO as a site and an occasion for practical lessons in the exercise of power relationships applicable to the physical and social world and capable, perhaps, of effecting a gradual transformation of these relationships.

In 1994, Laura, Steve, and I offered a graduate class at Diversity University MOO and circulated a notice to several graduate programs in rhetoric and composition inviting students to participate in our experiment. We offered a letter of congratulations for successful completion of the course but offered no credit for the class. We received responses from fourteen students and accepted all of them. We planned to meet in Steve's office at Diversity University MOO once a week for ten weeks. In an effort to simulate the conduct of a graduate class, provide substantial content for the course, and ensure some semblance of order, we asked our students to complete some readings each week, we asked one student to prepare a commentary on each week's readings and to circulate the commentary prior to our discussion, and we asked two students to serve as respondents on each week's commentary. We anticipated that following these formal proceedings, we would open the class to general discussion. In addition, Steve adopted the convention of displaying a sign with instructions on classroom behaviors and procedures. We felt that these measures were necessary to ensure that our discussions would not collapse into mere playfulness, idle chatter, or worse. We soon discovered, however, that our students not only challenged our position as figures of authority in the classroom but proved to be quite capable of monitoring their conduct on their own, with or without our intervention. Moreover, I believe that we all learned some lessons about relationships of power and authority that are equally valuable within or outside the classroom, in the physical and social world. As illustration, I offer a few brief passages from our discussions.

At the beginning of the course, our classroom procedures, drawn from our experience in traditional graduate classes, proved to be effective and useful, so we believed. Our students presented their commentaries, offered their responses, and participated in the general discussions. Steve provided instructions as necessary, and the discussions proved to be lively but also orderly and civil. The following illustration (typographics retained, as in the original) typifies these early discussions:

SteveDF holds up a BIG sign: | Laura? want to join the conversation? |

Laura_Gurak] nods yes.

Laura_Gurak] says, "I would like to pursue Lisa's skepticism."

Chris-B says, "I wanted to get one of my questions in before things go to chaos . . ."

Laura_Gurak] says, "The question she seems to be raising (waits for Chris's question . . .)"

Chris-B says, "I'll wait for Laura's answer."

. . . .

Geoffrey raises his hand. "May I ask a question, or is this for the panel only?"

Laura_Gurak] says, "Now the ? becomes, are these elctronic commuities good or bad . . ."

Chris-B says, "I get my question next."

Laura_Gurak] says, "for democracy?"

Geoffrey nods. "Sorry."

SteveDF says, "hold off for a sec, geoff"

Laura_Gurak] nods at Chris-B (Week 2 Log)[89]

At this stage (Week 2), students were courteous and tentative and displayed traditional classroom behaviors, such as raising their hands or requesting permission to speak. Steve used his sign to monitor the discussion and added verbal instructions to ensure orderly turn taking in the discussion. After only a few weeks, however, the tenor of the discussions changed dramatically, as the following illustration (typographics retained) suggests:

Laura_Gurak] says, "Why are we talking only about students/classrooms????"

. . . .

DonL says, "PRACTICALLY SPEAKING, WHAT ACTIONS SHOULD WE TAKE _OUTSIDE_ THE CLASSROOM TO ENACT THE DEMOCRATIC PUBLIC SPACES WE WISH TO HAVE IN CYBERSPACE."

SteveDF says, "and you touched on it earlier: can this space be used to further radical democracy—but not in cyberspace—in physical politicla world?"

Laura_Gurak] nods at Don's shout.

DonL is sorry for yelling again, but feels the need.

Chris-B says, "Big shouting Don and big sign Steve."

Logie says, "We have to begin with the understanding that cyber-space has been circumscribed.""

Laura_Gurak] [to Chris-B]: "BSD and BSS for short

Chris-B says, "Is it a testosterone thing?"

. . . .

Kim_W has big sign envy

Laura_Gurak] meant to 'continue' when she said 'go on' "

LisaM [to Kim_W]: "Kim??!!??

. . . .

DonL [to Chris-B]: Definitely a testosterone thing.

AheaP . o O (does that make KimW green with said envy?)

Laura_Gurak] feels a bit uncomfortable at how she forcefully sug-gested changing the thread. (Week 4 Log)[90]

In this segment of the discussion, Laura explicitly raises the issue of the poten-tial impact of the MOO experience in the physical world outside the classroom. Others fail to respond to her question, so one of the students restates the ques-tion in upper-case letters, the MOO equivalent of shouting. Students respond with playful commentary about the big shout and the big sign and explicitly remark upon the power relationships, and especially the traditional gender rela-tionships, implicit in these symbols. These few passages from our discussions, and others like them, show how the students contested traditional structures of classroom authority and traditional gender roles, how they helped us to see what we were unable to see for ourselves, and how the lessons that they (and we) learned in the MOO might apply to the physical and social world outside it. Thus they offer one kind of answer to the question that Laura sought (unsuc-cessfully) to explore. We can only speculate about the reasons for this suc-cessful challenge to traditional classroom authority, but we suspect that the process of self-selection of the participants contributed significantly to the out-come. Amy Bruckman explains that one of the key decisions in her conduct of Massachusetts Institute of Technology's MediaMOO was her decision to admit only people doing some kind of media research, a decision that parallels our own.[91] With Kolko, too, we can only speculate, hopefully, about the potential of digital discussions to effect gradual transformations of relationships of power and authority in the world outside the MOO.

CREATING A DIGITAL COMMUNITY
ACROSS A CULTURAL DIVIDE

Like other forms of digital media, the World Wide Web seems to offer unusual opportunities for dialogue—opportunities to explore and express one's self-identity, to test various versions of oneself, to contest traditional structures of authority, and to create new ideas in collaboration with others.[92] But the Web also seems to be increasingly attractive, and vulnerable, to mass-marketing efforts by large corporations, politicians, and special interests. Welch observes the power of large communication conglomerates—"new media robber barons"—to usurp and use the new digital media to "intellectually colonize" and "narcotize" the public, and Doheny-Farina notes the potential of the Web as a graphics delivery system to equip every political and special interest with its own printing and television services.[93] To counter these growing trends, some researchers have developed Web-based resources as a means of sharing information and ideas and encouraging creative collaborations. Welch describes a Web-based resource on feminist rhetoric (http://weather.ou.edu/~femrhets/, May 18, 2003), developed for the purpose of encouraging collaboration and mutual inquiry but open to strong disagreements and agonistic clashes of ideas.[94] Russian transculturist Mikhail N. Epstein describes a similar but broader venture, called InteLnet (http://www.emory.edu/INTELNET/, May 18, 2003), committed to creative collaboration across the whole range of humanistic disciplines on a global scale.[95] Doheny-Farina claims, nonetheless, that the new digital media tend to isolate individuals and to make them more dependent upon mass markets and globalized communication networks.[96] He therefore urges a redirection of the new media toward the needs of local communities, a development of wired neighborhoods grounded in geographically situated, physical communities and aimed at strengthening social commitments and enriching communal experiences at the local level.[97]

Motivated by concerns about the potential for mass marketing via the Web and inspired in part by Doheny-Farina's vision of the wired neighborhood, Teresa M. Harrison, Sibel Adali, and I have initiated the development of a youth-services information system, called Connected Kids (accessible at http://www.troyny.org/, under Community Resources, May 18, 2003), which will utilize sophisticated database and Web technologies to provide information about recreational , educational, and cultural opportunities to parents, teachers, and children in the City of Troy and Rensselaer County, New York.[98] Our work is based at Rensselaer Polytechnic Institute, a technological institution separated from its surrounding community by a deep cultural divide, dramatically illustrated in Ellen Cushman's portrait of the institution perched on a hill overlooking the city and connected to it by a vast staircase, for many years worn, neglected, and virtually impassable.[99] Although the staircase has recently been restored, the cultural divide remains. We nonetheless believe that this divide can be overcome through creative, collaborative efforts—efforts grounded in our belief that people working together can create better ideas and more useful outcomes than any one person or culture alone can produce. Such a belief is not self-evident and indeed has closer affinities to contemporary Russian transcultural thought than to American individualism and multiculturalism.

In Russian transcultural thought, individuals, and individual cultures, appear to be incomplete without each other. Epstein recalls Bakhtin's idea that the life of culture does not occur within but at the borders between cultures, for "only in the eyes of an alien culture, does another culture open itself in a fuller and deeper way."[100] Epstein therefore advocates a transcultural as opposed to a multicultural approach to the intellectual life of the global community. Transculture, Epstein explains, is "the site of interaction among all existing and potential cultures" and as such "is even richer than the totality of all known cultural traditions and practices."[101] Its goals are "to challenge the one-dimensionality of official culture" and "to ascend to a genuine totality that embraces a variety of modes of cultural thought."[102] In contrast to transculture, American multiculturalism is grounded in individualistic and pluralistic tendencies that support a multiplicity of distinct and separate minority cultures, which "may exist side by side without taking the slightest interest in one another."[103] American multiculturalism, Epstein claims, "proceeds from the assumption that every ethnic, sexual, or class culture is important and perfect in itself, while transculture proceeds from the assumption that every particular culture is incomplete and requires interaction with other cultures."[104] Epstein probably oversimplifies American multiculturalisms, which are themselves many rather than one, but his observations nonetheless invite us to test our own versions of ourselves, our own culture against other cultures, and thus to see, perhaps, what we could not otherwise see for ourselves.

Transculturists, following Bakhtin, believe that these interactions among cultures can produce richer outcomes than any one culture can produce by itself. Marina Timchenko finds interactions of this kind in adaptations of American films to Philippine or Indian culture and in adaptations of European films to American culture, and she describes the results as cultural "hybrids."[105] Epstein claims, however, that hybrids, even if considered merely as metaphors, "are still attached to the notion of species, stable essences as they are manifested in nature."[106] In place of hybridization, therefore, he advocates "improvisation," a process that, unlike self-centered creativity, requires both creativity and communication: "Somebody suggests a topic, unexpected for the improviser, whose task is to elaborate this topic unpredictably for the one who suggested it."[107] Improvisation therefore requires not one but two mutually stimulating consciousnesses.[108] To facilitate these "collective improvisations," Epstein created InteLnet, with the goals of advancing new ideas, investigating new connections among ideas, elaborating methodologies for a new humanistic metadiscipline suited to an electronic environment, designating electronic sites for new humanistic disciplines, and creating interactive texts as a collaboration of many minds.[109] As an illustration of one kind of electronic improvisation, Epstein recalls the assertion that "I know that I know nothing," attributed to the historical Socrates. Such a topic, he suggests, might be investigated in the opposite direction, with an assertion such as "I do not know what I know," attributable to an alternative Socrates.[110] Thus, improvisationally, we can envision both our own superiority over our ignorance and our inferiority to our own knowledge.[111] A case in point is the Socrates of *Protagoras,* who seems unaware, or perhaps unwilling to acknowledge, that some of what he knows he owes to Protagoras, the originator of the topic of the dialogue that bears his name.

Epstein's InteLnet project seeks to encourage creative intellectual collaborations—improvisations—with potentially global reach. In contrast, the Connected Kids project seeks to improve the quality of life for young people in a local community. The project is grounded in principles of creative collaboration similar to Epstein's but is situated in a physical community characterized by a deep cultural divide and therefore lacking a strong network of existing social relationships. As a consequence, it requires multiple and ongoing collaborations and improvisations encompassing a diversity of viewpoints and extending over a long period of time. The cultural divide in the City of Troy is documented in the *City of Troy Consolidated Plan 2000,* a recent report on Troy's future, which notes the City's extraordinary resources, on the one hand, and its growing economic plight, on the other. Troy was a major industrial, commercial, and transportation center in the middle of the nineteenth century, at the heart of America's industrial revolution. The *Consolidated Plan* recalls the City's proud history, its rich artistic and cultural heritage, its substantial technological capacity and workforce skills, and its strong tradition in education as the home of both Rensselear and Russell Sage College. But the report also notes the City's large number of vacant buildings, its declining and increasingly poorer population, and its growing minority population and declining average household size—which produce occasional cultural clashes and the special difficulties of single-parent families.

The Connected Kids project is based upon a set of creative collaborations among City of Troy and Rensselaer County officials, local school administrators and teachers, representatives from youth-services organizations, and, not least, Rensselaer graduate and undergraduate students, teenagers, and children. To orchestrate the collaborations among administrators and youth-services personnel, we have conducted a series of cooperative data-gathering and participatory-design sessions to facilitate an ongoing exchange of information and ideas and to support the development of the information system and the social network necessary to sustain it over the long term.[112] These collaborations include

Focus-group meetings with City, County, and youth-services administrators and staff to develop initial specifications for the database and World Wide Web interface.

Participatory-design meetings to test our understanding of the system specifications, developed in the focus-group meetings, to offer participants a preview of the database and solicit their responses, and to further develop our understanding of community needs.

Additional focus-group meetings with teachers, counselors, parents, and middle- and high-school students to develop specifications for the Web interface and the multimedia content.

On-site user tests with youth-services administrators and staff to begin to check the data-input functions and the Web interface.

These sessions have helped us to develop the initial specifications for the youth-services information system, to test our perceptions of the system against those of our collaborators, and to begin to build and test the system.

To orchestrate the collaborations among Rensselaer students, teenagers, and children, we have initiated computer maintenance and training activities to meet the special needs of young people with limited computing skills and to promote their participation in, and their sense of ownership of, the information system. To help young people to develop writing, drawing, computing, and multimedia design skills and to produce textual and visual content for the system, we have enlisted Rensselaer graduate and undergraduate students to

Set up networking equipment and establish cable connections at local Boys and Girls Clubs, with support from the 3Com Corporation and Time Warner Cable.

Rebuild computers—donated by Rensselaer—and equip them with Linux software for use in the after-school programs for children at the Troy Housing Authority's Martin Luther King and Taylor Apartments.[113]

Teach children at the Martin Luther King Apartments to use the computers and Linux software and to create stories and artwork for the database.

Offer instruction in Dreamweaver and Fireworks for high school seniors with an interest in science and technology in the Questar III New Visions program on the Rensselaer campus and work with these students to create Web-based information about issues and opportunities in science and technology as resources for middle- and high-school students.

Develop an archive of stories, artwork, and photographs of young people's activities to publicize both the students' work and the recreational, educational, and cultural activities available to them in Troy and Rensselaer County.

The computing and writing lessons have been particularly rich collaborations between Rensselaer students and children on the other side of the cultural divide.[114] Our students—most of them computer-science or information-technology majors—help children with limited computing skills to develop not only computing but also writing and drawing skills and to begin to understand themselves and their place in the world. Typically, the children have difficulty with abstract thought and complex structures, such as a Web-based make-your-own-adventure story, to which each child contributes a part. They respond more eagerly to requests to tell their own stories—though even these requests usually do not produce immediate results. Rather, our students need to assist the children by processes that resemble Bakhtin's anacrisis and syncrisis. To begin, they draw out the children's ideas about themselves, their families, their hopes and aspirations, sometimes by asking them to tell their stories orally and then to write them on paper and/or type them into the computer, sometimes by asking them to write and/or type simple lists of their activities and interests. In the process, perhaps inadvertently, they also help the children to express the conflicts and ambiguities in their lives, evident in their stories and in the juxtapositions of seemingly incongruous items in their lists of activities and interests. The children seem to be powerfully influenced by the mass media, and they frequently, and not unexpectedly, express hopes of becoming famous athletes, singers, or musicians. These hopes, for the children, as for most of us, conflict with the reality of our everyday lives. But we do not comment; we merely help the children to draw out and juxtapose these conflicts and inconsistencies. A girl writes that she wants to be a New York Yankee. A boy writes that he wants to be like Aaliyah. We encourage both of them to pursue their dreams. Another girl whose favorite subjects are math and science wants to be a singer. Surely she, too, should be encouraged to pursue her dream. But should she also be encouraged to pursue her interest in math or science? At the very least, should she be exposed to career opportunities in these fields? We hope that by developing computing, writing, and drawing skills she, and others, will begin to see new opportunities in fields such as computer science, information technology, technical writing, and graphic design. We hope, too, that by writing about themselves and their hopes and dreams the children will begin the process of actively testing their ideas, collaboratively creating new ideas, and courageously contesting old ideas (who can say whether a little girl can or cannot grow up to be a New York Yankee?). Deborah Mutnick tells us that in her work with basic-writing students she engages Bakhtin's concept of the chronotope (time/space) to help students to expand their world, and their writing, from their own experience to their neighborhood to a broader understanding of their past (memory and identity) and future (hopes and dreams) and their place in history, as represented in their readings.[115] In this way, they learn to situate their own experience in relation to the experience of their neighbors and that of the larger world in which they will live and work, sometimes modifying their own ideas, sometimes affirming and sometimes opposing others' ideas, as they learn to live in a world that is filled with ideas and people sometimes like, sometimes different from themselves. We believe that our collaborations are helping children to take some initial steps in this complex learning process.

Bakhtin objects to the formal analysis of rhetoric but envisions the possibility of a dialogized or dialogical rhetoric that admits other voices—voices that respond to the rhetor's discourse. Bakhtin might have realized this vision by reassessing the rhetorical genres themselves, but he turns instead to the Socratic dialogue, probably because he is more interested in tracing the lineage of the polyphonic novel than in reconstructing the rhetorical tradition. Nonetheless, his notion of the utterance as an exchange between speaking subjects and his rereading of the Socratic dialogue as a testing, contesting, and creating of ideas invites a rethinking of the traditional relationship between speaker and listener and speech, writer and reader and text, and thus invites a rethinking as well of the very meaning and purpose of public discourse. Bakhtin explains the Socratic dialogue not as an early stage in the development of the later Platonic monologue, and monological rhetoric, but as an early stage in the development of a kind of novelistic discourse characterized by a drawing forth and juxtaposing of ideas for the purpose of testing them each against the others, by a carnivalistic contesting of ideas for the purpose of transforming, not destroying, traditional languages and cultures, and by a collaborative creating of ideas that is reconstructive not only of people's ideas but also their lives. Bakhtin insists, moreover, upon reading texts in relation to other texts and to their extratextual historical context. Such a reading of the Socratic dialogue shows why the dialogic testing and contesting and creating of ideas is so important—because it challenges the monological rhetorical discourses of people who simultaneously hold conflicting cultural ideals—for example, self-regarding courage, on the one hand, and other-regarding justice, on the other—people whose thinking is thus at odds with itself. From such a perspective, the purpose of public discourse will not be to persuade but to participate in an ongoing exchange of ideas with other people and other cultures. Bakhtin's vision of a dialogized or dialogical rhetoric thus challenges traditional notions about public life and public discourse, about traditional power relationships, about our relationships with others. The possibility of a dialogical rhetoric in the context of print and digital media holds promise of extending this challenge from our limited oral exchanges with other people to our virtually unlimited exchanges with others, both globally and locally.

Notes

Chapter 1. Introduction

1. Meyer, "Dialectic and Questioning," 281–82, 287–89; Vitanza, "Three Countertheses," 162–63.

2. Conley, *Rhetoric in the European Tradition*, 8–17; Kennedy, *The Art of Persuasion*, 15–17, 74–79, 82–114; Kennedy, *Classical Rhetoric in Its Christian and Secular Tradition*, 53–93; Wardy, *The Birth of Rhetoric*, 52–138.

3. Evans, *Aristotle's Concept of Dialectic*, 7–30; Gulley, *The Philosophy of Socrates*, 8–22; Guthrie, *The Fifth-Century Enlightenment*, 349–59, 425–42; Robinson, *Plato's Earlier Dialectic*, 7–60.

4. Bakhtin, "Epic and Novel," 24–26; Bakhtin, *Problems of Dostoevsky's Poetics*, 109–12, 132–33; Buber, *I and Thou*, 115–16; Gadamer, *Dialogue and Dialectic*; Gadamer, *Truth and Method*, 362–79; *The Martin Buber-Carl Rogers Dialogue*.

5. Brickhouse and Smith, *Plato's Socrates*; Irwin, *Plato's Ethics*, 3–126; Penner, "Socrates and the Early Dialogues"; Vlastos, *Socrates, Ironist and Moral Philosopher*, 45–80; Yunis, *Taming Democracy*, 136–67.

6. Gadamer, *Dialogue and Dialectic*, 1–20, includes an essay on the *Lysis* but situates this dialogue in relation to the Platonic dialectic developed in the later dialogues. Likewise, Gadamer, *Truth and Method*, 367, clearly has in mind the later dialogues when he refers, for example, to "the reiterated yesses of the interlocutors in the Platonic dialogues."

7. Gadamer, *Truth and Method*, 362–69, 393–94. Meyer, *Rhetoric, Language, and Reason*, 1–2, 69, 71–74, takes Socrates as the starting-point of his effort to restore Socratic questioning to the rhetorical tradition in the form of a "problematological rhetoric."

8. Buber, *I and Thou*, 115–16; Czubaroff, "Dialogical Rhetoric," 170; Friedman, "Martin Buber and the Theater," 6–7.

9. Clark, "Martin Buber, Dialogue, and the Philosophy of Rhetoric," 232–40; Czubaroff, "Dialogical Rhetoric," 170–82.

10. Bakhtin, "Epic and Novel," 24–26; Bakhtin, *Problems of Dostoevsky's Poetics*, 109–12, 132–33; Morson and Emerson, *Mikhail Bakhtin*, 60–61, 461, 464.

Bakhtin, *Problems of Dostoevsky's Poetics*, 110, distinguishes "the Socratic notion of the dialogic nature of truth, and the dialogic nature of human thinking about truth," which he claims is characteristic of the earlier dialogues, from the "*official* monologism, which pretends to *possess a ready-made truth*" and which he claims is characteristic of the later dialogues.

11. Bakhtin, "Discourse in the Novel," 253–54. Clark, "Martin Buber, Dialogue, and the Philosophy of Rhetoric," 238–40; Czubaroff, "Dialogical Rhetoric," 172–82; and Halasek, "Starting the Dialogue," 98–99, use the phrase *dialogical* (or *dialogic*) *rhetoric* to refer to a particular kind or subset of rhetoric inspired by Buber, Bakhtin, and others. Bakhtin does not use this phrase, and he has, I believe, a far more radical vision for rhetorical discourse. Bakhtin believes that all rhetorical discourse is *dialogized* or dialogical, that is, that all rhetorical discourse is answerable and accountable to its prior speakers and future answerers—if only we would listen to them.

12. Kennedy, *Classical Rhetoric and Its Christian and Secular Tradition*, 59–61; Yunis, *Taming Democracy*, 119–29, 139–46.

13. Bakhtin, "Discourse in the Novel," 280–81, 284–85, 353–54.

14. Bakhtin, *Problems of Dostoevsky's Poetics*, 109–12.

15. Batstone, "Catullus and Bakhtin," 99–104; Nagy, "Reading Bakhtin Reading the Classics," 73, 80–82; and Tissol, "Herioc Parody and the Life of Exile," 137–42, observe Bakhtin's tendency toward overgeneralization in his readings of the classics. Harris, "Bakhtin, *Phaedrus*, and the Geometry of Rhetoric," 168–72, maps the multiplicity of voices in the *Phaedrus*. Kameen, *Writing/Teaching*, 149–50, 197–99, 218–30, citing Bakhtin's characterization of the Socratic dialogue, demonstrates how the multiplicity of voices in the *Phaedrus* effects a deference to, and a displacement from, the speakers' stated position at any given moment.

16. Clark and Holquist, *Mikhail Bakhtin*, 239–46, 299–305; Morson and Emerson, *Mikhail Bakhtin*, 146–61, 234–59, 314–15, 325–43, 443–48, 456–65.

17. Bakhtin, "Toward a Methodology for the Human Sciences," 162–63, 166–67.

18. Friedländer, *The Dialogues: First Period*, 5–91, 244–72; Friedländer, *The Dialogues: Second and Third Periods*, 63–140, 219–42; Irwin, *Plato's Ethics*, 31–44, 78–126, 169–297. Friedländer, *The Dialogues: First Period*, 50, suggests that the first book of the *Republic* was originally a separate, early dialogue.

19. Adkins, *Merit and Responsibility*, 10–85, 220–81; Irwin, *Classical Thought*, 6–19, 68–84; Irwin, *Plato's Ethics*, 31–44, 78–126; Kahn, "Drama and Dialectic in Plato's *Gorgias*"; North, *Sophrosyne*, 150–65; Schmid, *On Manly Courage*; Yunis, *Taming Democracy*, 117–71.

20. Bolter, *Writing Space*, 27–213; Harpold, "The Grotesque Corpus"; Lanham, *The Electronic Word*, 2–194; Tuman, *Word Perfect*, 1–108; Welch, *Electric Rhetoric*, 29–98, 101–89.

21. Schiappa, *The Beginnings of Rhetorical Theory in Classical Greece*, 14–29; Schiappa, "Did Plato Coin *Rhētorikē*?" Schiappa, "*Rhētorikē*: What's in a Name?"

22. Derrida, *The Post Card*; also Brickhouse and Smith, *Plato's Socrates*; Irwin, *Plato's Ethics*, 13–126; Nightingale, *Genres in Dialogue*, 79–92; Penner, "Socrates

and the Early Dialogues"; Vlastos, *Socrates, Ironist and Moral Philosopher*, 45–80; Yunis, *Taming Democracy*, 136–67.

23. Schiappa, *The Beginnings of Rhetorical Theory in Classical Greece*, 23–29; Schiappa, "Did Plato Coin *Rhētorikē?*" 463–70; Schiappa, "*Rhētorikē*: What's in a Name?" 8–11.

24. Schiappa, *The Beginnings of Rhetorical Theory in Classical Greece*, 27–28; Schiappa, "*Rhêtorikê*: What's in a Name?" 10–11.

25. Schiappa, "*Rhētorikē*: What's in a Name?" 8.

26. Schiappa, *The Beginnings of Rhetorical Theory in Classical Greece*, 28; Schiappa, "*Rhētorikē*: What's in a Name?" 11.

27. Gagarin, "Did the Sophists Aim to Persuade?"

28. Gagarin, "Did the Sophists Aim to Persuade?" 289–91.

29. Kerferd, *The Sophistic Movement*, 55–57. Kerferd, *The Sophistic Movement*, 59–60, notes that Zeno of Elea may have been the first to write dialogues but more likely was the first to appear as a speaker in dialogues written by others.

30. Benson, "Editor's Introduction," *Essays on the Philosophy of Socrates*, 3–6; Guthrie, *The Fifth-Century Enlightenment*, 325–488; Kahn, *Plato and the Socratic Dialogue*, 1–100; A. E. Taylor, *Socrates*; C. C. W. Taylor, *Socrates*; Vlastos, *Socrates, Ironist and Moral Philosopher*, 45–106.

31. Benson, "Editor's Introduction," *Essays on the Philosophy of Socrates*, 3–6; Brickhouse and Smith, *Plato's Socrates*, vii–ix; Penner, "Socrates and the Early Dialogues," 121–31; C. C. W. Taylor, *Socrates*, 32–40; Vlastos, *Socrates, Ironist and Moral Philosopher*, 45–80.

32. Guthrie, *The Fifth-Century Enlightenment*, 349.

33. Conley, *Rhetoric in the European Tradition*, 9.

34. Kennedy, *Classical Rhetoric and Its Christian and Secular Tradition*, 67.

35. Derrida, *The Post Card*, 144–47.

36. Bakhtin, *Problems of Dostoevsky's Poetics*, 109.

37. Bakhtin, *Problems of Dostoevsky's Poetics*, 109–12, 132.

38. Brickhouse and Smith, *Plato's Socrates*, vii–ix; Penner, "Socrates and the Early Dialogues," 121–31; Vlastos, *Socrates, Ironist and Moral Philosopher*, 45–80.

39. Brickhouse and Smith, *Plato's Socrates*, 13.

40. Adkins, *Merit and Responsibility*, 266–78; Kahn, "Drama and Dialectic in Plato's *Gorgias*," 94–96; Yunis, *Taming Democracy*, 139–61.

41. Nightingale, *Genres in Dialogue*, 70–71; Wardy, *The Birth of Rhetoric*, 85.

42. Brickhouse and Smith, *Plato's Socrates*, 23–29; Penner, "Socrates and the Early Dialogues," 126.

43. Penner, "Socrates and the Early Dialogues," 126.

44. Bender and Wellbery, "Rhetoricality," 19–20, 37; Bialostosky, "Dialogics as an Art of Discourse in Literary Criticism"; Dentith, "Bakhtin versus Rhetoric?" Farmer, *Saying and Silence*, 60–62; Farrell, *Norms of Rhetorical Culture*, 232–47; Halasek, *A Pedagogy of Possibility*, 24–26, 52–144; Halasek, "Starting the Dialogue"; Jasinski, "Heteroglossia, Polyphony, and *The Federalist Papers*"; Kent, "Hermeneutics and Genre"; Murphy, "Mikhail Bakhtin and the Rhetorical Tradition"; Schuster, "Mikhail Bakhtin as Rhetorical Theorist."

45. Farrell, *Norms of Rhetorical Culture*, 232–47; Murphy, "Mikhail Bakhtin and the Rhetorical Tradition."

46. Bender and Wellbery, "Rhetoricality," 37; Farmer, *Saying and Silence*, 60–62; Halasek, *A Pedagogy of Possibility*, 24–26, 52–82; Kent, "Hermeneutics and Genre," 34–41; Schuster, "Mikhail Bakhtin as Rhetorical Theorist," 2–6.

47. Halasek, *A Pedagogy of Possibility*, 58.

48. Emerson, "The Next Hundred Years of Mikhail Bakhtin," 14–16.

49. Bialostosky, "Bakhtin's 'Rough Draft,'" 16–23.

50. Emerson, "The Next Hundred Years of Mikhail Bakhtin," 17–19.

51. Bialostosky, "Dialogics as an Art of Discourse in Literary Criticism," 789–91.

52. Bialostosky, "Dialogics as an Art of Discourse in Literary Criticism," 789.

53. Clark, "Martin Buber, Dialogue, and the Philosophy of Rhetoric," 238–40; Czubaroff, "Dialogical Rhetoric," 172–82.

54. Cissna and Anderson, "Theorizing about Dialogic Moments," 64–65, 67; Czubaroff, "Dialogical Rhetoric," 182–84.

55. Dentith, "Bakhtin versus Rhetoric?" 311–14, 320–22.

56. Dentith, "Bakhtin versus Rhetoric?" 311–12.

57. Dentith, "Bakhtin versus Rhetoric?" 320–22.

58. Halasek, "Starting the Dialogue," 100–102.

59. Halasek, "Starting the Dialogue," 102–3.

60. Jasinski, "Heteroglossia, Polyphony, and *The Federalist Papers*," 26–27.

61. Jasinski, "Heteroglossia, Polyphony, and *The Federalist Papers*," 27.

62. Murphy, "Mikhail Bakhtin and the Rhetorical Tradition," 265–67.

63. Murphy, "Mikhail Bakhtin and the Rhetorical Tradition," 272, 274–75.

64. Farrell, *Norms of Rhetorical Culture*, 232–47.

65. Farrell, *Norms of Rhetorical Culture*, 234–35.

66. Farrell, *Norms of Rhetorical Culture*, 234–35.

67. Farrell, *Norms of Rhetorical Culture*, 17.

68. Farrell, *Norms of Rhetorical Culture*, 19–20, 22.

69. Farrell, *Norms of Rhetorical Culture*, 22–24.

70. Farrell, *Norms of Rhetorical Culture*, 31.

71. Farrell, *Norms of Rhetorical Culture*, 33.

72. Farrell, *Norms of Rhetorical Culture*, 236.

73. Farrell, *Norms of Rhetorical Culture*, 238, 241.

74. Farrell, *Norms of Rhetorical Culture*, 241–42.

75. Farrell, *Norms of Rhetorical Culture*, 238.

76. Farmer, *Saying and Silence*, 60–62; Halasek, *A Pedagogy of Possibility*, 52–82; Kent, "Hermeneutics and Genre," 34–41; Schuster, "Mikhail Bakhtin as Rhetorical Theorist," 2–6.

77. Morson and Emerson, *Mikhail Bakhtin*, 49, 235.

78. Côté, "Bakhtin's Dialogism Reconsidered through Hegel's 'Monologism,'" 24–27.

79. Gardiner, "'A Very Understandable Horror of Dialectics,'" 127–28, 139.

80. Morson and Emerson, *Mikhail Bakhtin*, 17–18.

81. Bialostosky, "Bakhtin and the Future of Rhetorical Criticism," 113.

82. Morson and Emerson, *Mikhail Bakhtin*, 130.

83. Morson and Emerson, *Mikhail Bakhtin*, 123–45.

84. Morson and Emerson, *Mikhail Bakhtin*, 125–26.

85. Morson and Emerson, *Mikhail Bakhtin*, 126.

86. Morson and Emerson, *Mikhail Bakhtin*, 127–29.

87. Morson and Emerson, *Mikhail Bakhtin*, 131–32.

88. Morson and Emerson, *Mikhail Bakhtin*, 132.

89. Morson and Emerson, *Mikhail Bakhtin*, 132.

90. Morson and Emerson, *Mikhail Bakhtin*, 139–45.

91. Morson and Emerson, *Mikhail Bakhtin*, 140–41.

92. Morson and Emerson, *Mikhail Bakhtin*, 143.

93. Emerson and Holquist, "Glossary," *The Dialogic Imagination*, 427.

94. Morson and Emerson, *Mikhail Bakhtin*, 128–29.

95. Schuster, "Mikhail Bakhtin as Rhetorical Theorist," 2.

96. Schuster, "Mikhail Bakhtin as Rhetorical Theorist," 2–3.

97. Halasek, *A Pedagogy of Possibility*, 26, 52–82.

98. Bender and Wellbery, "Rhetoricality," 37.

99. Farmer, *Saying and Silence*, 62.

100. Farmer, *Saying and Silence*, 62.

101. Halasek, *A Pedagogy of Possibility*, 58–59.

102. Emerson, "The Next Hundred Years of Mikhail Bakhtin," 14–15.

103. Emerson, "The Next Hundred Years of Mikhail Bakhtin," 19.

104. Emerson, "The Next Hundred Years of Mikhail Bakhtin," 19.

105. Bialostosky, "Bakhtin's 'Rough Draft,'" 18.

106. Bialostosky, "Bakhtin's 'Rough Draft,'" 18.

107. Bialostosky, "Bakhtin's 'Rough Draft,'" 19.

108. Bialostosky, "Bakhtin's 'Rough Draft,'" 20.

109. Irwin, *Classical Thought*, 7–8; Schmid, *On Manly Courage*, 20–21, 70–71, 101, 123–26, 168–70. Both Irwin, *Classical Thought*, 7; and Schmid, *On Manly Courage*, 101, identify *aretē* with the courage and skill of the warrior. Schmid, *On Manly Courage*, xvi, explains *andreia* as *manly courage* or *courage* (sometimes with *or manliness* added to emphasize the root meaning of the word, i.e., *andro,* male).

110. Irwin, *Classical Thought*, 72–81. North, *Sophrosyne*, 150, explains *sōphrosunē* as "the all-embracing order and the morality of restraint and limitation which the *polis* demanded." Martin, *Ancient Greece,* 171, 181, explains that both Socrates and Plato seemed to believe that men and women had the same capacity for virtue, including those virtues required to rule and defend the state. Annas, *An Introduction to Plato's "Rebublic,"* 172–78, 181–85, observes, however, that the principle of equality did not apply in practice.

111. Brandwood, *A Word Index to Plato*, 227–28; Kahn, *Plato and the Socratic Dialogue*, 292–309; Kerferd, *The Sophistic Movement*, 59–60; Liddell and Scott, *A Greek-English Lexicon*. Kahn, *Plato and the Socratic Dialogue*, 60–61, 298–99, 302–3, explains that *dialegesthai* in early dialogues such as the *Gorgias* and the *Protagoras* refers either to Socrates' conversations or to his technique of question and answer and that *dialektikē* in later dialogues such as the *Republic* and the *Phaedrus* refers to the correlative processes of collection and division. Kahn, *Plato and the Socratic Dialogue*, 302, claims that the "philosophically marked" use of the verb *dialegesthai* signals the emergence of the concept of dialectic.

112. Schiappa, "*Rhētorikē*: What's in a Name?" 8.

113. Meyer, "Dialectic and Questioning," 281–82.

114. Morson and Emerson, *Mikhail Bakhtin*, 130–31, explain that Bakhtin uses the term *dialogue* in at least three senses: as a global concept, "a view of truth and the world"; as a universal concept applicable to "*every* utterance"; and as a way of distinguishing dialogic from monologic discourse. In *Problems of Dostoevsky's Poetics*, 110, 132, Bakhtin distinguishes the Socratic dialogue from the Platonic monologue and the rhetorical dialogue (sense three) but he also describes it as a way of searching for truth (sense one), between people, in the process of dialogic interaction (sense two).

115. Gadamer, *Truth and Method*, 367–69; Morson and Emerson, *Mikhail Bakhtin*, 241–43.

116. Bolter, *Writing Space*, 102–20; Welch, *Electric Rhetoric*, 53–74, 101–12.

117. Bolter, *Writing Space*, 77–160; Tuman, *Word Perfect*, 62–66, 72–78, 87–99; Welch, *Electric Rhetoric*, 177–89.

CHAPTER 2. THE TRADITIONAL SOCRATES: DIALOGUE, RHETORIC, AND DIALECTIC

1. Mailloux, *Reception Histories*, 4–6; Miller, "Stevens' Rock and Criticism as Cure, II," 335–38; Rossetti, "The Rhetoric of Socrates"; Sosnoski, "Postmodern Teachers in Their Postmodern Classrooms," 207–8; Vitanza, *Negation, Subjectivity, and the History of Rhetoric*, 240–45, 254–61; Vitanza, "Three Countertheses," 162–63.

2. Brickhouse and Smith, *Plato's Socrates*, 3–29, 137–41; Kennedy, *Classical Rhetoric and Its Christian and Secular Tradition*, 58–66; Penner, "Socrates and the Early Dialogues," 122–31; Vlastos, *Socrates, Ironist and Moral Philosopher*, 45–80.

3. Adkins, *Merit and Responsibility*, 259–315; Havelock, *The Greek Concept of Justice*, 308–334; Irwin, *Classical Thought*, 6–19, 68–84; Irwin, *Plato's Ethics*, 31–126; Kahn, "Drama and Dialectic in Plato's *Gorgias*"; Yunis, *Taming Democracy*, 117–71.

4. Conley, *Rhetoric in the European Tradition*, 8–13; Enos, *Greek Rhetoric before Aristotle*, 91–101; Kennedy, *Classical Rhetoric and Its Christian and Secular Tradition*, 58–74; Yunis, *Taming Democracy*, 161–210.

5. Evans, *Aristotle's Concept of Dialectic*, 7–30; Gulley, *The Philosophy of Socrates*, 8–22; Guthrie, *The Fifth-Century Enlightenment*, 349–59, 425–42; Robinson, *Plato's Earlier Dialectic*, 7–60.

6. Grote, *A History of Greece*, 205–302; Mill, "On Liberty," 251–52; Mill, *A System of Logic;* Turner, *The Greek Heritage in Victorian Britain*, 264–321.

7. Brickhouse and Smith, *Plato's Socrates*, 3–29, 137–41; Penner, "Socrates and the Early Dialogues," 122–31; Vlastos, *Socrates, Ironist and Moral Philosopher*, 45–80.

8. Adkins, *Merit and Responsibility*, 266–78; Dodds, "Commentary," *Gorgias*, 364; Irwin, *Classical Thought*, 72–81; Irwin, "Notes," *Gorgias*, 238–39; Irwin, *Plato's Ethics*, 33–35; Kahn, "Drama and Dialectic in Plato's *Gorgias*," 95–96; Yunis, *Taming Democracy*, 136–61.

9. Bakhtin, *Problems of Dostoevsky's Poetics*, 106–12.

10. Guthrie, *The Fifth-Century Enlightenment*, 325–416; Martin, *Ancient Greece*, 168–73; A. E. Taylor, *Socrates*, 37–129; C. C. W. Taylor, *Socrates*, 3–73, 102; Vlastos, *Socrates, Ironist and Moral Philosopher*, 81–106. In addition to the early dialogues, some of the most important sources are Aristophanes' *Clouds*, Aristotle's *Metaphysics*, and Xenophon's *Memorabilia*.

11. Bury, *A History of Greece to the Death of Alexander the Great*, 247–513; Fine, *The Ancient Greeks*, 244–525; Martin, *Ancient Greece*, 94–173.

12. Bury, *A History of Greece to the Death of Alexander the Great*, 250–58, 277–82; Fine, *The Ancient Greeks*, 284–87, 304–5; Martin, *Ancient Greece*, 100–101, 104–5.

13. Bury, *A History of Greece to the Death of Alexander the Great*, 271–77; Fine, *The Ancient Greeks*, 312–14; Martin, *Ancient Greece*, 103–4; Simonides, "The Greek Dead at Thermopylae," 232.

14. Martin, *Ancient Greece*, 104–5, 109–13, 162–63; Ober, *Mass and Elite in Democratic Athens*, 83–84; Sinclair, *Democracy and Participation in Athens*, 5–6, 14–15. Martin, *Ancient Greece*, 104–5, 162–63, explains that women, too, participated in warfare, usually in support roles and sometimes also in fighting, but unlike men did not, as a consequence, have a larger role in Athenian political life.

15. Bury, *A History of Greece to the Death of Alexander the Great*, 336–42, 352–58, 363–67, 390–513; Fine, *The Ancient Greeks*, 363–82, 442–525; Martin, *Ancient Greece*, 105–8, 113–16, 147–62.

16. Martin, *Ancient Greece*, 168–73; C. C. W. Taylor, *Socrates*, 3–20.

17. C. C. W. Taylor, *Socrates*, 8.

18. Bury, *A History of Greece to the Death of Alexander the Great*, 442–43; Martin, *Ancient Greece*, 169; C. C. W. Taylor, *Socrates*, 4, 7–8.

19. Kerferd, *The Sophistic Movement*, 18–22; Ober, *Mass and Elite in Democratic Athens*, 89–90.

20. Kerferd, *The Sophistic Movement*, 55–57; Martin, *Ancient Greece*, 168–70; C. C. W. Taylor, *Socrates*, 4–7.

21. C. C. W. Taylor, *Socrates*, 3.

22. C. C. W. Taylor, *Socrates*, 8–9.

23. Martin, *Ancient Greece*, 171; C. C. W. Taylor, *Socrates*, 9, 12–13.

24. Bury, *A History of Greece to the Death of Alexander the Great*, 466–84; Fine, *The Ancient Greeks*, 491–97; Martin, *Ancient Greece*, 158–59.

25. Martin, *Ancient Greece*, 171–72; C. C. W. Taylor, *Socrates*, 10, 12.

26. Martin, *Ancient Greece*, 172–73; C. C. W. Taylor, *Socrates*, 10–11.

27. Griswold, "Plato's Metaphilosophy," 143–67, 286–93; Hyland, "Why Plato Wrote Dialogues," 38–50; Kahn, "Did Plato Write Socratic Dialogues?"

28. Kahn, "Did Plato Write Socratic Dialogues?" Kahn, "On the Relative Date of the *Gorgias* and the *Protagoras*"; Kahn, *Plato and the Socratic Dialogue*; Irwin, *Plato's Ethics*, 11–13; Penner, "Socrates and the Early Dialogues," 122–31; Vlastos, *Socrates, Ironist and Moral Philosopher*, 45–106.

29. Irwin, *Plato's Ethics*, 11–13; Kahn, "Did Plato Write Socratic Dialogues?" 38–39; Kahn, *Plato and the Socratic Dialogue*, 46–48; Penner, "Socrates and the Early Dialogues," 124–25; Vlastos, *Socrates, Ironist and Moral Philosopher*, 46–47.

30. Irwin, *Plato's Ethics*, 12.

31. Irwin, *Plato's Ethics*, 13.

32. Penner, "Socrates and the Early Dialogues," 124–25, however, includes *Republic*, Book 1, but not *Cratylus*, *Symposium*, and *Phaedo* among the early dialogues and regards *Gorgias* and *Meno* as transitional to the later Plato. Vlastos, *Socrates, Ironist and Moral Philosopher*, 46–47, includes *Republic*, Book 1, and *Gorgias* in the first group of early dialogues and includes *Cratylus*, *Symposium*, and *Phaedo* in the middle group.

33. Kahn, "Did Plato Write Socratic Dialogues?" Kahn, "On the Relative Date of the *Gorgias* and the *Protagoras*"; Kahn, *Plato and the Socratic Dialogue*, 47–48.

34. Kahn, "Did Plato Write Socratic Dialogues?" 40, 42–44; Kahn, "On the Relative Date of the *Gorgias* and the *Protagoras*," 74–75, 96–97.

35. Kahn, "Did Plato Write Socratic Dialogues?" 42–44; Kahn, "On the Relative Date of the *Gorgias* and the *Protagoras*," 75–76, 97–98.

36. Griswold, "Plato's Metaphilosophy," 153; Hyland, "Why Plato Wrote Dialogues," 42–43.

37. Kahn, *Plato and the Socratic Dialogue*, 39–40, 66–67, 69–70.

38. Gadamer, *Truth and Method*, 366–69.

39. Gadamer, *Truth and Method*, 368.

40. Gadamer, *Truth and Method*, 369, 394, maintains, on the one hand, that Plato seeks to overcome the weakness of the written logos by placing words and concepts "back within the original movement of the conversation" and, on the other, that he seeks "to bring out the logos as such and in doing so often leaves behind the actual partner in the conversation." Crapanzano, *Hermes' Dilemma and Hamlet's Desire*, 196, 207, claims that Gadamer is not *critically* aware of the effect of the recontextualization of primary dialogues, such as conversations, in secondary dialogues, such as written texts: "We should recognize, as Socrates would surely have recognized, that Plato's compromise—the written dialogue—is indeed written and subject to all of the uses and misuses of the written, the quoted, word."

41. Kameen, *Writing/Teaching*, 150–57, 159–61, 173–78, 197–99, 218–30.

42. Kameen, *Writing/Teaching*, 155.

43. Penner, "Socrates and the Early Dialogues," 122–25; and Vlastos, *Socrates, Ironist and Moral Philosopher*, 45–46, 81, maintain that the Socrates who appears in the early Platonic dialogues represents the views of the historical Socrates. Brickhouse and Smith, *Plato's Socrates*, vii–ix; and Kahn, "Did Plato Write Socratic Dialogues?" 35–36, 46, are agnostic on this issue. Brickhouse and Smith, *Plato's Socrates*, viii, claim only that a distinct and consistent philosophy can be found in the early dialogues. Kahn, "Did Plato Write Socratic Dialogues?" 46, claims that the Socrates who appears in the earlier dialogues "*is* the historical Socrates" only in the sense that, if Plato's portrait is inaccurate, "we are in no position to correct it." Kahn, *Plato and the Socratic Dialogues*, 2–3, however, emphasizes "the imaginative and essentially fictional nature of Socratic literature," most especially Plato's: "Plato's success as a dramatist is so great that he has often been mistaken for an historian."

44. Conley, *Rhetoric in the European Tradition*, 8–13; Evans, *Aristotle's Concept of Dialectic*, 17–30; Guthrie, *The Fifth-Century Enlightenment*, 425–42; Kennedy,

Classical Rhetoric and Its Christian and Secular Tradition, 54–74; Robinson, *Plato's Earlier Dialectic*, 7–60.

45. Miller, "Stevens' Rock and Criticism as Cure, II," 335; Rossetti, "The Rhetoric of Socrates," 235–36; Vitanza, *Negation, Subjectivity, and the History of Rhetoric*, 241, 256.

46. Conley, *Rhetoric in the European Tradition*, 8–13; Enos, *Greek Rhetoric before Aristotle*, 91–101; Kennedy, *Classical Rhetoric and Its Christian and Secular Tradition*, 54–74.

47. Kennedy, *Classical Rhetoric and Its Christian and Secular Tradition*, 58–66.

48. Kennedy, *Classical Rhetoric and Its Christian and Secular Tradition*, 58–59.

49. Kennedy, *Classical Rhetoric and Its Christian and Secular Tradition*, 64.

50. Conley, *Rhetoric in the European Tradition*, 9–10.

51. Enos, , *Greek Rhetoric before Aristotle*, 95.

52. Plato, *Gorgias*, trans. Lamb, Loeb Classical Library. References to this edition are included in the text.

53. Kennedy, *Classical Rhetoric and Its Christian and Secular Tradition*, 59–61.

54. Conley, *Rhetoric in the European Tradition*, 12.

55. Kennedy, *Classical Rhetoric and Its Christian and Secular Tradition*, 61–63.

56. Allen, "Comment," *The Gorgias*, 197.

57. Kennedy, *Classical Rhetoric and Its Christian and Secular Tradition*, 63–65.

58. Conley, *Rhetoric in the European Tradition*, 11–13; Kennedy, *Classical Rhetoric and Its Christian and Secular Tradition*, 66–74.

59. Kennedy, *Classical Rhetoric and Its Christian and Secular Tradition*, 73.

60. Plato, *Phaedrus*, trans. Fowler, Loeb Classical Library. References to this edition are included in the text.

61. Murray, "Disputation, Deception, and Dialectic," 282–84.

62. Kennedy, *Classical Rhetoric and Its Christian and Secular Tradition*, 73.

63. Adkins, *Merit and Responsibility*, 283–93; Annas, *An Introduction to Plato's "Republic,"* 109–69; Havelock, *The Greek Concept of Justice*, 308–23; Irwin, *Plato's Ethics*, 203–61; North, *Sophrosyne*, 169–76; Plato, *The Republic*, trans. Shorey, Loeb Classical Library. Adkins, *Merit and Responsibility*, 285, explains how the virtues in each of the three classes of the state parallel the virtues in each of the three parts of the soul: in the state, each of the classes has its own special *aretē* or excellence—"the governors, *sophia*, wisdom; the defenders, *andreia*, courage; and the rest . . . *sophrosune*, moderation and self-restraint"—and "*dikaiosune* exists in a state when each class performs its own function and 'minds its own business'"; similarly, in the soul, each of the parts has its own special excellence—"the intellectual, *sophia*; the spirited, *andreia*; and the appetitive, *sophrosune*."

64. Annas, *An Introduction to Plato's "Republic,"* 104.

65. Havelock, *The Greek Concept of Justice*, 321.

66. Yunis, *Taming Democracy*, 164.

67. Yunis, *Taming Democracy*, 165.

68. Evans, *Aristotle's Concept of Dialectic*, 7–30; Gulley, *The Philosophy of Socrates*, 8–22; Guthrie, *The Fifth-Century Enlightenment*, 349–59, 425–42; Robinson, *Plato's Earlier Dialectic*, 7–60.

69. Aristotle, *The Metaphysics*, trans. Tredennick, Loeb Classical Library.

70. Evans, *Aristotle's Concept of Dialectic*, 20–21.

71. Evans, *Aristotle's Concept of Dialectic*, 17, 25.

72. Guthrie, *The Fifth-Century Enlightenment*, 429; also Conley, *Rhetoric in the European Tradition*, 14–15; Kennedy, *Classical Rhetoric and Its Christian and Secular Tradition*, 82–86.

73. Conley, *Rhetoric in the European Tradition*, 14–15; Kennedy, *Classical Rhetoric and Its Christian and Secular Tradition*, 82–83.

74. Aristotle, *Topica*, trans. Forster, Loeb Classical Library. References to this edition are included in the text.

75. Aristotle, *The "Art" of Rhetoric*, trans. Freese, Loeb Classical Library; Aristotle, *On Rhetoric*, trans. Kennedy. Reference is to the Loeb edition and Kennedy's English translation.

76. Gulley, *The Philosophy of Socrates*, 9–11; Robinson, *Plato's Earlier Dialectic*, 49–50.

77. Robinson, *Plato's Earlier Dialectic*, 50–51.

78. Robinson, *Plato's Earlier Dialectic*, 52–53.

79. Guthrie, *The Fifth-Century Enlightenment*, 426–28.

80. Robinson, *Plato's Earlier Dialectic*, 33.

81. Plato, *Protagoras*, trans. Lamb, Loeb Classical Library.

82. C. C. W. Taylor, "Commentary," *Protagoras*, 152.

83. Gulley, *The Philosophy of Socrates*, 20–21.

84. Conley, *Rhetoric in the European Tradition*, 9–10.

85. Evans, *Aristotle's Concept of Dialectic*, 22–24.

86. Miller, "Stevens' Rock and Criticism as Cure, II," 335.

87. Vitanza, *Negation, Subjectivity, and the History of Rhetoric*, 241, 256.

88. Rossetti, "The Rhetoric of Socrates," 231–33, 235–36.

89. Sosnoski, "Postmodern Teachers in Their Postmodern Classrooms," 198, 207–8.

90. C. C. W. Taylor, *Socrates*, 86–99; Turner, *The Greek Heritage in Victorian Britain*, 264–321.

91. C. C. W. Taylor, *Socrates*, 86–88; Turner, *The Greek Heritage in Victorian Britain*, 274–78.

92. Kierkegaard, *The Concept of Irony with Continual Reference to Socrates*, 211; C. C. W. Taylor, *Socrates*, 88–92.

93. Kaufmann, "Nietzsche's Attitude toward Socrates," 123–28; C. C. W. Taylor, *Socrates*, 92–99; Turner, *The Greek Heritage in Victorian Britain*, 308–9.

94. Turner, *The Greek Heritage in Victorian Britain*, 292–97.

95. Grote, *A History of Greece*, 205–302. References to this edition are included in the text.

96. Mill, "Grote's History of Greece [5]."

97. Mill, "On Liberty" and *A System of Logic*. References to these works are included in the text. Cherwitz and Hikins, "John Stuart Mill's Doctrine of Assurance as a Rhetorical Epistemology," 73–74; and Cherwitz and Hikins, "John Stuart Mill's *On Liberty*," 16–20, explain that Mill's rhetoric of public discussion requires of participants three elements or precepts that together constitute his "doctrine of assurance": access to one's opinions, defense of those opinions, and actual correction of them.

98. McRae, "Introduction," *A System of Logic*, 7:xxvii–xxxvii; Scarre, *Logic and Reality in the Philosophy of John Stuart Mill*, 65–103; Schollmeier, "A Classical Rhetoric."

99. Elsewhere in *A System of Logic*, Mill claims that all inference is from particulars to other particulars, that is, "from our experience of John, Thomas, &c., who once were living, but are now dead," to "the mortality of the Duke of Wellington" (7:187). Schollmeier, "A Classical Rhetoric," 209–212, believes that Mill considers inferences from particulars to particulars to be the essence of inductive reasoning. McRae, "Introduction," *A System of Logic*, 7:xxviii–xxix; and Scarre, *Logic and Reality in the Philosophy of John Stuart Mill*, 80, however, maintain that Mill supposes such inferences to lead to universal propositions (concerning, e.g., the mortality of humans). McRae, "Introduction," *A System of Logic*, 7:xxviii, claims that Mill regards these universal propositions as empirical generalizations only, not as necessary principles; and Scarre, *Logic and Reality in the Philosophy of John Stuart Mill*, 75, 80, claims that Mill regards these so-called "*universal* propositions" as mere memoranda or records of "the direction which our inductive projection from particulars [to other particulars] has so far been taking."

100. Lowe, "What *Is* the 'Problem of Induction'?" McRae, "Introduction," *A System of Logic*, 7:xxxiv–xxxvi; Scarre, *Logic and Reality in the Philosophy of John Stuart Mill*, 80–103; and Stove, *The Rationality of Induction*, 30–43, review and assess the problem of induction. Stove, *The Rationality of Induction*, 3, 13, explains that the inductive inference from "All the many observed ravens have been black" to "All ravens are black" seemed to Hume to depend upon the presupposition that nature is uniform, a presupposition that "cannot be rationally inferred by induction." McRae, "Introduction," *A System of Logic*, 7:xxxiv–xxxvi, maintains that Mill, unlike Hume, did not seek to justify induction but simply to explain it.

101. Scarre, *Logic and Reality in the Philosophy of John Stuart Mill*, 95–97, calls these "local uniformity principles" but notes that they are mere "approximations to the

truth" that depend upon other universal propositions such as the principle of uniformity in the course of nature. He concludes that since Mill refuses "to allow universal propositions to function as premises" and insists that "'real' inference is always from particulars to particulars," he is left "without any effective criterion for distinguishing rational inductive projections from irrational ones."

102. Bhabha, "The Commitment to Theory"; Bhabha, "Sly Civility."

103. Bhabha, "The Commitment to Theory," 23.

104. Bhabha, "The Commitment to Theory," 23.

105. Bhabha, "The Commitment to Theory," 23–24.

106. Bhabha, "Sly Civility," 94–95; Moore-Gilbert, *Postcolonial Theory*, 119–20.

107. Derrida, *The Post Card*, 144, 146; Norris, *Derrida*, 187; Ulmer, *Applied Grammatology*, 141–42.

108. Derrida, *The Post Card*, 9–10, 251; Neel, *Plato, Derrida, and Writing*, 15–17.

109. Derrida, *The Post Card*, 10, 146.

110. Adkins, *Merit and Responsibility*, 259–315; Brickhouse and Smith, *Plato's Socrates*, 3–29, 137–41; Havelock, *The Greek Concept of Justice*; Irwin, *Classical Thought*, 6–19; Irwin, *Plato's Ethics*, 33–35; Kahn, "Drama and Dialectic in Plato's Gorgias," 95–96; Penner, "Socrates and the Early Dialogues," 122–31; Vlastos, *Socrates, Ironist and Moral Philosopher*, 45–80; Yunis, *Taming Democracy*, 136–71.

111. Vlastos, *Socrates, Ironist and Moral Philosopher*, 47–49, 53–80.

112. Vlastos, *Socrates, Ironist and Moral Philosopher*, 48.

113. Penner, "Socrates and the Early Dialogues," 125.

114. Brickhouse and Smith, *Plato's Socrates*, 13.

115. Adkins, *Merit and Responsibility*, 195–243; Irwin, *Classical Thought*, 6–19; Irwin, *Plato's Ethics*, 33–35; Kahn, "Drama and Dialectic in Plato's Gorgias," 95–96; Yunis, *Taming Democracy*, 136–50.

116. Irwin, *Plato's Ethics*, 41–44, 79–81, 84–85; Penner, "The Unity of Virtue"; Vlastos, "The Unity of the Virtues in the *Protagoras*."

117. Irwin, *Plato's Ethics*, 80–81.

118. Adkins, *Merit and Responsibility*, 32–33, 37–38.

119. Adkins, *Merit and Responsibility*, 221–23, 225, 227–28.

120. Adkins, *Merit and Responsibility*, 225.

121. Adkins, *Merit and Responsibility*, 235.

122. Liddell and Scott, *A Greek-English Lexicon*.

123. Derrida, "Plato's Pharmacy," 95; also Culler, *On Deconstruction*, 142–44; Neel, *Plato, Derrida, and Writing*, 79–80; Norris, *Derrida*, 37–38, 41–43.

124. Derrida, "Plato's Pharmacy," 97–98, 117, 130.

125. Brickhouse and Smith, *Plato's Socrates*, 5.

126. Irwin, *Plato's Ethics*, 17–19.

127. Irwin, *Plato's Ethics*, 19.

128. Penner, "Socrates and the Early Dialogues," 126.

129. Brickhouse and Smith, *Plato's Socrates*, 23–25.

130. Bakhtin, *Problems in Dostoevsky's Poetics*, 109–12.

131. Brickhouse and Smith, *Plato's Socrates*, 5.

132. Brickhouse and Smith, *Plato's Socrates*, 13.

133. Brickhouse and Smith, *Plato's Socrates*, 14.

134. Burnyeat, "Socratic Midwifery, Platonic Inspiration," 53, 60–61.

135. Burnyeat, "Socratic Midwifery, Platonic Inspiration," 55, 60–61.

136. Brickhouse and Smith, *Plato's Socrates*, 14.

137. Brickhouse and Smith, *Plato's Socrates*, 19.

CHAPTER 3. MIKHAIL M. BAKHTIN, DIALOGICAL RHETORIC, AND THE SOCRATIC DIALOGUE

1. Bakhtin, "Epic and Novel"; Bakhtin, *Problems of Dostoevsky's Poetics*, 106–37. References to Bakhtin's works, unless otherwise noted, are included in the text.

2. Bakhtin, "Discourse in the Novel," 267–69, 279–81, 336–55; Bialostosky, "Bakhtin and the Future of Rhetorical Criticism," 113; Morson and Emerson, *Mikhail Bakhtin*, 17–18, 130.

3. Bakhtin, "Discourse in the Novel," 348, 353–54.

4. Bakhtin, "The Problem of Speech Genres," 67–76; Kent, "Hermeneutics and Genre," 34–42; Morson and Emerson, *Mikhail Bakhtin*, 125–30.

5. Bakhtin, "Discourse in the Novel," 269–75, 288–96. Morson and Emerson, *Mikhail Bakhtin*, 130–31, 139–45, observe that Bakhtin uses the term *dialogue* in at least three senses and explain dialogue in its first sense as a universal concept applicable to every utterance.

6. Bakhtin, "Discourse in the Novel," 280, 353–54.

7. Bakhtin, *Problems of Dostoevsky's Poetics*, 109–12, 132–33.

8. Bakhtin, *Problems of Dostoevsky's Poetics*, 5–100; Bakhtin, *Rabelais and His World*, 4–11, 159–74, 452–54, 465–73; Mihailovic, *Corporeal Words*, 183–211; Morson and Emerson, *Mikhail Bakhtin*, 231–59, 443–56.

9. Bakhtin, "Toward a Methodology for the Human Sciences," 159–67.

10. Clark and Holquist, *Mikhail Bakhtin*, 16–62, 95–145, 253–74, 321–45, 353–58; Holquist, *Dialogism*, 1–13, 190–95; and Morson and Emerson, *Mikhail Bakhtin*, xiii–xv, xvii–xx, 63–100, review Bakhtin's life and works.

11. Kenez, *A History of the Soviet Union*, 14–183.

12. Bakhtin, "Author and Hero in Aesthetic Activity"; Bakhtin, *Toward a Philosophy of the Act*.

13. Bakhtin, *Problems of Dostoevsky's Poetics*, 273–302, includes selections from the 1929 edition and notes for the revision of the 1963 edition.

14. Clark and Holquist, *Mikhail Bakhtin*, 146–70; Emerson, *The First Hundred Years*, 74 n. 2; and Morson and Emerson, *Mikhail Bakhtin*, 101–19, assess the arguments for and against Bakhtin's authorship of these works.

15. Holquist, "Introduction," *The Dialogic Imagination*, xxvi; Holquist, "Introduction," *Speech Genres and Other Late Essays*, x–xi. Emerson and Holquist, "Glossary," *The Dialogic Imagination*, 427, explain that they translate the Russian word *slovo* as *discourse*, not *word*, to capture its meaning as both an individual word and a method of using words: "what interests Bakhtin is the sort of talk novelistic environments make possible, and how this type of talking threatens other more closed systems."

16. Emerson, *The First Hundred Years*, 48–72, 122–264.

17. Clark and Holquist, *Mikhail Bakhtin*, 21–23, 26–27.

18. Holquist, *Dialogism*, 20–21, 158–62.

19. Holquist, *Dialogism*, 20–21.

20. Clark and Holquist, *Mikhail Bakhtin*, 128–30.

21. Clark and Holquist, *Mikhail Bakhtin*, 129.

22. Mihailovic, *Corporeal Words*, 23, 30–31.

23. Clark and Holquist, *Mikhail Bakhtin*, 267–68, 306–13. Emerson, *The First Hundred Years*, 169–71, 189–95; and Mihailovic, *Corporeal Words*, 188–211, review arguments that link Bakhtin's concept of carnival more or less closely to Stalinism.

24. Clark and Holquist, *Mikhail Bakhtin*, 307–9.

25. Clark and Holquist, *Mikhail Bakhtin*, 267.

26. Bender and Wellbery, "Rhetoricality," 19–20, 37; Bialostosky, "Bakhtin and the Future of Rhetorical Criticism," 113–17; Farmer, *Saying and Silence*, 60–62; Halasek, *A Pedagogy of Possibility*, 23–26, 52–53, 57–66; Halasek, "Starting the Dialogue," 102–4; Schuster, "Mikhail Bakhtin as Rhetorical Theorist," 1–6.

27. Farrell, *Norms of Rhetorical Culture*, 233–41; Murphy, "Mikhail Bakhtin and the Rhetorical Tradition," 268–75.

28. Bialostosky, "Bakhtin and the Future of Rhetorical Criticism," 113; Morson and Emerson, *Mikhail Bakhtin*, 17–18; Perlina, "A Dialogue on the Dialogue," 534–35.

29. Bakhtin, "From Notes Made in 1970–71," 150.

30. Morson and Emerson, *Mikhail Bakhtin*, 130.

31. Kent, "Hermeneutics and Genre," 34–41; Morson and Emerson, *Mikhail Bakhtin*, 125–30.

32. Kent, "Hermeneutics and Genre," 35–36.

33. Kent, "Hermeneutics and Genre," 36, 41.

34. Bakhtin, "Discourse in the Novel," 270–75, 288–96.

35. Morson and Emerson, *Mikhail Bakhtin*, 139–45.

36. Emerson, "The Next Hundred Years of Mikhail Bakhtin," 14–15.

37. Bakhtin, "Response to a Question from the *Novy Mir* Editorial Staff," 7.

38. Morson and Emerson, *Mikhail Bakhtin*, 142–45, 309–17.

39. Morson and Emerson, *Mikhail Bakhtin*, 460–63.

40. Morson and Emerson, *Mikhail Bakhtin*, 59–62, 130–31, explain dialogue in its third sense as a global concept, a view of truth and the world.

41. Edwards, "Historicizing the Popular Grotesque," 46 n. 3; Morson and Emerson, *Mikhail Bakhtin*, 60–61, 461, 464; Nightingale, "Toward an Ecological Eschatology," 243 n. 3.

42. Batstone, "Catullus and Bakhtin," 99–104; Nagy, "Reading Bakhtin Reading the Classics," 73, 80–82; Tissol, "Heroic Parody and the Life of Exile," 137–42. Tissol, "Heroic Parody and the Life of Exile," 138, 142–54, claims that "dialogism, heteroglossia, and much that is taken to be the signifying practice of prose are just as important as features of poetry" and describes the rich and pervasive parody in Ovid's poetry. Nagy, "Reading Bakhtin Reading the Classics," 73, 80–91, claims exceptions to Bakhtin's generalizations about the epic and observes novelistic elements such as heteroglossia, centrifugal narrative, and a lack of finality in Homer's *Odyssey*. Batstone, "Catullus and Bakhtin," 104–32, posits a polyphonic self that is also a self-under-construction as two prerequisites of a dialogic lyric and demonstrates the dialogic potential of Catullus' poetry.

43. Harris, "Bakhtin, *Phaedrus*, and the Geometry of Rhetoric," 168–72, identifies many of these voices.

44. Kristeva, *Desire in Language*, 81.

45. Morson and Emerson, *Mikhail Bakhtin*, 60.

46. Bakhtin, *Problems of Dostoevsky's Poetics*, 132–33; Bakhtin, "Epic and Novel," 24–26; Morson and Emerson, *Mikhail Bakhtin*, 456–65.

47. Morson and Emerson, *Mikhail Bakhtin*, 465.

48. Morson and Emerson, *Mikhail Bakhtin*, 326.

49. Reed, "Reading Lermontov's *Geroj našego vremeni*," 304–73. Emerson, *The First Hundred Years*, 138–44, elaborates this argument.

50. Reed, "Reading Lermontov's *Geroj našego vremeni*," 316.

51. Reed, "Reading Lermontov's *Geroj našego vremeni*," 307–8.

52. Reed, "Reading Lermontov's *Geroj našego vremeni*," 313.

53. Reed, "Reading Lermontov's *Geroj našego vremeni*," 308, 316–17.

54. Emerson, *The First Hundred Years*, 141–42.

55. Emerson, *The First Hundred Years*, 144.

56. Emerson, *The First Hundred Years*, 154–55.

57. Morson and Emerson, *Mikhail Bakhtin*, 234, 256–57.

58. Clark and Holquist, *Mikhail Bakhtin*, 239–46; Morson and Emerson, *Mikhail Bakhtin*, 234–59.

59. Morson and Emerson, *Mikhail Bakhtin*, 234–37.

60. Morson and Emerson, *Mikhail Bakhtin*, 237–43, 249.

61. Morson and Emerson, *Mikhail Bakhtin*, 243–59.

62. Morson and Emerson, *Mikhail Bakhtin*, 241–42.

63. Morson and Emerson, *Mikhail Bakhtin*, 242.

64. Bakhtin, "Toward a Reworking of the Dostoevsky Book," *Problems of Dostoevsky's Poetics*, Appendix II, 299.

65. Clark and Holquist, *Mikhail Bakhtin*, 244–45; Emerson, *The First Hundred Years*, 150–51, 154–56; Morson and Emerson, *Mikhail Bakhtin*, 240, 254–55.

66. Morson and Emerson, *Mikhail Bakhtin*, 314–15, 325–43.

67. Morson and Emerson, *Mikhail Bakhtin*, 130–31, 146–61, explain dialogue in its second and restricted sense as distinct from monologue.

68. Morson and Emerson, *Mikhail Bakhtin*, 149–50.

69. Morson and Emerson, *Mikhail Bakhtin*, 149–59.

70. Morson and Emerson, *Mikhail Bakhtin*, 151.

71. Morson, "Parody, History, and Metaparody," 67.

72. Emerson, *The First Hundred Years*, 179–95; Mihailovic, *Corporeal Words*, 188–208, review and assess this literature.

73. Ryklin, "Bodies of Terror," 51.

74. Ryklin, "Bodies of Terror," 57–58, 68–69.

75. Ryklin, "Bodies of Terror," 51–53.

76. Mihailovic, *Corporeal Words*, 199–208. Kenez, *A History of the Soviet Union*, 104–5, explains the show trials as a culmination of the violence and terror that had long been a part of Soviet life.

77. Mihailovic, *Corporeal Words*, 201.

78. Mihailovic, *Corporeal Words*, 201.

79. Mihailovic, *Corporeal Words*, 208–10.

80. Eagleton, *Walter Benjamin or Towards a Revolutionary Criticism*, 148.

81. Stallybrass and White, *The Politics and Poetics of Transgression*, 13.

82. Stallybrass and White, *The Politics and Poetics of Transgression*, 201.

83. Morson and Emerson, *Mikhail Bakhtin*, 443–48.

84. Morson and Emerson, *Mikhail Bakhtin*, 446.

85. Mihailovic, *Corporeal Words*, 150.

86. Mihailovic, *Corporeal Words*, 166–82.

87. Dentith, "Bakhtin's Carnival," 74.

88. Dentith, "Bakhtin's Carnival," 68–70, explains the "tripes," the stomach and bowels of cattle, as "at once food to be devoured and the devouring belly itself, the flagrant embodiment of corporeality which points to death and the means of sustenance which point to life."

89. Mihailovic, *Corporeal Words*, 170–76. Mihailovic's close reading unpacks these dense, rich passages.

90. Kristeva, *Desire in Language*, 64–66; Kristeva, *Revolution in Poetic Language*, 59–60. Dentith, "Bakhtin and Contemporary Criticism," 89, 93–98; Holquist, *Dialogism*, 88–89; and Morson, "Parody, History, and Metaparody," 63–67, review and assess Bakhtin/Kristeva's concept of intertextuality.

91. Culler, *On Deconstruction*, 89–134; Leitch, *Deconstructive Criticism*, 55–163.

92. Culler, *On Deconstruction*, 121–28; Leitch, *Deconstructive Criticism*, 115–22, 157–63.

93. Dentith, "Bakhtin and Contemporary Criticism," 95–97.

94. Kristeva, *Desire in Language*, 66.

95. Kristeva, *Revolution in Poetic Language*, 59–60.

96. Dentith, "Baktin and Contemporary Criticism," 97.

97. Kent, "Hermeneutics and Genre," 41–42; Morson and Emerson, *Mikhail Bakhtin*, 290–94.

98. Morson and Emerson, *Mikhail Bakhtin*, 291.

CHAPTER 4. CULTURAL CONFLICT AND THE TESTING OF PERSONS AND IDEAS IN THE *LACHES*

1. Bakhtin, *Problems of Dostoevsky's Poetics*, 111–12.

2. Bakhtin, "Response to a Question from the *Novy Mir* Editorial Staff" 2–7; Bakhtin, "Toward a Methodology for the Human Sciences," 159–65.

3. Benardete, *The Rhetoric of Morality and Philosophy*; Conley, *Rhetoric in the European Tradition*, 8–17; Cushman, *Therapeia*, 211–41; Griswold, *Self-Knowledge in Plato's "Phaedrus,"* 157–201; Kennedy, *The Art of Persuasion*, 15–17, 74–79, 82–114; Kennedy, *Classical Rhetoric and Its Christian and Secular Tradition*, 53–93; Murray, "Disputation, Deception, and Dialectic"; Wardy, *The Birth of Rhetoric*, 52–138.

4. Benardete, *The Rhetoric of Morality and Philosophy*, 2–3, 5–7, 103–5; Conley, *Rhetoric in the European Tradition*, 9–13; Cushman, *Therapeia*, 219–33; Gris-

wold, *Self-Knowledge in Plato's "Phaedrus,"* 168–86; Kennedy, *The Art of Persuasion*, 15–17, 74–79; Kennedy, *Classical Rhetoric and Its Christian and Secular Tradition*, 58–74; Murray, "Disputation, Deception, and Dialectic," 84–87. Jaeger, *In Search of the Divine Centre*, 107–73, however, traces Plato's quest for knowledge from the *Protagoras* through the *Gorgias* to the *Meno*.

5. Wardy, *The Birth of Rhetoric*, 88–96.

6. Yunis, *Taming Democracy*, 136–67, reads the *Gorgias* as a response to Thucydides' Pericles rather than to the historical Pericles. Svoboda, in a review of *Taming Democracy*, 332–33, points out, however, that Plato may not actually have *read* Thucydides.

7. Bakhtin, *Problems of Dostoevsky's Poetics*, 73; Bakhtin, "Toward a Reworking of the Dostoevsky Book," *Problems of Dostoevsky's Poetics*, Appendix II, 299.

8. Benardete, *The Rhetoric of Morality and Philosophy*, 11; Griswold, *Self-Knowledge in Plato's "Phaedrus,"* 176; Kahn, *Plato and the Socratic Dialogue*, 60, 302–9; and Kerferd, *The Sophistic Movement*, 59–60, trace the meanings of *dialegesthai* as ordinary conversation and as a question-and-answer method of discussion from the early dialogues through the *Phaedrus*.

9. Adkins, *Merit and Responsibility*, 30–85; Havelock, *The Greek Concept of Justice*, 123–92; Irwin, *Classical Thought*, 6–19; Irwin, *Plato's Ethics*, 33–35; Jaeger, *Archaic Greece*, 3–34.

10. Irwin, *Classical Thought*, 7–8, 72–81, traces the range of meanings of *aretē* (which he renders variously as *goodness*, *excellence*, or *virtue*), from the Homeric association of excellence with noble birth, wealth, and social status and, in the warrior or leader, with strength, skill, and courage to the Socratic (and Platonic) examination of courage in its relationship to justice, in particular, and to virtue as a whole. Snell, *The Discovery of the Mind*, 158–59, observes, however, that even for Homer *aretē* had a tendency toward the moral because it designated qualities—"nobility, achievement, success and reputation"— by which one might earn respect within one's community. Schmid, *On Manly Courage*, 61–62, 101–2, 104–5, 123–26, 168–70, describes the complex of meanings associated with *andreia* in the *Laches*, from "the manly physical courage of the ancient he-man" to the true courage that is joined to rational intention, civic responsibility, and civic justice. Havelock, *The Greek Concept of Justice*, 308–23, recounts Plato's exploration of *dikaiosunē* in the *Republic* as a set of social rules, as a virtue within the individual soul, and as an abstract conceptual entity. North, *Sophrosyne*, 152, explains Plato's development of *sōphrosunē* from the early Socratic conception of virtue as knowledge to the later transformation of the popular meaning of the term as "restraint of appetite" into his own distinctive concept of virtue as "orderly arrangement within the soul."

11. Adkins, *Merit and Responsibility*, 235–36.

12. Friedländer, *The Dialogues: First Period*, 5–49, 244–72; Irwin, *Plato's Ethics*, 35–44, 78–92, 111–21, 95–121, 124–26.

13. Schmid, *On Manly Courage*, 70–71. Schmid, *On Manly Courage*, 71, explains Laches' and Nicias' notions of *andreia*: "Laches' emphasis on nature, the actual prasutice of war and the modest aversion to disgrace is as characteristically Spartan as Nicias' emphasis on art, learning, and the daring appetite for the noble is Athenian."

14. Schmid, *On Manly Courage*, 20–21, 66. Schmid, *On Manly Courage*, 123–26, 168–70, maintains that Socrates challenges both of these notions with his own view of courage joined to civic responsibility and civic justice.

15. Self, "Rhetoric and *Phronesis*," 142, explains that in Aristotle's *Rhetoric phronēsis* or practical wisdom seeks not merely to exert power over others but also to deliberate well in the interest of the self, the family, and the state. But Callicles clearly has no such interest in the welfare of others. Thus Lamb, trans., in Plato, *Gorgias*, Loeb Classical Library, renders *phronēsis* as *intelligence* rather than *practical wisdom* (492a).

16. Kristeva, *Desire in Language*, 81.

17. Havelock, *The Greek Concept of Justice*, 106–22; Havelock, *Preface to Plato*, 36–96; Jaeger, *Archaic Greece*, 35–56.

18. Havelock, *Preface to Plato*, 42–43.

19. Havelock, *Preface to Plato*, 44–45.

20. Havelock, *Preface to Plato*, 3–4, 36–37, 197–233.

21. Irwin, *Plato's Ethics*, 79–81, distinguishes the self-regarding from the other-regarding virtues. Adkins, *Merit and Responsibility*, 61, designates the other-regarding virtues as "quieter" values or virtues.

22. Adkins, *Merit and Responsibility*, 259–60.

23. Adkins, *Merit and Responsibility*, 283–93; Annas, *An Introduction to Plato's "Republic,"* 109–69; Havelock, *The Greek Concept of Justice*, 308–23; Irwin, *Plato's Ethics*, 203–61; North, *Sophrosyne*, 169–76.

24. Griswold, *Self-Knowledge in Plato's "Phaedrus,"* 88, 90; North, *Sophrosyne*, 176–81; Vlastos, *Socrates, Ironist and Moral Philosopher*, 77–78. North, *Sophrosyne*, 179, identifies the moral virtues with the Platonic Forms. But Griswold, *Self-Knowledge in Plato's "Phaedrus,"* 88, 90, points out that they are not specifically so named.

25. *The Iliad*, Oxford Library of Classical Texts; *The Iliad of Homer*, trans. Lattimore. References to the Oxford edition and Lattimore's translation are included in the text.

26. Havelock, *The Greek Concept of Justice*, 123–38.

27. Havelock, *The Greek Concept of Justice*, 124–25.

28. Adkins, *Merit and Responsibility*, 33–34; Irwin, *Classical Thought*, 8.

29. Havelock, *The Greek Concept of Justice*, 125–26.

30. Havelock, *The Greek Concept of Justice*, 123–24, 319–21.

31. Havelock, *The Greek Concept of Justice*, 126–35.

32. Havelock, *The Greek Concept of Justice*, 99–100, 128, 133.

33. Kennedy, *Classical Rhetoric and Its Christian and Secular Tradition*, 5–12.

34. Reyes, "Sources of Persuasion in the *Iliad*," 29–31.

35. Havelock, *The Greek Concept of Justice*, 123–24, 135–38.

36. Havelock, *The Greek Concept of Justice*, 125.

37. Havelock, *The Greek Concept of Justice*, 125–26.

38. Nagy, *The Best of the Achaeans*, 260–61, notes the use of the word *tharsaleos* with the sense of reproach or blame in the *The Odyssey*.

39. *The Odyssey*, Oxford Library of Classical Texts; *The Odyssey of Homer*, trans. Lattimore. References to the Oxford edition and Lattimore's translation are included in the text.

40. Havelock, *The Greek Concept of Justice*, 139–49.

41. Havelock, *The Greek Concept of Justice*, 150–92.

42. Havelock, *The Greek Concept of Justice*, 155–76.

43. Havelock, *The Greek Concept of Justice*, 143–45.

44. Havelock, *The Greek Concept of Justice*, 139–42, 145–47.

45. Nagy, *The Best of the Achaeans*, 260–61, explains that Odysseus, in his disguise as a beggar, seems to the suitors to be bold *(tharsaleos)* merely for making a simple request for food.

46. Friedländer, *The Dialogues: First Period*, 38–91; Friedländer, *The Dialogues: Second and Third Periods*, 63–67; Irwin, *Plato's Ethics*, 35–44, 169–80; Jaeger, *In Search of the Divine Centre*, 87–106; Kahn, *Plato and the Socratic Dialogue*, 148–257.

47. Friedländer, *The Dialogues: First Period*, 38–49, 67–91; Irwin, *Plato's Ethics*, 35–44; Kahn, *Plato and the Socratic Dialogue*, 164–70, 188–91, 194–203.

48. Friedländer, *The Dialogues: First Period*, 50–66; Friedländer, *The Dialogues: Second and Third Periods*, 63–140, 145–89; Irwin, *Plato's Ethics*, 169–80.

49. Friedländer, *The Dialogues: First Period*, 75–76; North, *Sophrosyne*, 153–58.

50. Friedländer, *The Dialogues: First Period*, 47; Schmid, *On Manly Courage*, 93–176.

51. Devereux, "Courage and Wisdom in Plato's *Laches*"; Devereux, "The Unity of the Virtues in Plato's *Protagoras* and *Laches*"; Kahn, *Plato and the Socratic Dialogue*, 167–68; O'Brien, *The Socratic Paradoxes,* 110–17; O'Brien, "The Unity of the *Laches*." Schmid, *On Manly Courage*, 42–45, surveys the history of this approach to interpretation of the *Laches*.

52. O'Brien, *The Socratic Paradoxes,* 110–17; O'Brien, "The Unity of the *Laches*," 305–12.

53. O'Brien, *The Socratic Paradoxes*, 110–14.

54. O'Brien, *The Socratic Paradoxes*, 113–14, 117.

55. Schmid, *On Manly Courage*, 6–15, 20–21, 55–59, 63–72, 93–176.

56. Schmid, *On Manly Courage*, 55–59.

57. Schmid, *On Manly Courage*, 70–71, 123–26. Schmid, *On Manly Courage*, 101, argues that Laches' definition of courage is nothing less than the traditional Greek notion of *aretē*.

58. Schmid, *On Manly Courage*, 20–21, 66, 168–70.

59. Plato, *Laches*, trans. Lamb, Loeb Classical Library. References to this edition are included in the text.

60. Bury, *A History of Greece to the Death of Alexander the Great*, 390–513; Fine, *The Ancient Greeks*, 442–525; Hornblower, *The Greek World 479–323 BC*, 127–80; Martin, *Ancient Greece*, 147–68.

61. Connor, *Thucydides*, 25–26, 181–84; De Romilly, *Thucydides and Athenian Imperialism*, 58–104, 110–55; Fine, *The Ancient Greeks*, 311–43; Martin, *Ancient Greece*, 105–8.

62. Thucydides, *History of the Peloponnesian War*, trans. Smith, Loeb Classical Library. References to this edition are included in the text. Connor, *Thucydides*, 12–15, explains that we know little about when and how the *History of the Peloponnesian War* became available to its Greek audience but argues that the text apparently was aimed at an intelligent and sophisticated audience and was intended to explore and challenge, not simply to affirm and reinforce, its basic values. O'Brien, *The Socratic Paradoxes*, 114–17; and Schmid, *On Manly Courage*, 6–15, cite parallels between Thucydides' and Plato's portraits of Laches and Nicias but do not claim that Plato had direct knowledge of Thucydides' *History of the Peloponnesian War*. Bury, *A History of Greece to the Death of Alexander the Great* , 458–63, describes the events surrounding the Battle of Mantinea and the battle itself.

63. Schmid, *On Manly Courage*, 14–15.

64. Bury, *A History of Greece to the Death of Alexander the Great*, 466–84; Fine, *The Ancient Greeks*, 491–97; Hornblower, *The Greek World 479–323 BC*, 140–44; and Martin, *Ancient Greece*, 158–59, describe the Sicilian expedition and related events. Hornblower, *The Greek World 479–323 BC*, 140, 143–44, argues that Thucydides greatly exaggerates the importance of the expedition for the outcome of the war.

65. Schmid, *On Manly Courage*, 9–10.

66. Connor, *Thucydides*, 13–14; and Fine, *The Ancient Greeks*, 442–45, note the wide currency of concepts of power and self-interest and of the right of the strong to dominate the weak, which they attribute in part to the influence of the sophists. Plato's portraits of Gorgias, Polus, and Callicles in the *Gorgias* suggest that he, too, attributed these concepts to the sophists, but his re-creation of Protagoras' Great Speech in the *Protagoras* seems to credit Protagoras with an alternative concept of civic virtue, based upon justice and temperance.

67. Bury, *A History of Greece to the Death of Alexander the Great*, 322–30; Fine, *The Ancient Greeks*, 329–63; Hornblower, *The Greek World 479–323 BC*, 15–31; Martin, *Ancient Greece*, 105–6.

68. Bury, *A History of Greece to the Death of Alexander the Great*, 330–45; Fine, *The Ancient Greeks*, 363–82; Hornblower, *The Greek World 479–323 BC*, 32–47; Martin, *Ancient Greece*, 106–8.

69. Also Thucydides, *History of the Peloponnesian War*, 2.36.1; 2.40.4; 2.42.2; 2.43.1; 2.45.1.

70. Yunis, *Taming Democracy*, 144, claims that this statement "provides the entire justification for Pericles' policy early in the war, a policy that Thucydides endorses." Connor, *Thucydides*, 74, however, maintains that within the context of the *History of the Peloponnesian War* as a whole "the view that greatness is self-justifying, not dependent upon its social or human effects or its conformity to justice or any other moral standard . . . is explored, subverted, and finally repudiated."

71. Both interpretations are vigorously defended. The parts/whole interpretation is proposed by Vlastos, "The Unity of the Virtues in the *Protagoras*" (a reprint of a 1972 essay), and is elaborated by Brickhouse and Smith, *Plato's Socrates*, 60–72; Devereaux, "Courage and Wisdom in Plato's *Laches*"; Devereaux, "The Unity of the Virtues in Plato's *Protagoras* and *Laches*"; and Kraut, *Socrates and the State*, 258–67. The identity/unity interpretation is proposed by Penner, "The Unity of Virtue" (a reprint of a 1973 essay), and is supported by Ferejohn, "The Unity of Virtue and the Objects of Socratic Inquiry"; Irwin, *Plato's Ethics*, 42–44, 81–92; Penner, "What Laches and Nicias Miss"; and C. C. W. Taylor, "Commentary," *Protagoras*, 103–8, 221–24. Vlastos, "Socrates on 'the Parts of Virtue,'" presents further support for his parts/whole interpretation.

72. Vlastos, "The Unity of the Virtues in the *Protagoras*," 232–33; Penner, "The Unity of Virtue," 162, 178.

73. Devereaux, "Courage and Wisdom in Plato's *Laches*"; Devereaux, "The Unity of the Virtues in Plato's *Protagoras* and *Laches*," 771–89; Kraut, *Socrates and the State*, 258–62; Vlastos, "The Unity of the Virtues in the *Protagoras*," 266–69; Vlastos, "Socrates on 'the Parts of Virtue.'"

74. Irwin, *Plato's Ethics*, 41–44, 81–92; Penner, "The Unity of Virtue," 175–77; Penner, "What Laches and Nicias Miss," 1–6.

75. Brickhouse and Smith, *Plato's Socrates*, 71; Vlastos, "The Unity of the Virtues in the *Protagoras*," 232–33.

76. Penner, "The Unity of Virtue," 162–63, 173–75; Penner, "What Laches and Nicias Miss," 5–6.

77. Devereaux, "The Unity of the Virtues in Plato's *Protagoras* and *Laches*," 777–78, claims that "a courageous person is just because courage requires wisdom and possession of wisdom guarantees possession of justice" but notes that, since only wisdom is manifested by all virtuous actions, "Some courageous actions might be just, but not all need be."

78. Kahn, "On the Relative Date of the *Gorgias* and the *Protagoras*," 74–76, 96–98, maintains, therefore, that the *Gorgias* must be earlier than both the *Laches* and the *Protagoras*.

79. O'Brien, *The Socratic Paradoxes,* 110–17; O'Brien, "The Unity of the *Laches*."

80. Schmid, *On Manly Courage*, 123–26, 168–70.

81. Martin, *Ancient Greece*, 104–5, 162–63, explains women's role in warfare during this period.

82. Schmid, *On Manly Courage*, 65–66.

83. Schmid, *On Manly Courage*, 66–67.

84. Schmid, *On Manly Courage*, 70–71.

85. Schmid, *On Manly Courage*, 70.

86. Schmid, *On Manly Courage*, 70.

87. Schmid, *On Manly Courage*, 104–5. Bury, *A History of Greece to the Death of Alexander the Great*, 272–77, 289–95; and Fine, *The Ancient Greeks*, 304–5, 319–20, describe the battles at Thermopylae and Plataea. At Thermopylae, three-hundred Spartans stood fast for several days against the invading Persian army before being overwhelmed and destroyed, thus permitting the rest of the Spartan forces to escape. At Plataea, the Spartans engaged in a series of maneuvers attempting to gain the advantage of position against the Persians but were attacked while attempting to change position and thus were forced to fight.

88. Schmid, *On Manly Courage*, 112–16.

89. Gulley, *The Philosophy of Socrates*, 157–58, argues that the *Laches* in this passage (192b ff.) disassociates wisdom from professional skill and from the prudential calculus of risks and in a later passage (194d ff.) associates wisdom rather with what is and is not to be feared, which is the province not of professional skill but of judgments of value.

90. Vlastos, "The *Protagoras* and the *Laches*," 109–14, argues that such a distinction between moral and technical knowledge is precisely what Socrates is seeking.

91. Schmid, *On Manly Courage*, 112, 115–16. Similarly, Kahn, *Plato and the Socratic Dialogue*, 165, suggests that although Laches' notion of intelligent perseverance is formally correct because it specifies a character trait guided by intelligence or understanding, it does not specify what kind of intelligence is needed: "we need to know what kind of intelligence: intelligence *in regard to what?*"

92. Schmid, *On Manly Courage*, 117–19.

93. Schmid, *On Manly Courage*, 123–26.

94. Devereaux, "Courage and Wisdom in Plato's *Laches*," 138–39; Devereaux, "The Unity of the Virtues in Plato's *Protagoras* and *Laches*," 171–73; and Kraut, *Socrates and the State*, 258–61, argue that Nicias and Socrates must uphold their initial agreement that courage is but a part of virtue. Irwin, *Plato's Ethics*, 43–44; Penner, "The Unity of Virtue," 175–76; and Penner, "What Laches and Nicias Miss," 3–4, argue, to the contrary, that Nicias and Socrates may accept their later agreement that courage is equivalent to the whole of virtue.

95. Gulley, *The Philosophy of Socrates*, 158, argues that the *Laches* in this passage (194d ff.) explicitly associates wisdom with judgments of value beyond the province of professional skill.

96. Schmid, *On Manly Courage*, 143–44.

97. Schmid, *On Manly Courage*, 168–69.

98. Kahn, *Plato and the Socratic Dialogue*, 166–67, suggests, however, that Nicias' definition of courage as knowledge of all things good and evil is essentially

Socrates' own definition of virtue and, moreover, that Nicias' definition completes the definition offered by Laches and thus provides "a perfectly respectable definition of courage: perseverance and toughness of soul guided by the knowledge of what is good and what is bad, what is and is not to be feared."

99. Schmid, *On Manly Courage*, 173–76, 178–80.

100. Havelock, *Preface to Plato*, 197–233.

101. Evans, *Aristotle's Concept of Dialectic*, 7–30; Gulley, *The Philosophy of Socrates*, 8–22; Guthrie, *The Fifth-Century Enlightenment*, 349–59, 425–42; Robinson, *Plato's Earlier Dialectic*, 7–60.

Chapter 5. Truth as Dialogic: Creating a Cultural Hybrid in the *Protagoras*

1. Benitez, "Argument, Rhetoric, and Philosophic Method," 235, 240.

2. Benitez, "Argument, Rhetoric, and Philosophic Method," 237.

3. Gulley, *The Philosophy of Socrates*, 18–20, 93–126, 151–64; Rossetti, "The Rhetoric of Socrates"; Santas, *Socrates*, 196–217. Gulley, *The Philosophy of Socrates*, 19–20, 155–57; and Santas, *Socrates*, 207, note weaknesses in Socrates' arguments at particularly decisive moments, such as the arguments in support of the unity of courage and wisdom (349e–51b) and in support of hedonism (351b–58d).

4. Guthrie, "Introduction," *"Protagoras" and "Meno,"* 22.

5. Schiappa, *Protagoras and* Logos, 6.

6. Bakhtin, *Problems of Dostoevsky's Poetics*, 6–8, 16, 81, 110. Burnyeat, "Socratic Midwifery, Platonic Inspiration," 53, 60, maintains that the image of Socrates as midwife (in *Theaetetus* 148e–51d) is not a characterization of the historical Socratic but a metaphor for Plato's own theory of knowledge.

7. Bakhtin, "Discourse in the Novel, 358–62.

8. The parts/whole interpretation of the *Protagoras* is presented in Brickhouse and Smith, *Plato's Socrates*, 69–71; Irwin, *Plato's Ethics*, 80–81; Kraut, *Socrates and the State*, 262–67; and Vlastos, "The Unity of the Virtues in the *Protagoras*." The identity/unity interpretation of the *Protagoras* is presented in Ferejohn, "The Unity of Virtue and the Objects of Socratic Inquiry"; Irwin, *Plato's Ethics*, 81–92; Kahn, *Plato and the Socratic Dialogue*, 216–24; Penner, "The Unity of Virtue," 169–75; and C. C. W. Taylor, "Commentary," *Protagoras*, 103–8, 221–24. Kahn, *Plato and the Socratic Dialogue*, 222, concludes, however, that "Plato in the *Protagoras* has deliberately left the thesis of unity indeterminate and open for further discussion."

9. Havelock, *The Liberal Temper in Greek Politics*, 206–30; Schiappa, *Protagoras and* Logos, 186.

10. Kerferd, *The Sophistic Movement*, 140–48; and Schiappa, *Protagoras and* Logos, 180–87, explain Protagoras' contributions to democratic theory.

11. Hemmenway, "Sophistry Exposed," 2, claims that the Protagoras of the dialogue is portrayed as holding "an ignoble and corrupting doctrine of virtue—one typical of the sophists," a doctrine of virtue as "the instrument of political success . . . primarily associated with courage and wisdom," a doctrine expressed with greater candor by Thrasymachus and Callicles.

12. Irwin, *Plato's Ethics*, 79–80, maintains that Socrates offers arguments in support of both the reciprocity and the identity/unity interpretations of the virtues.

13. Gosling and Taylor, *The Greeks on Pleasure*, 45–68; Irwin, *Plato's Ethics*, 81–92; and Rudebusch, "Plato, Hedonism, and Ethical Protagoreanism," 27–40, argue that the hedonism expressed in the *Protagoras* is Plato's own. Kahn, *Plato and the Socratic Dialogue*, 224–53, argues, to the contrary, that the hedonism of the *Protagoras* cannot be Socrates' or Plato's own since it conflicts with the Socratic paradox (which Plato accepts) that no one who knows what is good does what is bad. McCoy, "Protagoras on Human Nature, Wisdom, and the Good," 37; and Zeyl, "Socrates and Hedonism," 15, suggest that Socrates' hedonism is merely an argumentative strategy that he uses clarify Protagoras' position and to defend his own. Weiss, "Hedonism in the *Protagoras* and the Sophist's Guarantee," 19, claims that Socrates' hedonism is the foundation upon which he fashions "a craft for the sophists to hawk."

14. C. C. W. Taylor, "Commentary," *Protagoras*, 132–35, explains that the expression "good for" is a relational expression meaning "good for x," "good for y," and so forth.

15. McCoy, "Protagoras on Human Nature, Wisdom, and the Good," 31–32, reads this passage as humorous but nonetheless serious in intent. Hemmenway, "Sophistry Exposed," 18, describes it as "a rhetorical diversion." Havelock, *The Liberal Temper*, 203–4; and C. C. W. Taylor, "Commentary," *Protagoras*, 133, read it as a serious exposition on the relational character of the good.

16. Bakhtin, "Discourse in the Novel," 364.

17. Kerferd, *The Sophistic Movement*, 104–10; Ostwald, *From Popular Sovereignty to the Sovereignty of Law*, 240–42; Schiappa, *Protagoras and* Logos, 126–30, 166. Schiappa, *Protagoras and* Logos, 128, explains Protagoras' conception of relativity as frame of reference "as being or becoming *for someone*, or *of something* or *towards something*."

18. Allen, "Comment," *The Protagoras*, 114–15; C. C. W. Taylor, "Commentary," *Protagoras*, 144–45, 147–48.

19. Bowra, *Greek Lyric Poetry*, 326–36, 340–41, 345–49, 368–69; Jaeger, *Archaic Greece*, 213–14; C. C. W. Taylor, "Commentary," *Protagoras*, 141–42.

20. Bakhtin, *Problems of Dostoevsky's Poetics*, 73.

21. Havelock, *The Liberal Temper*, 163–230; Jaeger, *Archaic Greece*, 299–300, 308–11; Kerferd, *The Sophistic Movement*, 132–38, 140–48; Maranhão, *Therapeutic Discourse and Socratic Dialogue*, 162–68; Schiappa, *Protagoras and* Logos, 157–62, 168–71, 180–87.

22. Havelock, *The Liberal Temper*, 206–30.

23. Havelock, *The Liberal Temper*, 206, 208–9.

24. Havelock, *The Liberal Temper*, 222–23, 230.

25. Schiappa, *Protagoras and* Logos, 157–62, 180–87.

26. Schiappa, *Protagoras and* Logos, 161.

27. Schiappa, *Protagoras and* Logos, 180.

28. Schiappa, *Protagoras and* Logos, 181–85.

29. Benitez, "Argument, Rhetoric, and Philosophic Method"; Irwin, *Plato's Ethics*, 78–94.

30. Benitez, "Argument, Rhetoric, and Philosophic Method," 239–45.

31. Irwin, *Plato's Ethics*, 92–93.

32. Vlastos, *Platonic Studies*, 232–33.

33. Vlastos, *Platonic Studies*, 224–34.

34. Irwin, *Plato's Ethics*, 79–80.

35. Gosling and Taylor, *The Greeks on Pleasure*, 45–68; Irwin, *Plato's Ethics*, 81–92.

36. Kerferd, *The Sophistic Movement*, 4–5.

37. Irwin, *Plato's Ethics*, 80–81.

38. Schiappa, *Protagoras and* Logos, 6.

39. Havelock, *The Liberal Temper*, 206; Kerferd, *The Sophistic Movement*, 136.

40. Bakhtin, "Epic and Novel," 24; Bakhtin, *Problems of Dostoevsky's Poetics*, 109.

41. Gosling and Taylor, *The Greeks on Pleasure*, 52. Kerferd, *The Sophistic Movement*, 135–36, claims, however, that "conditioning in social mores" is itself a kind of knowledge. Of course, the kind of social conditioning that leads Protagoras to believe that a person can be courageous but unjust is precisely the kind of conditioning that Socrates wants to protest.

42. Irwin, *Plato's Ethics*, 127–47; Jaeger, *In Search of the Divine Centre*, 160–73; Kerferd, *The Sophistic Movement*, 136–37; Vlastos, "Socrates on 'the Parts of Virtue.'"

43. Plato, *Protagoras*, trans. Lamb, Loeb Classical Library. References to this edition are included in the text.

44. Allen, "Comment," *The Protagoras*, 114, for example, suggests that this interlude is merely a kind of comic relief, like the clowns in Shakespeare's plays.

45. Kerferd, *The Sophistic Movement*, 19, 42–54, provides background on the individual sophists.

46. Jaeger, *In Search of the Divine Centre*, 111–12, points out that Protagoras reverses the usual relationship between the poets and the sophists: whereas the sophists were accustomed to trading upon the prestige of the great poets, Protagoras identifies the poets as ancestors of the art of sophistry, who concealed their identity by calling themselves poets.

47. Schiappa, *Protagoras and* Logos, 184–85.

48. Irwin, *Plato's Ethics*, 79–81.

49. Adkins, *Merit and Responsibility*, 222–23, 227–28.

50. Adkins, *Merit and Responsibility*, 223.

51. Kerferd, *The Sophistic Movement*, 142–48; Schiappa, *Protagoras and* Logos, 180–87.

52. McCoy, "Protagoras on Human Nature, Wisdom, and the Good," 29–30; Schiappa, *Protagoras and* Logos, 180; C. C. W. Taylor, "Commentary," *Protagoras*, 81–83; Weiss, "Hedonism in the *Protagoras* and the Sophist's Guarantee," 17–18.

53. C. C. W. Taylor, "Commentary," *Protagoras*, 81, explains that *dikē* and *aidōs* are poetic forms of *dikaiosunē* and *sōphrosunē*, suited to the context of the myth.

54. Schiappa, *Protagoras and* Logos, 180–87.

55. Schiappa, *Protagoras and* Logos, 181.

56. Schiappa, *Protagoras and* Logos, 181.

57. Schiappa, *Protagoras and* Logos, 182–83.

58. Schiappa, *Protagoras and* Logos, 183–84.

59. Irwin, *Plato's Ethics*, 79.

60. Schiappa, *Protagoras and* Logos, 181–82;

61. Havelock, *The Liberal Temper*, 87–88, doubts that the Great Speech is Protagoras' own. Schiappa, *Protagoras and* Logos, 180, however, believes that the speech probably represents Protagoras' thoughts if not his own words. C. C. W. Taylor, "Commentary," *Protagoras*, 81–82, suggests that Protagoras' omits wisdom, conceived as practical wisdom or intelligence, because he simply presumes it as given.

62. Havelock, *Preface to Plato*, 39, notes that the *Protagoras* (325e) attests to the teaching of writing in the schools.

63. Irwin, *Plato's Ethics*, 44–48, claims that Socrates consistently holds that every virtue is good, all things considered, both for the agent and for other people.

64. Brickhouse and Smith, *Plato's Socrates*, 69–71, maintain that Socrates endorses the gold/parts-of-gold analogy and explain that the relationship between wisdom and the individual virtues is like the relationship between a generalized discipline and its specialized applications (as triangulation can be applied to coastal navigation or surveying, for example, the same skill producing different products).

65. Irwin, *Plato's Ethics*, 80.

66. Irwin, *Plato's Ethics*, 81.

67. Irwin, *Plato's Ethics*, 81.

68. C. C. W. Taylor, "Commentary," *Protagoras*, 132–35.

69. C. C. W. Taylor, "Commentary," *Protagoras*, 133.

70. C. C. W. Taylor, "Commentary," *Protagoras*, 133–34.

71. Kerferd, *The Sophistic Movement*, 104–10; Schiappa, *Protagoras and* Logos, 126–30.

72. Schiappa, *Protagoras and* Logos, 126.

73. Ostwald, *From Popular Sovereignty to the Sovereignty of Law*, 240.

74. Irwin, *Plato's Ethics*, 113–14.

75. Benitez, "Argument, Rhetoric, and Philosophic Method," 239–45; Havelock, *The Liberal Temper*, 206–30; Irwin, *Plato's Ethics*, 92–94; Schiappa, *Protagoras and* Logos, 157–62, 186.

76. Havelock, *The Liberal Temper*, 222–23, 229–30; Schiappa, *Protagoras and* Logos, 160–62.

77. Schiappa, *Protagoras and* Logos, 161.

78. C. C. W. Taylor, "Commentary," *Protagoras*, 144–45, 147–48.

79. Kameen, *Writing/Teaching*, 173–76; McCoy, "Socrates on Simonides," 349–58.

80. McCoy, "Socrates on Simonides," 352–53, 357.

81. Kameen, *Writing/Teaching*, 173–76.

82. C. C. W. Taylor, "Commentary," *Protagoras*, 141–42, explains how the poem might be reconstructed on the basis of the lines recorded in the *Protagoras*.

83. Jaeger, *Archaic Greece*, 213.

84. Jaeger, *Archaic Greece*, 213–14.

85. Bowra, *Greek Lyric Poetry*, 326–32.

86. Bowra, *Greek Lyric Poetry*, 332–36.

87. Adkins, *Merit and Responsibility*, 165–68, 196–97.

88. Gosling and Taylor, *The Greeks on Pleasure*, 52.

89. Irwin, *Plato's Ethics*, 81–85, 90–92.

90. Irwin, *Plato's Ethics*, 81–85; Penner, "The Unity of Virtue," 169–75.

91. Gulley, *The Philosophy of Socrates*, 157–58, claims that the two arguments conflict and that the argument of the *Protagoras* is therefore not to be taken seriously.

92. Gosling and Taylor, *The Greeks on Pleasure*, 53–54; and Irwin, *Plato's Ethics*, 92–93, hold this position. Kahn, *Plato and the Socratic Dialogue*, 237–38, maintains, to the contrary, that the sleight-of-hand trick by which Socrates is able to transform courage and cowardice into wisdom and ignorance reflects Plato's own view that "one cannot get from hedonism to morality as ordinarily understood without invoking a fundamentally different standard for moral approval and disapproval."

93. Gulley, *The Philosophy of Socrates*, 18–21, 154–62; C. C. W. Taylor, "Commentary," *Protagoras*, 150–61.

94. Gulley, *The Philosophy of Socrates*, 18–19; C. C. W. Taylor, "Commentary," *Protagoras*, 152–61.

95. C. C. W. Taylor, "Commentary," *Protagoras*, 152.

96. Gulley, *The Philosophy of Socrates*, 19; C. C. W. Taylor, "Commentary," *Protagoras*, 156. Kahn, *Plato and the Socratic Dialogue*, 166, claims that Protagoras sees what Laches failed to see, that "in some circumstances confidence is not a moral virtue, and hence not a mark of courage."

97. Gulley, *The Philosophy of Socrates*, 19–20, 157–58.

98. Irwin, *Plato's Ethics*, 92–93.

99. Irwin, *Plato's Ethics*, 324–28, 332–35.

100. Allen, trans., *The Protagoras*, 220 n. 43.

101. Kahn, *Plato and the Socratic Dialogue*, 236.

102. Irwin, *Plato's Ethics*, 85.

103. Irwin, *Plato's Ethics*, 85.

104. Gosling and Taylor, *The Greeks on Pleasure*, 52.

105. Kerferd, *The Sophistic Movement*, 136.

CHAPTER 6. DIALOGUE AS CARNIVAL: CONTESTING CULTURAL AND RHETORICAL PRACTICES IN THE *GORGIAS*

1. Allen, "Comment," *The Gorgias*, 192–201, 211–12, 224–25; Benardete, *The Rhetoric of Morality and Philosophy*; Conley, *Rhetoric in the European Tradition*, 8–13; Enos, *Greek Rhetoric before Aristotle*, 91–101; Kennedy, *The Art of Persuasion*, 15–17, 62–63, 74–79; Kennedy, *Classical Rhetoric and Its Christian and Secular Tradition*, 53–74; Murray, "Disputation, Deception, and Dialectic"; Plochmann and Robinson, *A Friendly Companion to Plato's "Gorgias."*

2. Allen, "Comment," *The Gorgias*, 193–94, 196–98, 224–25; Conley, *Rhetoric in the European Tradition*, 9; Enos, *Greek Rhetoric before Aristotle*, 98–99; Kennedy, *The Art of Persuasion*, 15–17; Kennedy, *Classical Rhetoric and Its Christian and Secular Tradition*, 59–65.

3. Irwin, *Plato's Ethics*, 95–126; Kahn, "Drama and Dialectic in Plato's Gorgias"; Kerferd, *The Sophistic Movement*, 78–82, 93–100; Nightingale, *Genres in Dialogue*, 79–92; Schiappa, *The Beginnings of Rhetorical Theory in Classical Greece*, 72–73, 114–52; Wardy, *The Birth of Rhetoric*, 25–85; Yunis, *Taming Democracy*, 117–61. Kahn, *Plato and the Socratic Dialogue*, 127, 129–31, argues, however, that the *Gorgias* resembles the *Apology* and the *Republic* rather than early aporetic dialogues such as the *Laches* and the *Protagoras* because it defends Socratic morality and offers a portrait of the true political artist who will become the philosopher-king of the *Republic*.

4. Bakhtin, "Epic and Novel," 25–26; Bakhtin, *Problems of Dostoevsky's Poetics*, 132.

5. Bakhtin, *Rabelais and His World*, 470–71.

6. Bakhtin, *Rabelais and His World*, 167.

7. Allen, "Comment," *The Gorgias*, 228–29; Nightingale, *Genres in Dialogue*, 82–85; Yunis, *Taming Democracy*, 153–61.

8. Nightingale, *Genres in Dialogue*, 85–87; Wardy, *The Birth of Rhetoric*, 84–85.

9. Bakhtin, *Problems of Dostoevsky's Poetics*, 111.

10. Kahn, "Drama and Dialectic in Plato's *Gorgias*," 95–98; Schmid, *On Manly Courage*, 20–21, 66. Schmid, 20–21, explains the transformation of the traditional Homeric ideal of courage into the contemporary Athenian ideal of courage guided by intelligence and technical skill.

11. Irwin, *Plato's Ethics*, 101–21; Kahn, "Drama and Dialectic in Plato's *Gorgias*," 104–10.

12. Dodds, "Commentary," *Gorgias*, 316.

13. Kahn, "Drama and Dialectic in Plato's *Gorgias*," 95.

14. Yunis, *Taming Democracy*, 136–37, 142–46.

15. Yunis, *Taming Democracy*, 144. Yunis, *Taming Democracy*, 136–39; and Svoboda, in a review of Yunis' *Taming Democracy*, 332–33, speculate about whether or not Plato actually *read* Thucydides.

16. Dodds, "Introduction," *Gorgias*, 15, 32–33; Kahn, "Drama and Dialectic in Plato's *Gorgias*," 95–96; Schmid, *On Manly Courage*, 20–21, 66.

17. Allen, "Comment," *The Gorgias*, 197; Conley, *Rhetoric in the European Tradition*, 9; Enos, *Greek Rhetoric before Aristotle*, 98–99; Kennedy, *Classical Rhetoric and Its Christian and Secular Tradition*, 66–67, 69, 71; Plochmann and Robinson, *A Friendly Companion to Plato's "Gorgias,"* xlii, 362 n. 49.

18. Kennedy, *Classical Rhetoric and Its Christian and Secular Tradition*, 54, 58–74.

19. Kennedy, *Classical Rhetoric and Its Christian and Secular Tradition*, 59–61.

20. Kennedy, *Classical Rhetoric and Its Christian and Secular Tradition*, 61–63.

21. Kennedy, *Classical Rhetoric and Its Christian and Secular Tradition*, 63–65.

22. Kennedy, *Classical Rhetoric and Its Christian and Secular Tradition*, 70–71.

23. Benardete, *The Rhetoric of Morality and Philosophy*, 2, 7, 104.

24. Plochmann and Robinson, *A Friendly Companion to Plato's "Gorgias,"* xxxiii.

25. Plochmann and Robinson, *A Friendly Companion to Plato's "Gorgias,"* xxiv, 67.

26. Plochmann and Robinson, *A Friendly Companion to Plato's "Gorgias,"* xxvii–xxviii, xlii, 67, 97.

27. Allen, "Comment," *The Gorgias*, 197.

28. Kerferd, *The Sophistic Movement*, 78–82, 93–100; Schiappa, *The Beginnings of Rhetorical Theory in Classical Greece*, 72–73, 114–52; Wardy, *The Birth of Rhetoric*, 25–51.

29. Schiappa, *The Beginnings of Rhetorical Theory in Classical Greece*, 72–73, 126–29.

30. Schiappa, *The Beginnings of Rhetorical Theory in Classical Greece*, 128–29.

31. Kerferd, *The Sophistic Movement*, 80–81, 93, 97–100.

32. Schiappa, *The Beginnings of Rhetorical Theory in Classical Greece*, 138–43, 148–52.

33. Fussi, "Why Is the *Gorgias* so Bitter?" 55.

34. Kahn, "Drama and Dialectic in Plato's *Gorgias*," 79–121.

35. Kahn, "Drama and Dialectic in Plato's *Gorgias*," 80, 96–97, 105–7.

36. Kahn, "Drama and Dialectic in Plato's *Gorgias*," 79–84.

37. Kahn, "Drama and Dialectic in Plato's *Gorgias*," 84–97, 110–17.

38. Kahn, "Drama and Dialectic in Plato's *Gorgias*," 97–110, 117–21.

39. Bakhtin, "Epic and Novel," 25–26; Bakhtin, *Problems of Dostoevsky's Poetics*, 132.

40. Bakhtin, "Epic and Novel," 25; Kennedy, *Classical Rhetoric and Its Christian and Secular Tradition*, 61–62.

41. Nightingale, *Genres in Dialogue*, 91.

42. Yunis, *Taming Democracy*, 136–61.

43. Yunis, *Taming Democracy*, 136–53.

44. Yunis, *Taming Democracy*, 141.

45. Yunis, *Taming Democracy*, 150–51.

46. Yunis, *Taming Democracy*, 142–46, 151–52.

47. Yunis, *Taming Democracy*, 145–46, 155–56.

48. Wardy, *The Birth of Rhetoric*, 65, 84–85.

49. Nightingale, *Genres in Dialogue*, 70–71, 82–87.

50. Kennedy, *Classical Rhetoric and Its Christian and Secular Tradition*, 58.

51. Bakhtin, *Problems of Dostoevsky's Poetics*, 132.

52. Berman, "How Polus Was Refuted"; Irwin, *Plato's Ethics*, 99–101; Kahn, "Drama and Dialectic in Plato's *Gorgias*," 84–92; Santas, *Socrates*, 221–54; Vlastos, *Socrates: Ironist and Moral Philosopher*, 139–48; and Vlastos, "Was Polus Refuted?" 454–60, explain the difficulties in Socrates' argument with Polus, for example—the most troublesome in the dialogue.

53. Enos, *Greek Rhetoric before Aristotle*, 93.

54. Enos, *Greek Rhetoric before Aristotle*, 95, 99.

55. Nightingale, *Genres in Dialogue*, 82–83, 85–86.

56. Nightingale, *Genres in Dialogue*, 86–87.

57. Bakhtin, *Problems of Dostoevsky's Poetics*, 111.

58. Brickhouse and Smith, *Plato's Socrates*, 19–22.

59. Brickhouse and Smith, *Plato's Socrates*, 13–14, 22–23.

60. Brickhouse and Smith, *Plato's Socrates*, 19.

61. Plato, *Gorgias*, trans. Lamb, Loeb Classical Library. References to this edition are included in the text. Allen, "Comment," *The Gorgias*, 192–230; Kennedy, *Classical Rhetoric and Its Christian and Secular Tradition*, 58–66; and others divide the dialogue into a series of exchanges with different speakers. Irwin, *Plato's Ethics*, 95–126, however, approaches the dialogue as a series of discussions on specific issues or topics rather than with particular speakers.

62. Fine, *The Ancient Greeks*, 292–93, 375–76; and Martin, *Ancient Greece*, 104, 108, 116–21, explain the building programs undertaken by Themistocles, Cimon, and Pericles.

63. Irwin, *Plato's Ethics*, 97, thus reconstructs the argument.

64. Kennedy, *Classical Rhetoric and Its Christian and Secular Tradition*, 60.

65. Kennedy, *Classical Rhetoric and Its Christian and Secular Tradition*, 60.

66. Kerferd, *The Sophistic Movement*, 78–82, 93–100; Schiappa, *The Beginnings of Rhetorical Theory in Classical Greece*, 72–73, 114–52.

67. Schiappa, *The Beginnings of Rhetorical Theory in Classical Greece*, 14–29.

68. Kahn, "Drama and Dialectic in Plato's *Gorgias*," 84.

69. Kennedy, *Classical Rhetoric and Its Christian and Secular Tradition*, 60.

70. Irwin, *Plato's Ethics*, 99.

71. Bakhtin, *Problems of Dostoevsky's Poetics*, 111.

72. Kennedy, *Classical Rhetoric and Its Christian and Secular Tradition*, 61–62.

73. Bakhtin, "Epic and Novel," 25–26.

74. Bakhtin, *Problems of Dostoevsky's Poetics*, 132.

75. Kahn, "Drama and Dialectic in Plato's *Gorgias*," 84.

76. Kahn, "Drama and Dialectic in Plato's *Gorgias*," 95–98.

77. Schmid, *On Manly Courage*, 20; Yunis, *Taming Democracy*, 142–46.

78. Allen, trans., *The Gorgias*, 257, renders *dialegesthai* as *dialectic* (471d). But Socrates is here contrasting Polus' attempt to refute him in rhetorical fashion with his own attempt to refute Polus—or permit Polus to refute him—by rendering and receiving accounts in discussion.

79. Kahn, "Drama and Dialectic in Plato's *Gorgias*," 95–97.

80. Bakhtin, *Problems of Dostoevsky's Poetics*, 132.

81. Irwin, *Plato's Ethics*, 100.

82. Vlastos, *Socrates: Ironist and Moral Philosopher*, 139–48; Vlastos, "Was Polus Refuted?" Berman, "How Polus Was Refuted," 272–77; Irwin, *Plato's Ethics*, 100–101; and Kahn, "Drama and Dialectic in Plato's *Gorgias*," 86–92, review and respond to Vlastos' argument.

83. Vlastos, *Socrates: Ironist and Moral Philosopher*, 139–44; Vlastos, "Was Polus Refuted?" 456–58.

84. Irwin, *Plato's Ethics*, 100; Kahn, "Drama and Dialectic in Plato's *Gorgias*," 89–92.

85. Berman, "How Polus Was Refuted," 271.

86. Self, "Rhetoric and *Phronesis*," 142, explains that in Aristotle's *Rhetoric* *phronēsis* or practical wisdom is never simply self-serving but "concerns itself with one's self, one's family, and the state because the individual's welfare is bound up with that of others." But Lamb, trans., in Plato, *Gorgias*, Loeb Classical Library, renders *phronēsis* as *intelligence* (492a)—for Callicles affirms only his own interest, not the interest of others.

87. Kahn, "Drama and Dialectic in Plato's *Gorgias*," 105–7.

88. Irwin, *Plato's Ethics*, 106–8; Kahn, "Drama and Dialectic in Plato's *Gorgias*," 107–10.

89. Kahn, "Drama and Dialectic in Plato's *Gorgias*," 97–98.

90. Irwin, *Plato's Ethics*, 111–14; Kahn, "Drama and Dialectic in Plato's *Gorgias*," 104–10.

91. Kahn, "Drama and Dialectic in Plato's *Gorgias*," 104–5.

92. Irwin, *Plato's Ethics*, 114, suggests that Plato may have reconsidered the arguments for hedonism expressed in the *Protagoras* and therefore revisited and revised them in the *Gorgias*.

93. Kahn, "Drama and Dialectic in Plato's *Gorgias*," 109–10.

94. Irwin, *Plato's Ethics*, 113–14.

95. Dodds, "Commentary," *Gorgias*, 316, recalls that the Socrates of the *Protagoras* (357a–b) has sought a *technē* or *epistēmē* that will permit us to make the right choice of pleasures and pains required for our salvation in life but has deferred this search until another time. He claims that the *Gorgias* shows that this *technē* cannot be the skill of the *rhētōr* and that the solution to the problem lies rather in the *Republic* and the *Statesman*.

96. Irwin, *Plato's Ethics*, 109–10; Kahn, "Drama and Dialectic in Plato's *Gorgias*," 98, 118–19; Kennedy, *Classical Rhetoric and Its Christian and Secular Tradition*, 64–65.

97. Nightingale, *Genres in Dialogue*, 70–71; Wardy, *The Birth of Rhetoric*, 65, 84–85; Yunis, *Taming Democracy*, 117–61. But Yunis, *Taming Democracy*, 156–60, claims that Socrates withdraws entirely from politics and from political discourse.

98. Kahn, "Drama and Dialectic in Plato's *Gorgias*," 96; Kennedy, *Classical Rhetoric and Its Christian and Secular Tradition*, 64–65.

99. Kahn, "Drama and Dialectic in Plato's *Gorgias*," 119; Nightingale, *Genres in Dialogue*, 70–71, 82–87; Wardy, *The Birth of Rhetoric*, 65, 85.

100. North, *Sophrosyne*, 161–64, points out that in this passage Socrates introduces a new concept of the soul brought to fulfillment in the *Republic* and the *Laws*— the need for good order and harmony in the parts of the soul.

101. Dodds, "Commentary," *Gorgias*, 355–56, 360–61, 364; Irwin, "Notes," *Gorgias*, 234–39; Wardy, *The Birth of Rhetoric*, 84–85; Yunis, *Taming Democracy*, 146–53.

102. Kahn, *Plato and the Socratic Dialogue*, 129–31, maintains, however, that Socrates' "true art of politics" is a political art fully realized not in the philosopher of the *Gorgias*—Socrates himself—but in the philosopher-king of the *Republic*.

103. Kahn, "Drama and Dialectic in Plato's *Gorgias*," 96.

104. Kennedy, *Classical Rhetoric and Its Christian and Secular Tradition*, 62–63, 65.

105. Yunis, *Taming Democracy*, 117–18, 167, 171.

106. Yunis, *Taming Democracy*, 117–18.

107. Thucydides, *History of the Peloponnesian War*, trans. Smith, Loeb Classical Library, 2.63.2–3; Yunis, *Taming Democracy*, 144.

108. Yunis, *Taming Democracy*, 144.

109. Yunis, *Taming Democracy*, 145.

110. Yunis, *Taming Democracy*, 145–46.

111. Yunis, *Taming Democracy*, 163–65, 168, 171.

112. Brickhouse and Smith, *Plato's Socrates*, 19.

113. Yunis, *Taming Democracy*, 156–60.

114. Yunis, *Taming Democracy*, 157–58.

115. Yunis, *Taming Democracy*, 158.

116. Nightingale, *Genres in Dialogue*, 70–72.

117. Wardy, *The Birth of Rhetoric*, 85.

118. Allen, "Comment," *The Gorgias*, 224–25, 227–30; Dodds, "Commentary," *Gorgias*, 375; Nightingale, *Genres in Dialogue*, 82–83.

119. Bakhtin, *Problems of Dostoevsky's Poetics*, 61, 73, 111–12.

120. Bakhtin, *Problems of Dostoevsky's Poetics*, 111.

121. Bakhtin, *Problems of Dostoevsky's Poetics*, 111–12.

122. Allen, "Comment," *The Apology*, 63–69; Brickhouse and Smith, *Socrates on Trial*, 37–47, 49–53; De Strycker, *Plato's Apology of Socrates*, 11, 21–25, 28–40; Kennedy, *Classical Rhetoric and Its Christian and Secular Tradition*, 55–58.

123. Brickhouse and Smith, *Socrates on Trial*, 37–39, 52–53.

124. Allen, "Comment," *The Apology*, 68–69; De Strycker, *Plato's Apology of Socrates*, 11, 21–25, 37–39; Kennedy, *Classical Rhetoric and Its Christian and Secular Tradition*, 55–56. Kennedy, *Classical Rhetoric and Its Christian and Secular Tradition*, 56, identifies the following parts of Socrates' defense: proemium; statement of the case (Socrates' denial of the charges against him); narration (Socrates' explanation of the prejudice against him); refutation of the charges; and epilogue.

125. Allen, "Comment," *The Apology*, 69.

126. Bakhtin, *Problems of Dostoevsky's Poetics*, 128.

127. Plato, *Apology*, trans. Fowler, Loeb Classical Library. References to this edition are included in the text.

128. Brickhouse and Smith, *Socrates on Trial*, 219–20.

129. Bakhtin, *Problems of Dostoevsky's Poetics*, 61, 73.

130. Nightingale, *Genres in Dialogue*, 82–83.

131. Allen, "Comment," *The Gorgias*, 228–29.

132. Yunis, *Taming Democracy*, 155–56.

133. Nightingale, *Genres in Dialogue*, 70–71, 82–87.

134. Nightingale, *Genres in Dialogue*, 85–86.

135. Nightingale, *Genres in Dialogue*, 86–87.

EPILOGUE. DIALOGICAL RHETORIC IN PRINT AND DIGITAL MEDIA

1. Bialostosky, "Bakhtin's 'Rough Draft,'" 6–7, 18–23.

2. Kahn, "Drama and Dialectic in Plato's *Gorgias*," 95–96, 110–21; Yunis, *Taming Democracy*, 139–46, 153–61. Yunis, *Taming Democracy*, 153–56, maintains, however, that Socrates' art of dialogue proves to be no more successful than Pericles' rhetoric as an art of improving people's lives.

3. Wardy, *The Birth of Rhetoric*, 67–68, 84–85; Yunis, *Taming Democracy*, 139–46.

4. Bolter, *Writing Space*, 27–76, 161–213; Harpold, "The Grotesque Corpus"; Lanham, *The Electronic Word*, 24, 104–9, 121–36, 170–79; Tuman, *Word Perfect*, 5–22, 35–47; Welch, *Electric Rhetoric*, 101–12.

5. Bolter, *Writing Space*, 77–160; Harpold, "The Grotesque Corpus," 5–7; Lanham, *The Electronic Word*, 56–62, 71–72, 112; Tuman, *Word Perfect*, 62–66, 72–78, 87–99; Welch, *Electric Rhetoric*, 177–89.

6. Welch, *Electric Rhetoric*, 53–74.

7. Welch, *Electric Rhetoric*, 67.

8. Adkins, *Merit and Responsibility*, 283–93; Annas, *An Introduction to Plato's "Republic,"* 109–69; Griswold, *Self-Knowledge in Plato's "Phaedrus,"* 88, 90; Havelock, *The Greek Concept of Justice*, 308–23; Irwin, *Plato's Ethics*, 203–61; North, *Sophrosyne*, 169–81; Vlastos, *Socrates, Ironist and Moral Philosopher*, 77–78.

9. Benardete, *The Rhetoric of Morality and Philosophy*, 103–5; Griswold, *Self-Knowledge in Plato's "Phaedrus,"* 138–65; Harris, "Bakhtin, *Phaedrus*, and the Geometry of Rhetoric"; Kahn, *Plato and the Socratic Dialogue*, 371–76; Kameen, *Writing/Teaching*, 149–50, 197–99, 218–30; Kastely, "Respecting the Rupture"; Kennedy, *Classical Rhetoric in Its Christian and Secular Tradition*, 66–74.

10. Plato, *Phaedrus*, trans. Fowler, Loeb Classical Library. References to this edition are included in the text.

11. Griswold, *Self-Knowledge in Plato's "Phaedrus,"* 138; Kahn, *Plato and the Socratic Dialogue*, 372.

12. Griswold, *Self-Knowledge in Plato's "Phaedrus,"* 164–65.

13. Benardete, *The Rhetoric of Morality and Philosophy*, 104–5.

14. Kennedy, *Classical Rhetoric in Its Christian and Secular Tradition*, 70. Kahn, *Plato and the Socratic Dialogue*, 373, observes this balance but argues that the division between the two parts reflects "the shift in Plato's own literary work, from the dramatic dialogue focused on the personality of Socrates to the more didactic compositions of later years."

15. Kastely, "Respecting the Rupture," 148–50.

16. Kastely, "Respecting the Rupture," 151.

17. Harris, "Bakhtin, *Phaedrus*, and the Geometry of Rhetoric," 15–21; Kameen, *Writing/Teaching*, 218–30.

18. Harris, "Bakhtin, *Phaedrus*, and the Geometry of Rhetoric," 17.

19. Harris, "Bakhtin, *Phaedrus*, and the Geometry of Rhetoric," 17–18.

20. Kameen, *Writing/Teaching*, 225.

21. Kameen, *Writing/Teaching*, 227.

22. Bolter, *Writing Space*, 102–20; Lanham, *The Electronic Word*, 56–62, 71–72, 112; Tuman, *Word Perfect*, 76, 89–91; Welch *Electric Rhetoric*, 104–9, 184–87.

23. Bolter, *Writing Space*, 81–98, 203–13; Lanham, *The Electronic Word*, 24, 105, 124, 132; Tuman, *Word Perfect*, 11–22, 35–39.

24. Lanham, *The Electronic Word*, 24.

25. Bolter, *Writing Space*, 81–83.

26. Bolter, *Writing Space*, 83–87, 91–93.

27. Tuman, *Word Perfect*, 36–37.

28. Bolter, *Writing Space*, 102–20, 203–13; Lanham, *The Electronic Word*, 56–62, 71–72, 112; Tuman, *Word Perfect*, 89–91; Welch, *Electric Rhetoric*, 104–9, 184–87.

29. Lanham, *The Electronic Word*, 60.

30. Lanham, *The Electronic Word*, 61, 71, 112.

31. Bolter, *Writing Space*, 102–6.

32. Bolter, *Writing Space*, 203–8.

33. Welch, *Electric Rhetoric*, 104–5, 184–87.

34. Tuman, *Word Perfect*, 90–91.

35. Tuman, *Word Perfect*, 90–91.

36. Turkle, *Life on the Screen*, 217–18; Welch, *Electric Rhetoric*, 186, 188–89. Turkle, *Life on the Screen*, 217, describes *flaming* as "the practice of trading angry and often *ad hominem* remarks on any given topic." Welch, *Electric Rhetoric*, 186, noting that *flaming* is so frequently sexist and racist, labels it "*argumentum ad feminam et hominem.*"

37. Bolter, *Writing Space*, 107–9.

38. Bolter, *Writing Space*, 108–9.

39. Clifford, *The Predicament of Culture*, 21–54; Crapanzano, *Hermes' Dilemma and Hamlet's Desire*, 188–215; Dwyer, "Preface," *Moroccan Dialogues*, xv–xxiii; Hess, *Science in the New Age*, 13–16, 157–76; Mannheim and Tedlock, "Introduction," *The Dialogic Emergence of Culture*, 1–32; Marcus and Fischer, *Anthropology as Cultural Critique*, 17–76.

40. Clifford, *The Predicament of Culture*, 26–37; Mannheim and Tedlock, "Introduction," *The Dialogic Emergence of Culture*, 15; Marcus and Fischer, *Anthropology as Cultural Critique*, 54–57. Marcus and Fischer, *Anthropology as Cultural Critique*, 45–73, review a variety of psychodynamic, realist, and modernist (including dialogic) approaches to ethnography. Clifford, *The Predicament of Culture*, 21–54, contrasts experiential (scientific) and interpretive, dialogical, and polyphonic approaches.

41. Bakhtin, *Problems of Dostoevsky's Poetics*, 110–11; Clifford, *The Predicament of Culture*, 41–42, 46–47; Dwyer, "Preface," *Moroccan Dialogues*, xvi–xix; Hess, *Science in the New Age*, 160–61; Mannheim and Tedlock, "Introduction," *The Dialogic Emergence of Culture*, 15–16; Marcus and Fischer, *Anthropology as Cultural Critique*, 30–31.

42. Martin, *Flexible Bodies*, 227–50.

43. Bakhtin, *Problems of Dostoevsky's Poetics*, 73; Dwyer, *Moroccan Dialogues*.

44. Marcus and Fischer, *Anthropology as Cultural Critique*, 69–70.

45. Dwyer, "Preface," *Moroccan Dialogues*, xvii–xix.

46. Clifford, *The Predicament of Culture*, 43–44; Crapanzano, *Hermes' Dilemma and Hamlet's Desire*, 205–7.

47. Crapanzano, *Hermes' Dilemma and Hamlet's Desire*, 207.

48. Clifford, *The Predicament of Culture*, 41–42.

49. Clifford, *The Predicament of Culture*, 46–47.

50. Mannheim and Tedlock, "Introduction," *The Dialogic Emergence of Culture*, 15–16.

51. Mannheim and Tedlock, "Introduction," *The Dialogic Emergence of Culture*, 15–16, 34.

52. Hess, *Science in the New Age*, 15–16, 160–61, 167, 172.

53. Hess, *Science in the New Age*, 176.

54. Martin, *Flexible Bodies*, 143–44, 150, 158–59, 232–37.

55. Martin, *Flexible Bodies*, 14–16, 21–250.

56. Martin, *Flexible Bodies*, 21–63.

57. Martin, *Flexible Bodies*, 23–27.

58. Martin, *Flexible Bodies*, 29.

59. Martin, *Flexible Bodies*, 71–81, 88–90, 107–12.

60. Martin, *Flexible Bodies*, 14–16.

61. Martin, *Flexible Bodies*, 143–225.

62. Martin, *Flexible Bodies*, 236.

63. Martin, *Flexible Bodies*, 233.

64. Martin, *Flexible Bodies*, 249–50.

65. Bolter, *Writing Space*, 113–17; Bruckman, "Finding One's Own in Cyberspace"; Faigley, *Fragments of Rationality*, 163–99; Howard, *A Rhetoric of Electronic Communities*, 85–167; Kolko, "Bodies in Place"; Tuman, *Word Perfect*, 87–99; Turkle, *Life on the Screen*, 177–209, 255–69.

66. Faigley, *Fragments of Rationality*, 163–99; Howard, *A Rhetoric of Electronic Communities*, 85–167; Tuman, *Word Perfect*, 87–99.

67. Bolter, *Writing Space*, 116; Kolko, "Bodies in Place."

68. Bolter, *Writing Space*, 116; Kolko, "Bodies in Place," 262–63.

69. Zappen, Gurak, and Doheny-Farina, "Rhetoric, Community, and Cyberspace."

70. Turkle, *Life on the Screen*, 179–80, 185–86, 258–62, 268–69.

71. Bolter, *Writing Space*, 116.

72. Faigley, *Fragments of Rationality*, 167, 191.

73. Faigley, *Fragments of Rationality*, 182–83, 185.

74. Tuman, *Word Perfect*, 90–91

75. Tuman, *Word Perfect*, 91.

76. Faigley, *Fragments of Rationality*, 185; Tuman, *Word Perfect*, 91.

77. Howard, *A Rhetoric of Electronic Communities*, 101–48.

78. Howard, *A Rhetoric of Electronic Communities*, 150–55, 159–60.

79. Stallybrass and White, *The Politics and Poetics of Transgression*, 201.

80. Wills, "Upsetting the Public," 141.

81. Wills, "Upsetting the Public," 141, 149.

82. Faigley, *Fragments of Rationality*, 167.

83. Howard, *A Rhetoric of Electronic Communities*, 125–28, 138–45.

84. Howard, *A Rhetoric of Electronic Communities*, 160.

85. Kolko, "Bodies in Place," 262–63.

86. Kolko, "Bodies in Place," 262–63.

87. Kolko, "Bodies in Place," 262–63.

88. Zappen, Gurak, and Doheny-Farina, "Rhetoric, Community, and Cyberspace," 405–15.

89. Zappen, Gurak, and Doheny-Farina, "Rhetoric, Community, and Cyberspace," 406.

90. Zappen, Gurak, and Doheny-Farina, "Rhetoric, Community, and Cyberspace," 411–12.

91. Bruckman, "Finding One's Own in Cyberspace," 16–17, 19.

92. Bolter, *Writing Space*, 116–20, 205–8; Turkle, *Life on the Screen*, 258–59.

93. Doheny-Farina, *The Wired Neighborhood*, 79; Welch, *Electric Rhetoric*, 188–89.

94. Welch, *Electric Rhetoric*, 177–84, 186.

95. Epstein, "InteLnet."

96. Doheny-Farina, *The Wired Neighborhood*, 6–7.

97. Doheny-Farina, *The Wired Neighborhood*, 6–7, 15–16.

98. Adali, Harrison, and Zappen, "Connected Kids." The Connected Kids project is supported by the City of Troy; Rensselaer County; Academic and Research Computing, the School of Humanities and Social Sciences, and the School of Science at Rensselaer; the 3Com Urban Challenge Program; the National Science Foundation; Time Warner Cable; the Rubin Community Fellows Program; and private donors. This material is based upon work supported by the National Science Foundation under Grant No. 0091505. Any opinions, findings, and conclusions or recommendations expressed in this material are those of the author and do not necessarily reflect the views of the National Science Foundation.

99. Cushman, "The Rhetorician as an Agent of Social Change," 8–11.

100. Bakhtin, "Response to a Question from the *Novy Mir* Editorial Staff," 7; Epstein, *After the Future*, 298, 304.

101. Epstein, *After the Future*, 299.

102. Epstein, *After the Future*, 299.

103. Epstein, *After the Future*, 301.

104. Epstein, *After the Future*, 303.

105. Timchenko, "Transition," 139.

106. Epstein, "From Difference to Interference," 94.

107. Epstein, "Improvisational Community," 202.

108. Epstein, "Improvisational Community," 203.

109. Epstein, "InteLnet," 276–77.

110. Epstein, "The Interactive Anthology of Alternative Ideas," 298.

111. Epstein, "The Interactive Anthology of Alternative Ideas," 298.

112. Harrison and Zappen, "Methodological and Theoretical Frameworks for the Design of Community Information Systems." Bakhtin's contemporary Lev Vygotsky (1896–1934), in *Mind and Society* and *Thought and Language*, develops a sociocultural theory of language and cognition on principles similar to Bakhtin's. Wertsch, *Vygotsky and the Social Formation of Mind*, 224–30, finds parallels in Bakhtin's and Vygotsky's theories of language. Wells, *Dialogic Inquiry*, 21–25, explains some of the basic principles of Vygotsky's theory of cognition: that learning is based on interactions with others in mutual cooperative activity, that collaborative learning is more productive of positive outcomes than individual learning, and that learning is more productive if it is relevant to the learner's own purposes. Cole and Engeström, "A Cultural-Historical Approach to Distributed Cognition"; Engeström, "Innovative Learning in Work Teams"; Engeström and Miettinen, "Introduction," *Perspectives on Activity Theory*; and John-Steiner and Meehan, "Creativity and Collaboration in Knowledge Construction," among others, engage Vygotskyian principles to explain the dynamics of culturally situated creative problem-solving and design projects. Our data-gathering and participatory-design activities are based upon this work.

113. Tuthill, "Troy Housing Authority Narrows Digital Divide with Help from RPI," 20.

114. Hart-Davidson, Zappen, and Halloran, "On the Formation of Democratic Citizens," describe some of these collaborations.

115. Mutnick, "Through the Gates of the Chronotope."

Works Cited

Adali, Sibel, Teresa M. Harrison, and James P. Zappen. "Connected Kids: Community Information System Design and Development." In *Proceedings of the Second National Conference on Digital Government Research, May 20–22, 2002, Los Angeles, California*, 301–7. University of Southern California and Columbia University: Digital Government Research Center, 2002.

Adkins, Arthur W. H. *Merit and Responsibility: A Study in Greek Values*. Oxford: Clarendon Press, 1960.

Allen, R. E. "Comment." *The Apology*, by Plato. In *Euthyphro, Apology, Crito, Meno, Gorgias, Menexenus*, trans. R. E. Allen, 61–78. Vol. 1 of *The Dialogues of Plato*. New Haven, Connecticut: Yale University Press, 1984.

———. "Comment." *The Gorgias*, by Plato. In *Euthyphro, Apology, Crito, Meno, Gorgias, Menexenus*, trans. R. E. Allen, 189–230. Vol. 1 of *The Dialogues of Plato*. New Haven, Connecticut: Yale University Press, 1984.

———. "Comment." *The Protagoras*, by Plato. In *Ion, Hippias Minor, Laches, Protagoras*, trans. R. E. Allen, 89–168. Vol. 3 of *The Dialogues of Plato*. New Haven, Connecticut: Yale University Press, 1996.

———, trans. *The Gorgias*, by Plato. In *Euthyphro, Apology, Crito, Meno, Gorgias, Menexenus*, 231–316. Vol. 1 of *The Dialogues of Plato*. New Haven, Connecticut: Yale University Press, 1984.

———, trans. *The Protagoras*, by Plato. In *Ion, Hippias Minor, Laches, Protagoras*, 169–223. Vol. 3 of *The Dialogues of Plato*. New Haven, Connecticut: Yale University Press, 1996.

Annas, Julia. *An Introduction to Plato's "Republic."* Oxford: Clarendon Press, 1981.

Aristotle. *The "Art" of Rhetoric*. Trans. John Henry Freese. Loeb Classical Library, vol. 193. London: William Heinemann, 1926.

———. *The Metaphysics*. In *The Metaphysics*, trans. Hugh Tredennick; *The Oeconomica* and *The Magna Moralia*, trans. G. Cyril Armstrong, 1:1–473; 2:1–320. 2 vols. Loeb Classical Library. London: William Heinemann, 1933; Cambridge, Massachusetts: Harvard University Press, 1935.

———. *On Rhetoric: A Theory of Civic Discourse*. Trans. George A. Kennedy. New York: Oxford University Press, 1991.

———. *Topica*. In *Posterior Analytics*, trans. Hugh Tredennick; *Topica*, trans. E. S. Forster, 263–739. Loeb Classical Library, vol. 391. London: William Heinemann, 1960.

Bakhtin, M[ikhail]. M. "Author and Hero in Aesthetic Activity." In *Art and Answerability: Early Philosophical Essays*, ed. Michael Holquist and Vadim Liapunov, trans. Vadim Liapunov, 4–256. University of Texas Press Slavic Studies, no. 9. Austin: University of Texas Press, 1990.

———. "Discourse in the Novel." In *The Dialogic Imagination: Four Essays*, ed. Michael Holquist, trans. Caryl Emerson and Michael Holquist, 259–422. University of Texas Press Slavic Series, no. 1. Austin: University of Texas Press, 1981.

———. "Epic and Novel: Toward a Methodology for the Study of the Novel." In *The Dialogic Imagination: Four Essays*, ed. Michael Holquist, trans. Caryl Emerson and Michael Holquist, 3–40. University of Texas Press Slavic Series, no. 1. Austin: University of Texas Press, 1981.

———. "From Notes Made in 1970–71." In *Speech Genres and Other Late Essays*, ed. Caryl Emerson and Michael Holquist, trans. Vern W. McGee, 132–58. University of Texas Press Slavic Series, no. 8. Austin: University of Texas Press, 1986.

———. *Problems of Dostoevsky's Poetics*. Ed. and trans. Caryl Emerson. Theory and History of Literature, vol. 8. Minneapolis: University of Minnesota Press, 1984.

———. "The Problem of Speech Genres." In *Speech Genres and Other Late Essays*, ed. Caryl Emerson and Michael Holquist, trans. Vern W. McGee, 60–102. University of Texas Press Slavic Series, no. 8. Austin: University of Texas Press, 1986.

———. *Rabelais and His World*. Trans. Hélène Iswolsky. 1968. Reprint, Bloomington: Indiana University Press, Midland Book, 1984.

———. "Response to a Question from the *Novy Mir* Editorial Staff." In *Speech Genres and Other Late Essays*, ed. Caryl Emerson and Michael Holquist, trans. Vern W. McGee, 1–9. University of Texas Press Slavic Series, no. 8. Austin: University of Texas Press, 1986.

———. "Toward a Methodology for the Human Sciences." In *Speech Genres and Other Late Essays*, ed. Caryl Emerson and Michael Holquist, trans. Vern W. McGee, 159–72. University of Texas Press Slavic Series, no. 8. Austin: University of Texas Press, 1986.

———. *Toward a Philosophy of the Act*. Ed. Vadim Liapunov and Michael Holquist. Trans. Vadim Liapunov. University of Texas Press Slavic Series, no. 10. Austin: University of Texas, 1993.

Batstone, William W. "Catullus and Bakhtin: The Problems of a Dialogic Lyric." In *Bakhtin and the Classics*, ed. R. Bracht Branham, 99–136. Rethinking Theory. Evanston, Illinois: Northwestern University Press, 2002.

Benardete, Seth. *The Rhetoric of Morality and Philosophy: Plato's "Gorgias" and "Phaedrus."* Chicago: University of Chicago Press, 1991.

Bender, John, and David E. Wellbery. "Rhetoricality: On the Modernist Return of Rhetoric." In *The Ends of Rhetoric: History, Theory, Practice*, ed. John Bender and David E. Wellbery, 3–39. Stanford, California: Stanford University Press, 1990.

Benitez, Eugenio. "Argument, Rhetoric, and Philosophic Method: Plato's *Protagoras.*" *Philosophy and Rhetoric* 25 (1992): 222–52.

Benson, Hugh H. "Editor's Introduction." In *Essays on the Philosophy of Socrates*, ed. Hugh H. Benson, 3–13. New York: Oxford University Press, 1992.

Berman, Scott. "How Polus Was Refuted: Reconsidering Plato's *Gorgias* 474c–475c." *Ancient Philosophy* 11 (1991): 265–84.

Bhabha, Homi K. "The Commitment to Theory." In *The Location of Culture*, 19–39. London: Routledge, 1994.

———. "Sly Civility." In *The Location of Culture*, 93–101. London: Routledge, 1994.

Bialostosky, Don [H]. "Bakhtin and the Future of Rhetorical Criticism: A Response to Halasek and Bernard-Donals." In *Landmark Essays on Bakhtin, Rhetoric, and Writing*, ed. Frank Farmer, 111–17. Landmark Essays, vol. 13. Mahwah, New Jersey: Lawrence Erlbaum Associates, Hermagoras Press, 1998.

———. "Bakhtin's 'Rough Draft': *Toward a Philosophy of the Act*, Ethics, and Composition Studies." *Rhetoric Review* 18 (1999): 6–25.

———. "Dialogics as an Art of Discourse in Literary Criticism." *Publications of the Modern Language Association* 101 (1986): 788–97.

Bolter, Jay David. *Writing Space: Computers, Hypertext, and the Remediation of Print.* 2nd ed. Mahwah, New Jersey: Lawrence Erlbaum Associates, 2001.

Bowra, C. M. *Greek Lyric Poetry: From Alcman to Simonides.* Oxford: Clarendon Press, 1961.

Brandwood, Leonard. *A Word Index to Plato.* Leeds, England: W. S. Maney and Son, 1976.

Brickhouse, Thomas C., and Nicholas D. Smith. *Plato's Socrates.* New York: Oxford University Press, 1994.

———. *Socrates on Trial.* Princeton, New Jersey: Princeton University Press, 1989.

Bruckman, Amy. "Finding One's Own in Cyberspace." In *High Wired: On the Design, Use, and Theory of Educational MOOs*, ed. Cynthia Haynes and Jan Rune Holmevik, 15–24. Ann Arbor: University of Michigan Press, 1998.

Buber, Martin. *I and Thou.* Trans. Walter Kaufmann. New York: Simon and Schuster, Touchstone Book, 1970.

Burnyeat, Myles F. "Socratic Midwifery, Platonic Inspiration." In *Essays on the Philosophy of Socrates*, ed. Hugh H. Benson, 53–65. New York: Oxford University Press, 1992.

Bury, J. B. *A History of Greece to the Death of Alexander the Great.* 3rd ed. London: Macmillan and Company, 1951.

Cherwitz, Richard A., and James W. Hikins. "John Stuart Mill's Doctrine of Assurance as a Rhetorical Epistemology." In *Explorations in Rhetoric: Studies in Honor of Douglas Ehninger*, ed. Ray E. McKerrow, 69–84. Glenview, Illinois: Scott, Foresman and Company, 1982.

———. "John Stuart Mill's *On Liberty*: Implications for the Epistemology of the New Rhetoric." *Quarterly Journal of Speech* 65 (1979): 12–24.

Cissna, Kenneth N., and Rob Anderson, "Theorizing about Dialogic Moments: The Buber-Rogers Position and Postmodern Themes." *Communication Theory* 8 (1998): 63–104.

City of Troy Consolidated Plan 2000. Troy, New York: City of Troy, 2000.

Clark, Allen. "Martin Buber, Dialogue, and the Philosophy of Rhetoric." In *Philosophers on Rhetoric: Traditional and Emerging Views*, ed. Donald G. Douglas, 225–42. Skokie, Illinois: National Textbook Company, 1973.

Clark, Katerina, and Michael Holquist. *Mikhail Bakhtin*. Cambridge, Massachusetts: Harvard University Press, Belknap Press, 1984.

Clifford, James. *The Predicament of Culture: Twentieth-Century Ethnography, Literature, and Art*. Cambridge, Massachusetts: Harvard University Press, 1988.

Cole, Michael, and Yrjö Engeström. "A Cultural-Historical Approach to Distributed Cognition." In *Distributed Cognitions: Psychological and Educational Considerations*, ed. Gavriel Salomon, 1–46. Learning in Doing: Social, Cognitive, and Computational Perspectives. Cambridge: Cambridge University Press, 1993.

Conley, Thomas M. *Rhetoric in the European Tradition*. New York: Longman, 1990.

Connor, W. Robert. *Thucydides*. Princeton, New Jersey: Princeton University Press, 1984.

Côté, Jean-François. "Bakhtin's Dialogism Reconsidered through Hegel's 'Monologism': The Dialectical Foundation of Aesthetics and Ideology in Contemporary Human Sciences." In *Materializing Bakhtin: The Bakhtin Circle and Social Theory*, ed. Craig Brandist and Galin Tihanov, 20–42. St. Antony's Series. London: Macmillan Press, 2000.

Crapanzano, Vincent. *Hermes' Dilemma and Hamlet's Desire: On the Epistemology of Interpretation*. Cambridge, Massachusetts: Harvard University Press, 1992.

Culler, Jonathan. *On Deconstruction: Theory and Criticism after Structuralism*. Ithaca, New York: Cornell University Press, 1982; Cornell Paperbacks, 1983.

Cushman, Ellen. "The Rhetorician as an Agent of Social Change." *College Composition and Communication* 47 (1996): 7–28.

Cushman, Robert E. *Therapeia: Plato's Conception of Philosophy*. Chapel Hill: University of North Carolina Press, 1958.

Czubaroff, Jeanine. "Dialogical Rhetoric: An Application of Martin Buber's Philosophy of Dialogue." *Quarterly Journal of Speech* 86 (2000): 168–89.

De Romilly, Jacqueline. *Thucydides and Athenian Imperialism*. Trans. Philip Thody. Oxford: Basil Blackwell, 1963. Reprint, Salem, New Hampshire: Ayer Company Publishers, 1988.

De Strycker, E. *Plato's Apology of Socrates: A Literary and Philosophical Study with a Running Commentary*. Ed. and completed by S. R. Slings. Mnemosyne: Bibliotheca Classica Batava. Leiden, The Netherlands: E. J. Brill, 1994.

Dentith, Simon. "Bakhtin and Contemporary Criticism." In *Bakhtinian Thought: An Introductory Reader*, 88–102, 104. Critical Readers in Theory and Practice. London: Routledge, 1995.

———. "Bakhtin versus Rhetoric?" In *Face to Face: Bakhtin in Russia and the West*, ed. Carol Adlam, Rachel Falconer, Vitalii Makhlin, and Alastair Renfrew, 311–25. Sheffield, England: Academic Press, 1997.

———. "Bakhtin's Carnival." In *Bakhtinian Thought: An Introductory Reader*, 65–87, 103–4. Critical Readers in Theory and Practice. London: Routledge, 1995.

Derrida, Jacques. "Plato's Pharmacy." In *Dissemination*, trans. Barbara Johnson, 61–171. Chicago: University of Chicago Press, 1981.

———. *The Post Card: From Socrates to Freud and Beyond*. Trans. Alan Bass. Chicago: University of Chicago Press, 1987.

Devereux, Daniel T. "Courage and Wisdom in Plato's *Laches*." *Journal of the History of Philosophy* 15 (1977): 129–41.

———. "The Unity of the Virtues in Plato's *Protagoras* and *Laches*." *Philosophical Review* 101 (1992): 765–89.

Dodds, E. R. "Commentary." In *Gorgias*, by Plato, 188–386. Oxford: Clarendon Press, 1959; Clarendon Paperback, 1990.

———. "Introduction." In *Gorgias*, by Plato, 1–67. Oxford: Clarendon Press, 1959; Clarendon Paperback, 1990.

Doheny-Farina, Stephen. *The Wired Neighborhood*. New Haven, Connecticut: Yale University Press, 1996.

Dwyer, Kevin. *Moroccan Dialogues: Anthropology in Question*. 1982. Reprint, Prospect Heights, Illinois: Waveland Press, 1987.

———. "Preface." In *Moroccan Dialogues: Anthropology in Question*, xv–xxiii. 1982. Reprint, Prospect Heights, Illinois: Waveland Press, 1987.

Eagleton, Terry. *Walter Benjamin or Towards a Revolutionary Criticism*. London: Verso, 1981.

Edwards, Anthony T. "Historicizing the Popular Grotesque: Bakhtin's *Rabelais and His World* and Attic Old Comedy." In *Bakhtin and the Classics*, ed. R. Bracht Branham, 27–55. Rethinking Theory. Evanston, Illinois: Northwestern University Press, 2002.

Emerson, Caryl. *The First Hundred Years of Mikhail Bakhtin*. Princeton, New Jersey: Princeton University Press, 1997.

———. "The Next Hundred Years of Mikhail Bakhtin (The View from the Classroom)." *Rhetoric Review* 19 (2000): 12–27.

Emerson, Caryl, and Michael Holquist. "Glossary." In *The Dialogic Imagination: Four Essays*, ed. Michael Holquist, trans. Caryl Emerson and Michael Holquist,

423–34. University of Texas Press Slavic Series, no. 1. Austin: University of Texas Press, 1981.

Engeström, Yrjö. "Innovative Learning in Work Teams: Analyzing Cycles of Knowledge Creation in Practice." In *Perspectives on Activity Theory*, ed. Yrjö Engeström, Reijo Miettinen, and Raija-Leena Punamäki, 377–404. Learning in Doing: Social, Cognitive, and Computational Perspectives. Cambridge: Cambridge University Press, 1999.

Engeström, Yrjö, and Reijo Miettinen. "Introduction." In *Perspectives on Activity Theory*, ed. Yrjö Engeström, Reijo Miettinen, and Raija-Leena Punamäki, 1–16. Learning in Doing: Social, Cognitive, and Computational Perspectives. Cambridge: Cambridge University Press, 1999.

Enos, Richard Leo. *Greek Rhetoric before Aristotle*. Prospect Heights, Illinois: Waveland Press, 1993.

Epstein, Mikhail N. *After the Future: The Paradoxes of Postmodernism and Contemporary Russian Culture*. Trans. Anesa Miller-Pogacar. Critical Perspectives on Modern Culture. Amherst: University of Massachusetts Press, 1995.

———. "From Difference to Interference." In *Transcultural Experiments: Russian and American Models of Creative Communication*, by Ellen E. Berry and Mikhail N. Epstein, 91–101. New York: St. Martin's Press, 1999.

———. "Improvisational Community." In *Transcultural Experiments: Russian and American Models of Creative Communication*, by Ellen E. Berry and Mikhail N. Epstein, 201–13. New York: St. Martin's Press, 1999.

———. "InteLnet: Web Projects in the Humanities." In *Transcultural Experiments: Russian and American Models of Creative Communication*, by Ellen E. Berry and Mikhail N. Epstein, 276–89. New York: St. Martin's Press, 1999.

———. "The Interactive Anthology of Alternative Ideas: An Introduction." In *Transcultural Experiments: Russian and American Models of Creative Communication*, by Ellen E. Berry and Mikhail N. Epstein, 290–301. New York: St. Martin's Press, 1999.

Evans, J. D. G. *Aristotle's Concept of Dialectic*. Cambridge: Cambridge University Press, 1977.

Faigley, Lester. *Fragments of Rationality: Postmodernity and the Subject of Composition*. Pittsburgh Series in Composition, Literacy, and Culture. Pittsburgh: University of Pittsburgh Press, 1992.

Farmer, Frank. *Saying and Silence: Listening to Composition with Bakhtin*. Logan: Utah State University Press, 2001.

Farrell, Thomas B. *Norms of Rhetorical Culture*. New Haven, Connecticut: Yale University Press, 1993.

Ferejohn , Michael T. "The Unity of Virtue and the Objects of Socratic Inquiry." *Journal of the History of Philosophy* 20 (1982): 1–21.

Fine, John V. A. *The Ancient Greeks: A Critical History*. Cambridge, Massachusetts: Harvard University Press, Belknap Press, 1983.

Friedländer, Paul. *The Dialogues: First Period*, trans. Hans Meyerhoff. Vol. 2 of *Plato*. Bollingen Series, vol. 59, no. 2. New York: Random House, Pantheon Books, 1964.

————. *The Dialogues: Second and Third Periods*, trans. Hans Meyerhoff. Vol. 3 of *Plato*. Bollingen Series, vol. 59, no. 3. New York: Random House, Pantheon Books, 1969.

Friedman, Maurice. "Martin Buber and the Theater." In *Martin Buber and the Theater*, ed. and trans. Maurice Friedman, 3–25. New York: Funk and Wagnalls, 1969.

Fussi, Alessandra. "Why Is the *Gorgias* so Bitter?" *Philosophy and Rhetoric* 33 (2000): 39–58.

Gadamer, Hans-Georg. *Dialogue and Dialectic: Eight Hermeneutical Essays on Plato*. Trans. P. Christopher Smith. New Haven, Connecticut: Yale University Press, 1980.

————. *Truth and Method*. Trans. Joel Weinsheimer and Donald G. Marshall. 2nd, rev. ed. New York: Crossroad Publishing Corporation, 1990.

Gagarin, Michael. "Did the Sophists Aim to Persuade?" *Rhetorica: A Journal of the History of Rhetoric* 19 (2001): 275–91.

Gardiner, Michael. "'A Very Understandable Horror of Dialectics': Bakhtin and Marxist Phenomenology." In *Materializing Bakhtin: The Bakhtin Circle and Social Theory*, ed. Craig Brandist and Galin Tihanov, 119–41. St. Antony's Series. London: Macmillan Press, 2000.

Gosling, J. C. B., and C. C. W. Taylor. *The Greeks on Pleasure*. Oxford: Clarendon Press, 1982.

Griswold, Charles L. Jr. "Plato's Metaphilosophy: Why Plato Wrote Dialogues." In *Platonic Writings, Platonic Readings*, ed. Charles L. Griswold Jr., 143–67, 286–93. New York: Routledge, 1988.

————. *Self-Knowledge in Plato's "Phaedrus."* New Haven, Connecticut: Yale University Press, 1986.

Grote, George. *A History of Greece: From the Earliest Period to the Close of the Generation Contemporary with Alexander the Great*. New ed. Vol. 8. London: John Murray, 1884.

Gulley, Norman. *The Philosophy of Socrates*. London: Macmillan and Company, 1968.

Guthrie, W. K. C. *The Fifth-Century Enlightenment*. Vol. 3 of *A History of Greek Philosophy*. Cambridge: Cambridge University Press, 1969.

————. "Introduction." In *"Protagoras" and "Meno,"* trans. W. K. C. Guthrie, 7–25. Penguin Classics. London: Penguin Books, 1956.

Halasek, Kay. *A Pedagogy of Possibility: Bakhtinian Perspectives on Composition Studies*. Carbondale: Southern Illinois University Press, 1999.

————. "Starting the Dialogue: What Can We Do about Bakhtin's Ambivalence toward Rhetoric?" In *Landmark Essays on Bakhtin, Rhetoric, and Writing*, ed. Frank

Farmer, 97–105. Landmark Essays, vol. 13. Mahwah, New Jersey: Lawrence Erlbaum Associates, Hermagoras Press, 1998.

Harpold, Terence. "The Grotesque Corpus: Hypertext as Carnival." *Perforations* 1 (1992): 1–8.

Harris, R. Allen. "Bakhtin, *Phaedrus*, and the Geometry of Rhetoric." In *Landmark Essays on Bakhtin, Rhetoric, and Writing*, ed. Frank Farmer, 15–22. Landmark Essays, vol. 13. Mahwah, New Jersey: Lawrence Erlbaum Associates, Hermagoras Press, 1998.

Harrison, Teresa M., and James P. Zappen. "Methodological and Theoretical Frameworks for the Design of Community Information Systems." *Journal of Computer-Mediated Communication* 8, no. 3 (2003).

Hart-Davidson, William, James P. Zappen, and S. Michael Halloran. "On the Formation of Democratic Citizens: Rethinking the Rhetorical Tradition in a Digital Age." In *Viability of the Rhetorical Tradition*, ed. Richard Graff, Arthur Walzer, and Janet Atwill. Albany: State University of New York Press. Forthcoming.

Havelock, Eric A. *The Greek Concept of Justice: From Its Shadow in Homer to its Substance in Plato*. Cambridge, Massachusetts: Harvard University Press, 1978.

———. *The Liberal Temper in Greek Politics*. New Haven, Connecticut: Yale University Press, 1957.

———. *Preface to Plato*. Cambridge, Massachusetts: Harvard University Press, Belknap Press, 1963.

Hemmenway, Scott R. "Sophistry Exposed: Socrates on the Unity of Virtue in the *Protagoras*." *Ancient Philosophy* 16 (1996): 1–23.

Hess, David J. *Science in the New Age: The Paranormal, Its Defenders and Debunkers, and American Culture*. Science and Literature. Madison: University of Wisconsin Press, 1993.

Holquist, Michael. *Dialogism: Bakhtin and His World*. New Accents. London: Routledge, 1990.

———. "Introduction." In *The Dialogic Imagination: Four Essays*, ed. Michael Holquist, trans. Caryl Emerson and Michael Holquist, xv–xxxiii. University of Texas Press Slavic Series, no. 1. Austin: University of Texas Press, 1981.

———. "Introduction." In *Speech Genres and Other Late Essays*, ed. Caryl Emerson and Michael Holquist, trans. Vern W. McGee, ix–xxiii. University of Texas Press Slavic Series, no. 8. Austin: University of Texas Press, 1986.

Hornblower, Simon. *The Greek World 479–323 BC*. Rev. ed. Routledge History of the Ancient World. London: Routledge, 1991.

Howard, Tharon W. *A Rhetoric of Electronic Communities*. New Directions in Computer and Composition Studies. Greenwich, Connecticut: Ablex Publishing Corporation, 1997.

Hyland, Drew A. "Why Plato Wrote Dialogues." *Philosophy and Rhetoric* 1 (1968): 38–50.

The Iliad. Ed. David B. Monro and Thomas W. Allen. 3rd ed. Vols. 1 and 2 of *Homer's Works.* Oxford Library of Classical Texts. Oxford: Clarendon Press, n.d.

The Iliad of Homer. Trans. Richmond Lattimore. Chicago: University of Chicago Press, 1951; Phoenix Book, 1961.

Irwin, Terence. *Classical Thought.* Vol. 1 of *A History of Western Philosophy.* Oxford: Oxford University Press, Opus Book, 1989.

———. "Notes." In *Gorgias,* by Plato, trans. Terence Irwin, 109–250. Clarendon Plato Series. Oxford: Clarendon Press, 1979.

———. *Plato's Ethics.* New York: Oxford University Press, 1995.

Jaeger, Werner. *Archaic Greece: The Mind of Athens.* Trans. Gilbert Highet. 2nd ed. Vol. 1 of *Paideia: The Ideals of Greek Culture.* New York: Oxford University Press, 1945.

———. *In Search of the Divine Centre.* Trans. Gilbert Highet. Vol. 2 of *Paideia: The Ideals of Greek Culture.* New York: Oxford University Press, 1943.

Jasinski, James. "Heteroglossia, Polyphony, and *The Federalist Papers.*" *Rhetoric Society Quarterly* 27 (1997): 23–46.

John-Steiner, Vera P., and Teresa M. Meehan. "Creativity and Collaboration in Knowledge Construction." In *Vygotskian Perspectives on Literacy Research: Constructing Meaning through Collaborative Inquiry,* ed. Carol D. Lee and Peter Smagorinsky, 31–48. Learning in Doing: Social, Cognitive, and Computational Perspectives. Cambridge: Cambridge University Press, 2000.

Kahn, Charles H. "Did Plato Write Socratic Dialogues?" In *Essays on the Philosophy of Socrates,* ed. Hugh H. Benson, 35–52. New York: Oxford University Press, 1992.

———. "Drama and Dialectic in Plato's *Gorgias.*" *Oxford Studies in Ancient Philosophy* 1 (1983): 75–121.

———. "On the Relative Date of the *Gorgias* and the *Protagoras.*" *Oxford Studies in Ancient Philosophy* 6 (1988): 69–102.

———. *Plato and the Socratic Dialogue: The Philosophical Use of a Literary Form.* Cambridge: Cambridge University Press, 1996.

Kameen, Paul. *Writing/Teaching: Essays toward a Rhetoric of Pedagogy.* Pittsburgh Series in Composition, Literacy, and Culture. Pittsburgh: University of Pittsburgh Press, 2000.

Kastely, James L. "Respecting the Rupture: Not Solving the Problem of Unity in Plato's *Phaedrus.*" *Philosophy and Rhetoric* 35 (2002): 138–52.

Kaufmann, Walter. "Nietzsche's Attitude toward Socrates." In *Nietzsche: A Critical Reader,* ed. Peter R. Sedgwick, 123–43. Blackwell Critical Readers. Oxford: Blackwell Publishers, 1995.

Kenez, Peter. *A History of the Soviet Union from the Beginning to the End.* Cambridge: Cambridge University Press, 1999.

Kennedy, George [A.] *The Art of Persuasion in Greece.* Princeton, New Jersey: Princeton University Press, 1963.

———. *Classical Rhetoric and Its Christian and Secular Tradition from Ancient to Modern Times*. 2nd ed., rev. Chapel Hill: University of North Carolina Press, 1999.

Kent, Thomas. "Hermeneutics and Genre: Bakhtin and the Problem of Communicative Interaction." In *Landmark Essays on Bakhtin, Rhetoric, and Writing*, ed. Frank Farmer, 33–49. Landmark Essays, vol. 13. Mahwah, New Jersey: Lawrence Erlbaum Associates, Hermagoras Press, 1998.

Kerferd, G. B. *The Sophistic Movement*. Cambridge: Cambridge University Press, 1981.

Kierkegaard, Søren. *The Concept of Irony with Continual Reference to Socrates*. Ed. and trans. Howard V. Hong and Edna H. Hong. Vol. 2 of *Kierkegaard's Writings*. Princeton, New Jersey: Princeton University Press, 1989.

Kolko, Beth. "Bodies in Place: Real Politics, Real Pedagogy, and Virtual Space." In *High Wired: On the Design, Use, and Theory of Educational MOOs*, ed. Cynthia Haynes and Jan Rune Holmevik, 253–65. Ann Arbor: University of Michigan Press, 1998.

Kraut, Richard. *Socrates and the State*. Princeton, New Jersey: Princeton University Press, 1984.

Kristeva, Julia. *Desire in Language: A Semiotic Approach to Literature and Art*. Ed. Leon S. Roudiez. Trans. Thomas Gora, Alice Jardine, and Leon S. Roudiez. New York: Columbia University Press, 1980.

———. *Revolution in Poetic Language*. Trans. Margaret Waller. New York: Columbia University Press, 1984.

Lanham, Richard A. *The Electronic Word: Democracy, Technology, and the Arts*. Chicago: University of Chicago Press, 1993.

Leitch, Vincent B. *Deconstructive Criticism: An Advanced Introduction*. New York: Columbia University Press, 1983.

Liddell, Henry George, and Robert Scott. *A Greek-English Lexicon*. http://www.perseus.tufts.edu/, May 18, 2003.

Lowe, E. J. "What *Is* the 'Problem of Induction'?" *Philosophy* 62 (1987): 325–40.

Mailloux, Steven. *Reception Histories: Rhetoric, Pragmatism, and American Cultural Politics*. Ithaca, New York: Cornell University Press, 1998.

Mannheim, Bruce, and Dennis Tedlock. "Introduction." In *The Dialogic Emergence of Culture*, ed. Dennis Tedlock and Bruce Mannheim, 1–32. Urbana: University of Illinois Press, 1995.

Maranhão, Tullio. *Therapeutic Discourse and Socratic Dialogue*. Rhetoric of the Human Sciences. Madison: University of Wisconsin Press, 1986.

Marcus, George E., and Michael M. J. Fischer. *Anthropology as Cultural Critique: An Experimental Moment in the Human Sciences*. Chicago: University of Chicago Press, 1986.

The Martin Buber-Carl Rogers Dialogue: A New Transcript with Commentary. Transcribed by Rob Anderson and Kenneth N. Cissna. State University of New York

Series in Speech Communication. Albany: State University of New York Press, 1997.

Martin, Emily. *Flexible Bodies: Tracking Immunity in American Culture—From the Days of Polio to the Age of AIDS*. Boston: Beacon Press, 1994.

Martin, Thomas R. *Ancient Greece: From Prehistoric to Hellenistic Times*. New Haven, Connecticut: Yale University Press, 1996.

McCoy, Marina Berzins. "Protagoras on Human Nature, Wisdom, and the Good: The Great Speech and the Hedonism of Plato's *Protagoras*." *Ancient Philosophy* 18 (1998): 21–39.

———. "Socrates on Simonides: The Use of Poetry in Socratic and Platonic Rhetoric." *Philosophy and Rhetoric* 32 (1999): 349–67.

McRae, R. F. "Introduction." In *A System of Logic Ratiocinative and Inductive: Being a Connected View of the Principles of Evidence and the Methods of Scientific Investigation*, by John Stuart Mill, ed. J. M. Robson, xxi–xlviii. Vols. 7 and 8 of *Collected Works of John Stuart Mill*. Toronto: University of Toronto Press, 1974.

Meyer, Michel. "Dialectic and Questioning: Socrates and Plato." *American Philosophical Quarterly* 17 (1980): 281–89.

———. *Rhetoric, Language, and Reason*. Literature and Philosophy. University Park: Pennsylvania State University Press, 1994.

Mihailovic, Alexandar. *Corporeal Words: Mikhail Bakhtin's Theology of Discourse*. Studies in Russian Literature and Theory. Evanston, Illinois: Northwestern University Press, 1997.

Mill, John Stuart. "Grote's History of Greece [5]." In *Newspaper Writings: December 1847–July 1873*, ed. Ann P. Robson and John M. Robson, 1157–64. Vol. 25 of *Collected Works of John Stuart Mill*. Toronto: University of Toronto Press, 1986.

———. "On Liberty." In *Essays on Politics and Society*, ed. J. M. Robson, 213–310. Vol. 18 of *Collected Works of John Stuart Mill*. Toronto: University of Toronto Press, 1977.

———. *A System of Logic Ratiocinative and Inductive: Being a Connected View of the Principles of Evidence and the Methods of Scientific Investigation*. Ed. J. M. Robson. Vols. 7 and 8 of *Collected Works of John Stuart Mill*. Toronto: University of Toronto Press, 1974.

Miller, J. Hillis. "Stevens' Rock and Criticism as Cure, II." *Georgia Review* 30 (1976): 330–48.

Moore-Gilbert, Bart. *Postcolonial Theory: Contexts, Practices, Politics*. London: Verso, 1997.

Morson, Gary Saul. "Parody, History, and Metaparody." In *Rethinking Bakhtin: Extensions and Challenges*, ed. Gary Saul Morson and Caryl Emerson, 63–86, 271–74. Northwestern University Press Series in Russian Literature and Theory. Evanston, Illinois: Northwestern University Press, 1989.

Morson, Gary Saul, and Caryl Emerson. *Mikhail Bakhtin: Creation of a Prosaics*. Stanford, California: Stanford University Press, 1990.

Murphy, John M. "Mikhail Bakhtin and the Rhetorical Tradition." *Quarterly Journal of Speech* 87 (2001): 259–77.

Murray, James S. "Disputation, Deception, and Dialectic: Plato on the True Rhetoric (*Phaedrus* 261–266)." *Philosophy and Rhetoric* 21 (1988): 279–89.

Mutnick, Deborah. "Through the Gates of the Chronotope: Bakhtin and Composition Studies." Paper presented at the Bakhtin, Vygotsky, Composition, and Rhetoric Special Interest Group of the Conference on College Composition and Communication, New York, March 21, 2003.

Nagy, Gregory. *The Best of the Achaeans: Concepts of the Hero in Archaic Greek Poetry*. Rev. ed. Baltimore: Johns Hopkins University Press, 1999.

———. "Reading Bakhtin Reading the Classics: An Epic Fate for Conveyors of the Heroic Past." In *Bakhtin and the Classics*, ed. R. Bracht Branham, 71–96. Rethinking Theory. Evanston, Illinois: Northwestern University Press, 2002.

Neel, Jasper. *Plato, Derrida, and Writing*. Carbondale: Southern Illinois University Press, 1988.

Nightingale, Andrea Wilson. *Genres in Dialogue: Plato and the Construct of Philosophy*. Cambridge: Cambridge University Press, 1995.

———. "Toward an Ecological Eschatology: Plato and Bakhtin on Other Worlds and Times." In *Bakhtin and the Classics*, ed. R. Bracht Branham, 220–49. Rethinking Theory. Evanston, Illinois: Northwestern University Press, 2002.

Norris, Christopher. *Derrida*. Cambridge, Massachusetts: Harvard University Press, 1987.

North, Helen. *Sophrosyne: Self-Knowledge and Self-Restraint in Greek Literature*. Cornell Studies in Classical Philology, vol. 35. Ithaca, New York: Cornell University Press, 1966

Ober, Josiah. *Mass and Elite in Democratic Athens: Rhetoric, Ideology, and the Power of the People*. Princeton, New Jersey: Princeton University Press, 1989.

O'Brien, Michael J. *The Socratic Paradoxes and the Greek Mind*. Chapel Hill: University of North Carolina Press, 1967.

———. "The Unity of the *Laches*." In *Essays in Ancient Greek Philosophy*, ed. John P. Anton with George L. Kustas, 303–15. Albany: State University of New York Press, 1971.

The Odyssey. Ed. Thomas W. Allen. Rev. ed. Vols. 3 and 4 of *Homer's Works*. Oxford Library of Classical Texts. Oxford: Clarendon Press, n.d.

The Odyssey of Homer. Trans. Richmond Lattimore. New York: Harper and Row, 1965; Harper Colophon Books, 1975.

Ostwald, Martin. *From Popular Sovereignty to the Sovereignty of Law: Law, Society, and Politics in Fifth-Century Athens*. Berkeley: University of California Press, 1986.

Penner, Terry. "Socrates and the Early Dialogues." In *The Cambridge Companion to Plato*, ed. Richard Kraut, 121–69. Cambridge Companions. Cambridge: Cambridge University Press, 1992.

———. "The Unity of Virtue." In *Essays on the Philosophy of Socrates*, ed. Hugh H. Benson, 162–84. New York: Oxford University Press, 1992.

———. "What Laches and Nicias Miss—And Whether Socrates Thinks Courage Merely a Part of Virtue." *Ancient Philosophy* 12 (1992): 1–27.

Perlina, Nina. "A Dialogue on the Dialogue: The Baxtin-Vinogradov Exchange (1924–65)." *Slavic and East European Journal* 32 (1988): 526–41.

Plato. *Apology*. In *Euthyphro, Apology, Crito, Phaedo, Phaedrus*, trans. Harold North Fowler, 61–145. Vol. 1 of *Plato*. Loeb Classical Library, vol. 36. Cambridge, Massachusetts: Harvard University Press, 1914.

———. *Gorgias*. In *Lysis, Symposium, Gorgias*, trans. W. R. M. Lamb, 247–533. Vol. 3 of *Plato*. Loeb Classical Library, vol. 166. Cambridge, Massachusetts: Harvard University Press, 1925.

———. *Laches*. In *Laches, Protagoras, Meno, Euthydemus*, trans. W. R. M. Lamb, 1–83. Vol. 2 of *Plato*. Loeb Classical Library, vol. 165. Cambridge, Massachusetts: Harvard University Press, 1924.

———. *Phaedrus*. In *Euthyphro, Apology, Crito, Phaedo, Phaedrus*, trans. Harold North Fowler, 405–579. Vol. 1 of *Plato*. Loeb Classical Library, vol. 36. Cambridge, Massachusetts: Harvard University Press, 1914.

———. *Philebus*. In *The Statesman, Philebus*, trans. Harold North Fowler; *Ion*, trans. W. R. M. Lamb, 197–399. Vol. 8 of *Plato*. Loeb Classical Library, vol. 164. Cambridge, Massachusetts: Harvard University Press, 1925.

———. *Protagoras*. In *Laches, Protagoras, Meno, Euthydemus*, trans. W. R. M. Lamb, 85–257. Vol. 2 of *Plato*. Loeb Classical Library, vol. 165. Cambridge, Massachusetts: Harvard University Press, 1924.

———. *The Republic*. Trans. Paul Shorey. Vols. 5, rev. ed., and 6 of *Plato*. Loeb Classical Library, vols. 237 and 276. Cambridge, Massachusetts: Harvard University Press, 1930 (rev. 1937), 1935.

———. *The Statesman*. In *The Statesman, Philebus*, trans. Harold North Fowler; *Ion*, trans. W. R. M. Lamb, 1–195. Vol. 8 of *Plato*. Loeb Classical Library, vol. 164. Cambridge, Massachusetts: Harvard University Press, 1925.

———. *Theaetetus*. In *Theaetetus, Sophist*, trans. Harold North Fowler, 1–257. Vol. 7, rev. ed., of *Plato*. Loeb Classical Library, vol. 123. Cambridge, Massachusetts, 1921 (rev. 1928).

Plochmann, George Kimball, and Franklin E. Robinson. *A Friendly Companion to Plato's "Gorgias."* Carbondale: Southern Illinois University Press, 1988.

Reed, Natasha Alexandrovna. "Reading Lermontov's *Geroj našego vremeni*: Problems of Poetics and Reception." Ph.D. diss., Harvard University, 1994.

Reyes, G. Mitchell. "Sources of Persuasion in the *Iliad*." *Rhetoric Review* 21 (2002): 22–39.

Robinson, Richard. *Plato's Earlier Dialectic*. 2nd ed. Oxford: Clarendon Press, 1953.

Rossetti, Livio. "The Rhetoric of Socrates." *Philosophy and Rhetoric* 22 (1989): 225–38.

Rudebusch, George. "Plato, Hedonism, and Ethical Protagoreanism." In *Plato*, ed. John Anton and Anthony Preus, 27–40. Vol. 3 of *Essays in Ancient Greek Philosophy*. Albany: State University of New York Press, 1989.

Ryklin, Mikhail K. "Bodies of Terror: Theses toward a Logic of Violence." *New Literary History* 24 (1993): 51–74.

Santas, Gerasimos Xenophon. *Socrates: Philosophy in Plato's Early Dialogues*. Arguments of the Philosophers. London: Routledge and Kegan Paul, 1979.

Scarre, Geoffrey. *Logic and Reality in the Philosophy of John Stuart Mill*. Synthese Historical Library, vol. 34. Dordrecht, The Netherlands: Kluwer Academic Publishers, 1989.

Schiappa, Edward. *The Beginnings of Rhetorical Theory in Classical Greece*. New Haven, Connecticut: Yale University Press, 1999.

———. "Did Plato Coin *Rhētorikē?*" *American Journal of Philology* 111 (1990): 457–70.

———. *Protagoras and* Logos*: A Study in Greek Philosophy and Rhetoric*. Studies in Rhetoric/Communication. Columbia: University of South Carolina Press, 1991.

———. "*Rhētorikē*: What's in a Name? Toward a Revised History of Early Greek Rhetorical Theory." *Quarterly Journal of Speech* 78 (1992): 1–15.

Schmid, Walter T. *On Manly Courage: A Study of Plato's "Laches."* Philosophical Explorations. Carbondale: Southern Illinois University Press, 1992.

Schollmeier, Paul. "A Classical Rhetoric of Modern Science." *Philosophy and Rhetoric* 17 (1984): 209–20.

Schuster, Charles I. "Mikhail Bakhtin as Rhetorical Theorist." In *Landmark Essays on Bakhtin, Rhetoric, and Writing*, ed. Frank Farmer, 1–14. Landmark Essays, vol. 13. Mahwah, New Jersey: Lawrence Erlbaum Associates, Hermagoras Press, 1998.

Self, Lois S. "Rhetoric and *Phronesis*: The Aristotelian Ideal." *Philosophy and Rhetoric* 12 (1979): 130–45.

Simonides. "The Climb to Virtue." In *The Oxford Book of Greek Verse in Translation*, ed. T. F. Higham and C. M. Bowra, 236. Oxford: Clarendon Press, 1938.

———. "The Greek Dead at Thermopylae." In *The Oxford Book of Greek Verse in Translation*, ed. T. F. Higham and C. M. Bowra, 232. Oxford: Clarendon Press, 1938.

Sinclair, R. K. *Democracy and Participation in Athens*. Cambridge: Cambridge University Press, 1988.

Snell, Bruno. *The Discovery of the Mind in Greek Philosophy and Literature*. Trans. T. G. Rosenmeyer. 1953. Reprint, New York: Dover Publications, 1982.

Sosnoski, James J. "Postmodern Teachers in Their Postmodern Classrooms: Socrates Begone!" In *Contending with Words: Composition and Rhetoric in a Postmodern Age*, ed. Patricia Harkin and John Schilb, 198–219. New York: Modern Language Association of America, 1991.

Stallybrass, Peter, and Allon White. *The Politics and Poetics of Transgression.* Ithaca, New York: Cornell University Press, 1986.

Stove, D. C. *The Rationality of Induction.* Oxford: Clarendon Press, 1986.

Svoboda, Michael. Review of *Taming Democracy: Models of Political Rhetoric in Classical Athens,* by Harvey Yunis. *Rhetorica: A Journal of the History of Rhetoric* 17 (1999): 331–33.

Taylor, A. E. *Socrates: The Man and His Thought.* Beacon Press, 1952. Reprint, Garden City, New York: Doubleday and Company, Anchor Books, 1953.

Taylor, C. C. W. "Commentary." In *Protagoras,* by Plato, trans. C. C. W. Taylor, 64–215. Rev. ed. Clarendon Plato Series. Oxford: Clarendon Press, 1991.

———. *Socrates.* Past Masters. Oxford: Oxford University Press, 1998.

Thucydides. *History of the Peloponnesian War.* Trans. Charles Forster Smith. 4 vols. Loeb Classical Library. Cambridge, Massachusetts, Harvard University Press, 1919–23 (vol. 1 rev. 1928; vol. 2 rev. 1930).

Timchenko, Marina. "Transition: The State of Contemporary Artistic Culture." In *Re-Entering the Sign: Articulating New Russian Culture,* ed. Ellen E. Berry and Anesa Miller-Pogacar, 129–43. Ann Arbor: University of Michigan Press, 1995.

Tissol, Garth. "Heroic Parody and the Life of Exile: Dialogic Reflections on the Career of Ovid." In *Bakhtin and the Classics,* ed. R. Bracht Branham, 137–57. Rethinking Theory. Evanston, Illinois: Northwestern University Press, 2002.

Tuman, Myron C. *Word Perfect: Literacy in the Computer Age.* Pittsburgh Series in Composition, Literacy, and Culture. Pittsburgh: University of Pittsburgh Press, 1992.

Turkle, Sherry. *Life on the Screen: Identity in the Age of the Internet.* New York: Simon and Schuster, 1995.

Turner, Frank M. *The Greek Heritage in Victorian Britain.* New Haven, Connecticut: Yale University Press, 1981.

Tuthill, William. "Troy Housing Authority Narrows Digital Divide with Help from RPI." *Business Review* 28, no. 42 (18–24 January 2002): 20.

Ulmer, Gregory L. *Applied Grammatology: Post(e)-Pedagogy from Jacques Derrida to Joseph Beuys.* Baltimore: Johns Hopkins University Press, 1985.

Vitanza, Victor J. *Negation, Subjectivity, and the History of Rhetoric.* Albany: State University of New York Press, 1997.

———. "Three Countertheses: Or, A Critical In(ter)vention into Composition Theories and Pedagogies." In *Contending with Words: Composition and Rhetoric in a Postmodern Age,* ed. Patricia Harkin and John Schilb, 139–72. New York: Modern Language Association of America, 1991.

Vlastos, Gregory. "The *Protagoras* and the *Laches.*" In *Socratic Studies,* ed. Myles Burnyeat, 109–26. Cambridge: Cambridge University Press, 1994.

———. *Socrates, Ironist and Moral Philosopher.* Cornell Studies in Classical Philology. Ithaca, New York: Cornell University Press, 1991.

———. "Socrates on 'the Parts of Virtue.'" In *Platonic Studies*, 418–23. 2nd printing, with corrections. Princeton, New Jersey: Princeton University Press, 1981.

———. "The Unity of the Virtues in the *Protagoras*." In *Platonic Studies*, 221–69. 2nd printing, with corrections. Princeton, New Jersey: Princeton University Press, 1981.

———. "Was Polus Refuted?" *American Journal of Philology* 88 (1967): 454–60.

Vygotsky, L[ev]. S. *Mind in Society: The Development of Higher Psychological Processes*. Ed. Michael Cole, Vera John-Steiner, Sylvia Scribner, and Ellen Souberman. Cambridge, Massachusetts: Harvard University Press, 1978.

———. *Thought and Language*. Rev. and ed. Alex Kozulin. Cambridge, Massachusetts: Massachusetts Institute of Technology Press, 1986.

Wardy, Robert. *The Birth of Rhetoric: Gorgias, Plato and Their Successors*. Issues in Ancient Philosophy. London: Routledge, 1996.

Weiss, Roslyn. "Hedonism in the *Protagoras* and the Sophist's Guarantee." *Ancient Philosophy* 10 (1990): 17–39.

Welch, Kathleen E. *Electric Rhetoric: Classical Rhetoric, Oralism, and a New Literacy*. Digital Communication. Cambridge, Massachusetts: Massachusetts Institute of Technology Press, 1999.

Wells, Gordon. *Dialogic Inquiry: Toward a Sociocultural Practice and Theory of Education*. Learning in Doing: Social, Cognitive, and Computational Perspectives. Cambridge: Cambridge University Press, 1999.

Wertsch, James V. *Vygotsky and the Social Formation of Mind*. Cambridge, Massachusetts: Harvard University Press, 1985.

Wills, Clair. "Upsetting the Public: Carnival, Hysteria and Women's Texts." In *Bakhtin and Cultural Theory*, ed. Ken Hirschkop and David Shepherd, 130–51. Manchester, United Kingdom: Manchester University Press, 1989.

Yunis, Harvey. *Taming Democracy: Models of Political Rhetoric in Classical Athens*. Rhetoric and Society. Ithaca, New York: Cornell University Press, 1996.

Zappen, James P., Laura J. Gurak, and Stephen Doheny-Farina, "Rhetoric, Community, and Cyberspace." *Rhetoric Review* 15 (1997): 400–419.

Zeyl, Donald J. "Socrates and Hedonism: *Protagoras* 351b–358d." In *Plato*, ed. John Anton and Anthony Preus, 5–25. Vol. 3 of *Essays in Ancient Greek Philosophy*. Albany: State University of New York Press, 1989.

Index

Adali, Sibel, 156
adikos (unjust), 22, 80
Adkins, Arthur W. H., 6, 33, 71, 103,
    110, 172n63, 182n21
agathos (good, brave), 71–73, 75–76,
    106, 108–9
agōn (contest), 138–39
agora (assembly), 75
aidōs (respect, reverence), 103, 190n53
aischros (shameful, ugly), 131
Allen, R. E., 23, 114, 121, 138–39,
    189n44, 195n61, 195n78
anacrisis and syncrisis (drawing forth,
    juxtaposing), 13–14, 41, 45, 50, 76;
    and dialogical anthropology, 147; in
    digital communities, 160; in "Epic
    and Novel," 37; in the *Gorgias*, 127,
    131; in the *Laches*, 14, 47, 69, 81,
    83–84, 88, 90–91; in *Problems of
    Dostoevsky's Poetics*, 2, 37, 46
andreia (courage, *manliness*): in the
    early dialogues, 68–69, 85, 87, 91,
    106, 111, 120, 132, 168n109,
    181n10, 181n13; in Homer, 68; in the
    later dialogues, 172n63; in
    Simonides, 97, 110
Annas, Julia, 25, 168n110
aporia, 33–34, 84, 92, 101–2, 192n3
aretē (excellence, virtue): in Athenian
    culture, 33; in the early dialogues,
    13, 68–69, 71, 77–78, 83–85, 87, 90,
    93, 102, 117, 119–20, 122, 129–31,
    137, 181n10; in Homer, 3, 13, 68,
    71–77, 117, 119, 122, 130–31, 137,

168n109, 181n10; in the later dia-
    logues, 71, 76, 142–43, 172n63,
    181n10; in Protagoras' Great Speech,
    104; in the struggle against AIDS,
    147, 149; in Thucydides' *History*, 80
Aristophanes, 4; *Clouds*, 169n10
aristos (best, bravest), 73, 75, 84
Aristotle, 21, 25–28, 32; *The "Art" of
    Rhetoric*, 5, 26–27, 182n15, 196n86;
    The Metaphysics, 25, 27, 126,
    169n10; *Topica*, 26
Athenian empire, 1, 3, 6, 13–14, 18–19,
    33–34, 38, 50–51, 63, 68–70, 78–80,
    103, 115, 117–20, 122–25, 130,
    134–36, 141
authoritative discourse, 12, 42, 146, 151

Bakhtin, Mikhail M.: and the classics,
    38, 45, 164n15, 178n42; and contex-
    tual/extratextual methodology,
    63–66; life and works of, 38–40; and
    the novel, 51–63; and rhetoric, 1–4,
    6–15, 37–38, 40–45; and Socrates,
    1–3, 33–36; and Socratic dialogue,
    45–51
Bakhtin, Mikhail M., works by:
    Aesthetics of Verbal Creativity, 39
    "Author and Hero in Aesthetic
        Activity," 12, 38–39; empathy
        and detachment of individuals in,
        43;
    The Dialogic Imagination, 39
    "Discourse in the Novel," 39;
        authoritative discourse in, 42;